The Worldview Theme Song Book

Exploring The Feelings Behind Worldviews

by Stephen P. Cook

material found on the **Project Worldview** website
www.projectworldview.org
may enrich your experience with this book

The Worldview Theme Song Book: Exploring the Feelings Behind Worldviews can help you explore, make connections, make sense out of the confusion of existence, see the big picture and find meaning in life. It can help you cope with your own feelings and in your quest for a healthy worldview. Like its sister *www.projectworldview.org* website, it promises to be a good place to get unbiased help as you tackle life's big questions and expand your worldview. In this regard, we include the following:

Neutrality Pledge
"Your worldview should be uniquely yours...We won't force our beliefs on you! We will help you find your way in taking a free inquiry path to a worldview."

Acknowledgements
Thanks to friends who helped me wrestle with song lyrics—especially to "Lena". And to muses who inspired me in answering my unspoken request—which my have been something like "O divine Poesy, goddess-daughter of Zeus! Help me sing the story…" in *Doc* by Mary Doria Russell, author of *The Sparrow*

Dedication
This book is dedicated to the songwriters and musicians who have added so much to my life all these years.

The Worldview Theme Song Book: Exploring the Feelings Behind Worldviews

by Stephen P. Cook

copyright 2015 by Stephen P. Cook
ISBN: 978-0-9627349-4-6
manufactured in the USA
second printing
Library of Congress Control Number: 2015900171

publisher: **Parthenon Books**
Prescott, Arizona USA
parthenonbooks@projectworldview.org

Using the Front Cover to Set the Stage for the Book
Its two symbols provide a map for "exploring the feelings behind worldviews."

1) The global education symbol. Global education focuses on whole systems and emphasizes the interconnections and interdependencies that traditional, reductionist education often overlooks. It extends boundaries of concern, and strives to involve the whole person—seen as a thinking, feeling, joining, and doing creature. To me the globe in the symbol represents both our planet Earth and an individual human head striving to make sense of his or her world. This is done over many years by learning from experience. The result is a worldview: a conceptual framework and set of beliefs/values. Ideally it represents our view of the world we live in, facilitates our increasing understanding of it, and allows us to optimally function within it.

2) The strings of a lyre—an ancient musical instrument. Music manipulates emotions: it plays on our heartstrings. This symbol is built around an upside down capital Greek letter, the last one in the Greek alphabet: omega. Strong emotions can turn our lives upside down. Despite best efforts to steer lives in a direction guided by reason, and learn from interaction with other people and the surrounding environment, we often end up going where our feelings lead us. Our emotions have the last word!

An Invitation—To Select One of Two Ways to Read This Book

1) Of course you can start this book at the beginning. This is "a very good place to start," as Julie Andrews put it in the song "Do Re Mi" from one of the most beloved movies of all time: *The Sound of Music*. And you can then proceed to read straight through to the book's end, in Part III. This is recommended—especially if you are interested in how your brain works, more completely exploring the feelings behind worldviews, and deriving the most benefit from tools *Project Worldview* provides (some in this book, others freely available online) for doing this. And if you to want to better understand the book's ending: a worldview shaking true story involving a strange gift, another movie and another favorite song.

2) But if you wish to get to the songs sooner… You can just read the section that follows this one, look over the Table of Contents, read the Overview and Introduction in Part I, and then jump to Part II—where the songs begin. In offering this suggestion (and the preceding one), I'm trying to put myself in your shoes and consider what you're hoping to get from this book. Such empathizing with a particular person in mind not only shows respect, in a way it's like giving that person a gift. One gift we can give someone whose motives we might otherwise question is "the benefit of the doubt." With that said, let me invite those of you especially eager to get to the songs to start this book at the beginning of Part II (page 20). There the first song you'll find is one entitled "The Doubt." Note some songs are labeled "part of the author's personal story."

The Worldview Theme Songs as Respectful Music Parody

The eighty-one original songs you'll find in part II—one for each worldview theme—represent the heart of this book. Given their intent, and that they are to be sung to the tune of other songs—I think of them as "respectful music parody." Music parody typically involves writing new lyrics for a popular song, often with a mocking or humorous intent, but, in performing, reusing the music itself. Thus in the 1980s "Weird Al" Yankovic transformed Queen's "Another One Bites the Dust" into "Another One Rides the Bus," and Michael Jackson's "Beat It" into "Eat It." I've done something similar in this book's songs, but the intent is to educate, emotionally provoke and sometimes inspire, rather than mock or make fun. Indeed, many of these songs would fit nicely into church services (well, perhaps not any church service!) Thus use of "respectful" seems appropriate to better describe the music genre.

In this regard, consider the first song you'll find there on page 20 as Part II begins. It's to be sung to the tune of "The Weight" —a 1960s song from The Band. It's called "The Doubt" —and it's provided to help get at feelings associated with the accompanying worldview theme: Humbly Unsure (theme #1A).

Table of Contents

Part II   **Worldview Themes and Songs**

There are eighty-one worldview themes and new songs.
Each has its own page, containing the following:

a paragraph summarizing the theme with words
a new song, with notations ➔ notes that promote understanding
name / info about the original song upon which the new one is based
comments related to associated emotional armor / baggage / coping issues
relative thinking / feeling / joining / doing contributions ➔ TFJD code
an emotional volatility index VI
a link to the www.projectworldview.org theme page for lots more info

Part III   **Music, Emotional Volatility, Memes, Oracles, Strange Events**

Overview of This Book ➔ The Goal: Happiness and Self Actualization

It's the ultimate personal development state. Happy, self actualized people, according to psychologist Abraham Maslow, have achieved, "the full use and exploitation of talent, capacities, potentialities, etc." They are confident and find their way through life better partly due to a better understanding of themselves.

An Important Part of Reaching that Goal: A Healthy Worldview

Your beliefs.   Your Values.   Your Answers to Life's Big Questions.   Where You Fit In.
How You Treat Others. Your Framework for Making Sense Out of The World and Putting Meaning in Life.
Also, Emotional Intelligence, including the capacity to comfort yourself, is a key part of this foundation!

.

Problem: Many People Struggle Along the Road to Emotional Maturity

This is not surprising. As Maslow wrote, "The struggle between fear and courage, between defense and growth, between pathology and health is an eternal, intrapsychic struggle."

Along that road, "emotional armor" can protect us. Part I investigates how your brain functions to both protect you from stress /danger and reward you during "feel good" moments. In addition, we are typically comforted, motivated and inspired by beliefs and values we hold dear.	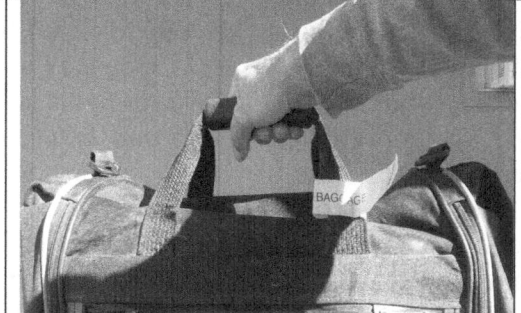	**What Beliefs and Values Provide You With Additional Emotional Armor?** Unfortunately these often fail, and we carry the scars of past disappointments, wrongs, and trauma around with us. **What Emotional Baggage Do You Carry?**

Problem: Some Worldviews Are Built Around Themes That, Taken Together, Can Result in People Going Through Life Singing a Sad Song

In Part II, for each of the eighty-one worldview themes used to characterize worldviews, you'll get a concise description, a TFJD code, a VI index, and related emotional armor / baggage / coping mechanism comments. **But words / numbers fall short—so to help get at the feelings behind them, a song is provided for each.**

Problem: Some Worldviews Are Built Around Themes With High Emotional Volatility—Invest Wisely!

Part III explains the importance of this (VI) index and how it is calculated. Investing in these themes can be risky. While the upside potential in terms of the best life has to offer is great, so is the downside potential!

Problem: Scientists Struggle to Understand How Our Brains Work

This book will help you appreciate this, including perhaps the biggest mystery of all: what is consciousness? Part III explores, "Analogous to a genetic code, is there a "memetic code" behind how memes propagate?

Problem: Trying to Explain Certain Events Can Shake Worldviews

By 1930 physicists managed to explain certain experimental findings, but in doing so they had replaced the cause & effect of classical Newtonian based physics, with assigning random events a key role in quantum mechanics. Einstein didn't like it, saying "God does not play dice!" In this, he may have been wrong…?

| Inspired by MIT physicist Kerson Huang, Part III discusses using oracles in decision-making, the random element in our lives, and presents a version of the *I Ching* oracle based on TFJD codes. | TFJD code = 3121

thinking / feeling / joining / doing | Those with worldviews built on the Scientific Materialism theme (with TFJD code 3121) write off strange Jungian synchronicities as coincidences. Are they? Part III ends with a bizarre true story! |

A. Introduction

The Personal Story Behind This Book

I've long tried to make sense of all human behavior in terms of four basic components: thinking, feeling, joining, and doing. Which of these is the most important? Which have I tried hardest to personally cultivate? For most of my adult life I'd have answered, "thinking." I would described this as valuing logic, reasoning, and analysis over faith. And noted the reasoning often involves formulating in abstract terms—that is, going beyond concrete expressions—in solving problems. And I would have linked it to being open to learning and thought-provoking new experience rather than preferring the comfortable expectancy of "same old, same old." (Figure #1)

But there have been brief periods in my life when my feelings obviously seemed most important. When I was emotionally distraught—after chinks in my emotional armor appeared and I'd been hurt, or after my unquestioning faith in someone had been shaken —my motivation to think, join, or do was severely affected. Unexpected problems—rather than presenting challenges to take in stride and meet with vigor—would become big anxiety-producing obstacles. Unhappy, with the confidence in my ability to make decisions and do a good job of running my life shaken, my tendency then was to retreat. I tended to seek the comfort and security of "same old" and not pursue new experience. So I'd miss out on learning adventures, meeting new people, etc.

In mid 2013, for the first time in fifteen years, I found myself alone and settling into such a state: I was suffering. Thinking back on that period, I agree with what David Brooks has recently written on this topic.[1] "Suffering gives people a more accurate sense of their own limitations, what they can control and cannot control. When people are thrust down into these deeper zones, they are forced to confront the fact they can't determine what goes on there. Try as they might, they just can't tell themselves to stop feeling pain, or to stop missing the one who has died or gone."

Fortunately I'd been there before and had some coping skills to draw on. Even so, how I managed to right my emotional ship of state was unexpected. For old songs I wrote new lyrics (a term from the Greek lyrikos meaning singing to the lyre.)

Thus "Sail With Serenity"—to be sung to the tune of "After the Gold Rush" by Neil Young—was born. So was "Grateful," to be sung to the tune of the old Temptations hit "My Girl," and many others. By the time I'd written just a few, and knew I was on the road to recovery, I had both a renewed appreciation of the importance of "feelings" and an idea. The idea was to continue writing songs and make them the heart of a book about exploring the feelings behind worldviews.

Worldview Themes, Personality Factors

One way to characterize, compare, and contrast worldviews is by using worldview themes. With a formal name and description, a theme describes the beliefs, thoughts, feelings, and behavior that come together in a way that is articulated in similar fashion by lots of people. Many such themes together describe a person's worldview.

Identifying these themes can be simple. When asked to discuss what's important to them, what they believe in, what they value, most people can make a good start in enunciating what they build their lives around. Listening to the comments of ordinary people when so queried, you'd hear a lot about God, family, treating other people right, their country, the work they do, making a good living, etc. But asked to provide a list of themes that taken together could characterize (in a general way) all human behavior, the way the world works, and everything that people can conceive of —obviously the challenge is much greater!

I started work making such a list of worldview themes over thirty years ago. Not surprisingly, it's gotten longer as the years have gone on. I've finally decided to cap it at a particular number: eighty-one. If it were longer, I decided, it would be too cumbersome. That number mathematically relates back to the thinking, feeling, joining, and doing starting point. Before I explain, let me first share the names of some of the themes in my list.

To facilitate that, imagine an interaction between two people with different worldviews. I might characterize one of those as built around themes such as "Secular Humanism," "Scientific Method," "Sustainability," and "Social Welfare Statism." Suppose the other person values themes like "Belief in a Personal God," "Religious Fundamentalism," "Self Reliant Nonconformity," and "Anthropocentrism." An interaction between these two folks, given the different nature of their worldviews, might be interesting—particularly if there was a need for substantive discussion!

In the game of life you constantly interact with people. The outcome of serious confrontations— constructive information exchange, compromise, dispute resolution, personal growth, or stubborn standoffishness, fighting, relationship breakdown, fear, etc.—often critically depends on how well the participants understand each other. In one on one interaction, good understanding involves not only knowledge of the other person's worldview, but also of the other's personality. Following Carver and Connor-Smith[2], we define this as, "the dynamic organization within the person of the psychological and physical systems that underlie that person's patterns of actions, thoughts, and feelings." And note that increasingly the academic psychology community uses a five factor model to facilitate discussion of individual personality differences. These five factors are: 1) openness to experience, 2) conscientiousness, 3) neuroticism, 4) agreeableness, and 5) extraversion.

We'll progress through this list with comments and make thinking, feeling, joining, doing connections as Part I continues. Note the first factor connects with the first choice identified in the list of Basic Choices in Figure #1. Some people are very open-minded and eager to seek out new experience; others are more likely to take refuge in the comfort of "same old, same old" thoughts, behaviors, places, etc. This list of basic choices presents a starting point for understanding, not just other people but yourself: your own feelings, personality, and worldview. What emotional armor / baggage do you carry? What mechanisms do you use to cope with stress? How open to experience, conscientious, neurotic, etc. are you? What worldview themes do you value? Before attempting answers, consider the following exercise.

A Simple Way of Describing Everything

Suppose we want to make sense of "everything" (i.e. all observed human behavior and the environment in which it occurs.) We seek a "big picture, low resolution" way of creating a model that facilitates an ultimate, long-term goal of attaining better understanding and making more useful predictions. While we'll need to more precisely define them and more fully probe their neuroscience basis, we decide that our model will ultimately rest on basic components of "Thinking," "Feeling," "Joining," and "Doing," and so called TFJD codes that we form from them.

Specifically, suppose we decide to build our model of everything (= reality) around what goes into eighty-one boxes. Each box has its own TFJD address based on the relative level—ranked with 1 (low) to 2 (average) to 3 (high) —that each of the four basic components contributes. (Technically our model is a four dimensional array A with 81 elements A_{ijkl} where allowed index values are 1, 2, and 3.) There are $3^4 = 81$ possible TFJD codes, from 1111 to 3333 (see Figure #2).

Figure #2 shows what I've put in those boxes: each has a specific worldview theme (those named and described in Part II) corresponding to a specific TFJD code. Settling on the particular themes (after years of deliberation!) to fill those eighty-one boxes was admittedly somewhat arbitrary. Coming up with them—giving names and writing descriptions—can be done in many different ways. But there are two main constraints: 1) the theme put in a particular box has to fit the numerical TFJD profile, and 2) taken as a whole, all of the eighty-one themes have to be able to generally account for all observed human behavior and the conceptual framework behind it.

The *Project Worldview* themes represent both a work in progress and a challenge: if you don't like them, fill in the boxes of this "big picture, low resolution" framework in a way that embodies your understanding and is personally more useful to you. Sure, this will involve your own personal preferences, but there is no arbitrariness in how the eighty-one TFJD code boxes are defined. As for naming / categorizing in general: it promotes good communication and better understanding!

Figure #1: Basic Choices (meta-theme pairs)
open-minded or values cognitive consistency ("same old")? values logic, reason, analysis or faith?
calm, restrainted, responsible or chaotic, problematic? intolerant pain or generosity, love?
values individualism or collectivism? hierarchical rigidity or egalitarian progressivism?
human-centered or nature-centered? values freedom from limits or values limits and ethics?

Figure #2: The 81 TFJD Code Boxes and the *Project Worldview* Theme Map

example: In box coded 1233 (1 on thinking, 2 on feeling, 3 on joining, 3 on doing) is Theme #7B Magic

notes: 1) As one proceeds from left to right in the table below, generally thinking becomes more evident.

2) As one proceeds from top to bottom, generally speaking, feeling becomes more evident.

3) There are no good or bad code scores: their meaning is loosely connected to activity in certain brain areas.

1111 #7A MYSTICISM	2111 #11B FREE WILL	3111 #18B DISPASSIONATE
1112 #20B AUTHORITARIANISM	2112 #29A THE SELF-RESTRAINED PERSON	3112 #30 INTELLECTUAL FREEDOM
1113 #33A SERVITUDE	2113 #35A SELF RELIANT NONCONFORMITY	3113 #46A TECHNOLOGICAL FIX MENTALITY
1121 #11A FATALISM	2121 #39A TOUGH LOVE	3121 #5A SCIENTIFIC MATERIALISM
1122 #47B PACIFISM	2122 #19A ECONOMIC INDIVIDUALISM	3122 #6 SCIENTIFIC METHOD
1123 #15 COLLECTIVE COGNITIVE IMPERATIVE	2123 #26A THE CONSUMERIST	3123 #22A EXPANSIONISM (ECONOMIC)
1131 #5B VITALISM	2131 #31 EDUCATION FOR DEMOCRACY	3131 #4 GLOBAL VISION: THE BIG PICTURE
1132 #23B ENOUGHNESS	2132 #47A ATTITUDINAL FIX MENTALITY	3132 #23A SUSTAINABILITY
1133 #37A PROUD IDENTIFICATION	2133 #48 CO-OPERATIVE SOCIETY ADVOCATE	3133 #19B CORPORATE CAPITALISM
1211 #9B APOCALYPTICISM	2211 #1A HUMBLY UNSURE	3211 #20A ELITISM
1212 #14A MORALISTIC GOD	2212 #52 INDEPENDENT LVG for SICK, DISABLED	3212 #28B HEALTHY ORIENTATION
1213 #26B THE MORE IS BETTER MENTALITY	2213 #25 ANTHROPOCENTRISM	3213 #45B WORK HARD, PAY AS YOU GO
1221 #14B REINCARNATION	2221 #17B GRATITUDE & FORGIVENESS	3221 #42 ETHICAL ORIENTATION
1222 #45A BORROWING MENTALITY	2222 #34 VALUING TRADITIONS & STATUS QUO	3222 #50A LIBERTARIAN
1223 #24 STRUGGLING WITH SUSTENANCE	2223 #3 FOCUSED VISION	3223 #13 DANCING WITH SYSTEMS
1231 #8A MONOTHEISM	2231 #32 VALUING HUMAN RIGHTS	3231 #49B SOCIALISM
1232 #8B BELIEF IN A PERSONAL GOD	2232 #16 GOLDEN RULE, MUTUAL HELP ETHIC	3232 #49A SOCIAL WELFARE STATISM
1233 #7B MAGIC	2233 #44B ANIMAL RIGHTS	3233 #40 ENVIRONMENTAL ECONOMICS
1311 #39B SCAPEGOATING	2311 #36B CONSPIRACISM	3311 #36A CYNICISM
1312 #33B ADDICTION	2312 #2B I KNOW WHAT'S BEST FOR YOU	3312 #1B SKEPTICISM
1313 #28A HEDONISTIC ORIENTATION	2313 #29B THE THREATENING PERSON	3313 #46B MILITARISM
1321 #9A RELIGIOUS FUNDAMENTALISM	2321 #44A SANCTITY & DIGNITY OF LIFE	3321 #10 SECULAR HUMANISM
1322 #17A BITTERNESS & VENGEANCE	2322 #50B LEFT ANARCHIST	3322 #22B IMPERIALISM
1323 #18A PASSIONATELY IMPULSIVE	2323 #41 STRUGGLING WITH SELF ESTEEM	3323 #43 SEEKING WEALTH AND POWER
1331 #2A THE TRUE BELIEVER	2331 #21A POPULISM	3331 #37B GLOBAL CITIZEN
1332 #38 VALUING FAMILY	2332 #21B SERVICE TO OTHERS	3332 #51 ETHICAL GLOBALIZATION
1333 #12 THE ARTISTIC WORLDVIEW	2333 #27 BELONGING TO NATURE	3333 #35B WORKING FOR CHANGE

More About the Songs in This Book

The songs I've written, one for each worldview theme, represent the heart of this book in Part II. They are based on songs that typically were popular in America during the 20th century. As noted at the bottom of each theme's page, many of them made "The 500 Greatest Songs of All Time" list compiled by *Rolling Stone* (Dec 9, 2004 issue.)

As I've mentioned, their existence can be traced to my suffering. I will spare you the details, except to say that eighteen of this book's eighty-one songs are either autobiographical or semiauto-biographical. They are labeled "author's personal story" in the SONG—NOTES /COMMENTS at the end of each song. Despite my background as a scientist, teacher, and writer, with songwriting I tried to cultivate the artist inside me. In this regard consider part of a worldview theme description you'll find in Part II for theme #12: Artistic Orientation. "As an artist... My work should arouse feelings and maximize my audience's emotional commitment. I offer my creation to others, serving as their intermediary. Its birth can be traced to my isolation, suffering, ego suppression, then awakening, connecting—sometimes by analogizing —and above all, my empathizing."

My suffering helped foster a creative state of mind. It led to wanting to identify certain feelings, put them in songs, and share the resulting product. In simpler terms, perhaps I started writing many of these songs as therapy to ease pain. And, if misery does love company, I suppose I was inviting others to share my experience and resulting songs.

So, perhaps at first, in the late summer of 2013, I was metaphorically wanting "to sing alchemically sorrow into joy again" (to use a phrase from *Singing the Soul Back Home: Shamanism in Daily Life*[3] author Caitlin Matthews). Once I healed to the extent where the song-writing therapy was no longer needed, I began to realize that writing song lyrics could also potentially do something else important to me. It could educate and arouse feelings in other people so as to affect positive change in the world.

As I realized this, I also grasped a complication if the songs were to be part of *Project Worldview*: the neutrality pledge (see inside front cover). Seems I couldn't keep this promise—and both advocate and attempt to passionately move people on behalf of some cause dear to my heart and strongly associated with valuing a particular worldview theme—unless I was willing and able to write songs on behalf of all eighty-one themes! Rather than deciding there was no way I'd pen lyrics on behalf of themes I was just pretending to value—when in fact I detest them—I decided instead to view this as a threefold challenge.

First, it would test the extent of my tolerance for beliefs and values I don't hold or share. Second, it would test my ability to empathize with other people. Could I do such a good job that my lyrics captured the passion those people felt for something important to them (that wasn't at all important to me or at worst was something I thoroughly disapproved of)? Third, it would test my talent as an artist seeking to "arouse feelings and maximize my audience's emotional commitment." Have I succeeded? If readers report singing a favorite song, with my lyrics substituted for the original ones, the answer will be yes!

Rounding Out The Book and a Confession

From "Overview of this Book" (page 1) and the two pages that precede it, you should have a pretty good idea as to what it's about. I won't say much more here. Except to add that your experience with it can be enhanced by material on the *Project Worldview* website. Besides thousands of "more to explore" links, targeted worldview analysis—of current events, of your own beliefs/values with computer programs you can use, etc. — you'll find simpler things. Like background term definitions and excerpts from the 2009 *The Worldview Literacy Book*[4] accompanying each of the worldview themes. Suffice it to say this book you've started reading goes beyond that 2009 book in exploring feelings aspects of worldviews and in other ways. It's certainly much more personal.

Finally, a confession. When I started writing, I had no idea that before I finished, I'd feel this was a book I was destined to write. That feeling goes beyond the inspiration of the recent past (thank you, Muses!) that went into writing eighty one songs. It goes back to a decision I made in 1973 in Santa Cruz, California: to try to both intellectually and experientially sample a big chunk of all life has to offer, not specialize and more narrowly confine myself. I like the choice I made. The book's ending will help you understand. Enjoy!

B. Your Brain: Concepts and Thinking
Concepts, Neurons, and Memory Formation

A concept refers to the abstract generalized ideas and understanding that replace a set of sensory experiences and memories. For example, a young girl handles different objects: rectangular blocks, orange, beach ball, tennis ball, toy cars, globe, etc. She forms a mental concept of "roundness" that some of the objects fit into, others don't. This observing, abstracting, recalling memories, discriminating, categorizing, etc. process is called conceptualization.

In recent years, scientists who study the brain and nervous system—neuroscientists—have gained a new understanding of this process. It seems that links are made between neurons—specialized conducting cells of brain, nerves and spinal cord. While some neurons are specialized for different functions, they all consist of branch-like extensions called dendrites that receive input signals from other neurons, and long fibrous axons that output signals to still others.

Figure #3: Neurons

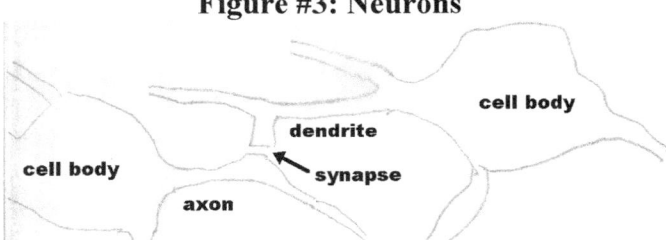

It seems that non-human brains form concepts as well. Consider the concept of a "bed." Certainly tired humans entering a hotel room at night can instantly recognize the presence of such an object. For a mouse, a related concept is "nest." Neuroscientist Joe Z. Tsien has extensively instrumented, monitored and investigated how the brains of mice work. He's described[1] one finding as follows. "We accidentally discovered that a small number of hippocampal neurons…appear to respond to the abstract concept of "nest." These cells react vigorously to all types of nests, regardless of whether they are round or square or triangular or made of cotton or plastic or wood. Place a piece of glass over the nest so the animal can see it but can no longer climb in, and the nest cells cease to react." Tsien found a linkage of neurons in the mouse brain that seemed to physically embody the key functionality behind the nest concept.

The hippocampus is a brain area that plays a key role in long-lasting memory formation and storage. Memories of specific perceptions or events—again in the form of links between neurons—precede forming of neural networks associated with concepts.

The complexity of the human brain is staggering: 100 billion neurons join together in making around 100 trillion connections! Electrical signals pulse through this web. Traversing the gap between where dendrites and axons meet, the synapse (Figure #3), requires the secretion and release of a brain chemical or neurotransmitter, and appropriate receptors. Successful chemical transport across the synapse typically triggers the neighboring neuron to fire (more like electrically discharge), and so on.

There is debate[2] as to how many neurons are needed to store a simple memory or recollection. Some neuroscientists believe only a handful are involved, while others assert that such storage is distributed over linkages involving hundreds of thousands to millions of cells. And there is debate over a related question: the amount of detail the neural linkage representing a concept codes for. Does our mental recollection of a long-dead grandfather, for example, depict him frowning and biting his tongue, hairs protruding from his nose, facial wrinkles and elaborately mapped body language consistent with that, or provide a much lower resolution, just sparsely filled in image?

One can use the size of the brain, its typical neuron numbers and response times, the fact that a typical person remembers no more than 10,000 concepts, and that sparse representations allow more rapid retrieval and associations with other memories and concepts, to argue for a "sparse to middling" position in which thousands or tens of thousands—not millions—of neurons or "concept cells" (as some call them) are employed.

Clearly there are key tasks our brains perform as they make sense of reality for us. They include information gathering and storage, relating new experiences to older ones, organizing knowledge, conceptualizing and mapping, responding to feed-back and learning. While this begins to happen soon after birth, we realize conceptual map development happens both concurrently with and is constrained by the development of our brains.

For example, typically our earliest memories are of events after we became three years old. Why? The hippocampus isn't mature enough to fully function until kids are three. Often when events occurring before that age are recalled, they are of a traumatic nature stored as "emotional memories" in the amygdala, which functions properly at birth.

How Our Brains Develop As We Grow Up

Roughly speaking, the lower and older (in evolutionary terms) parts of our brains mature sooner as we grow up as children. These include the brain stem (our primitive "Reptilean Brain") and the limbic system (our "Mammalian Brain"). While the latter (like the former) is still an "unconscious" part of our brain, it's directly connected to our evolutionarily younger and conscious cortex which sits with all that grey matter spread out, layered and folded above it.

Figure #4: The Human Brain

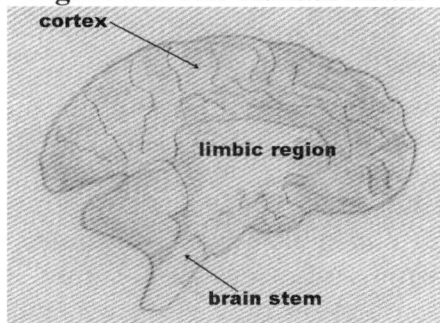

The cortex, with various subregions, plays a major role in perception, maintaining attention, encoding and retrieving memory, language, critical thinking and consciousness. The limbic system steadily feeds information to the cortex—including the emotional responses it generates, urges, etc. The amygdala, where fear is registered, is located there, as is the hippocampus, important to declarative memory. Long-term memory is either non-declarative or declarative. The former stores procedures and skills mastered unconsciously (like riding a bike), whereas declarative memory stores both factual information and specific personal memories of experiences. A key brain pathway is between the prefrontal cortex and the memory centered in the hippocampus.

Once children start school the number of concepts they've acquired grows from hundreds into thousands. Recent research has found that human brains, once thought to be done maturing by age twelve, don't reach maturity until twenty-five. This slow development explains much bizarre, impulsive, risky, thrill-seeking, lacking good judgment behavior typical of teen-age years!

Figure #5: The Limbic System

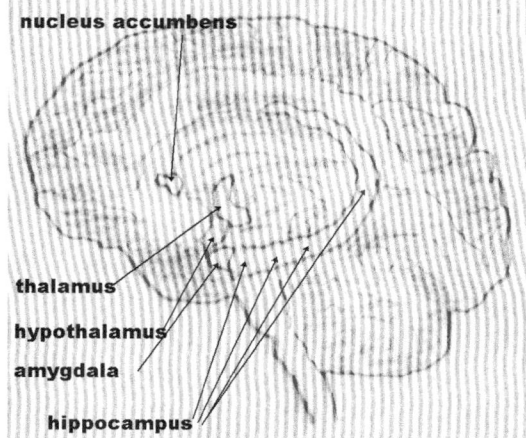

A list of key brain developments—based on a "The New Science of the Teenage Brain" report[3]—that occur as teens grow to adults include:
1) axons become better insulated with whitish, fatty myelin speeding up transmission of signals,
2) dendrites become thinner and connections to frequently firing synapses are stronger, while those not often firing become weaker and atrophy,
3) as this occurs the cortex becomes thinner, more capable, and operates faster / more efficiently in terms of handling more variables and agendas,
4) the corpus callosum connecting the brain's right (RB) and left hemispheres (LB) thickens (stay tuned for more on RB and LB specialization), and
5) the key pathway we've described between cortex and hippocampus becomes stronger, aiding incorporating of memory into decision-making.

The end product of all this is the full development of what are called executive functions of the brain. Typically centered in the prefrontal cortex, these include: 1) planning and top down management, 2) regulation, and control of attention (connection with the reticular formation in the brain stem plays a role here), 3) reasoning, employing a "working memory" under direct control of the cortex, and 4) reality testing/error monitoring that can uncover the need for novel or non-habitual/automatic type responses, and also inhibit inappropriate actions. Note: many descriptions of the second personality factor (in our Part Ia list) called conscientiousness include the determined planning, purposely striving for goals, and ability to control impulses associated with well developed executive brain function.

Thinking / Its Integration With Other Activities

In summary, we've discussed two key jobs the "Thinking" part of brains—what is to be associated with "T" in the TFJD codes—perform: #1 Making a conceptual map of reality based on processing and learning from information, #2 Decision-making worthy of a chief executive. As we turn our attention to the other parts of this code, we note that, in artificially dividing up functions of the highly integrated human brain into four activities, we have over-simplified a complex situation. Certainly sensory inputs to the brain are highly integrated. As one neuroscientist notes[4], "Our many different senses collaborate even more than we previously realized. What we hear depends a lot on what we see and feel." Something similar is true of output activities under the brain's guidance as well.

Back to those two things we're associating with the "thinking" part of brains. Certain experiences and situations involve both #1 and #2 and require making a choice between being receptive (open-minded?) to feedback and acting, or ignoring it. The latter can happen in two ways: a) based on signals from lower brain regions that suggest there is nothing out of the ordinary and the usual habitual/automatic response is fine, or b) higher brain level decision invoking the need for a certain cognitive consistency (facts, beliefs, values are consistent with each other.) Recall the Figure #1 choice, and note: unlike cognitive dissonance, which produces discomfort, those valuing cognitive consistency find comfort in not seeking out and/or ignoring facts, beliefs, values that would necessitate some revising of the relevant part of their worldview framework. Either way, instead of action, the result is passively doing nothing.

As we've suggested, thinking doesn't happen in isolation but connects with the other three of our four fundamental activities. Consider the thinking—doing connection first. Given that organisms were unconsciously moving long before they were consciously thinking, not surprisingly parts of the brain associated with actively doing something lay below the cortex (subcortical). Between it and the limbic system, in the center back of the brain, is the basal ganglia. This region of interconnected neuron clusters activates when we face a choice. It might be thought of as having the role of a trusted advisor.

Three important paths link the basal ganglia to other parts of the brain: 1) one to the pre-frontal cortex above is involved in selecting voluntary movements and has connections to motor and premotor cortical regions.; 2) one to the substantia nigra region of the brain stem below controls automatic (meaning without thinking) movements and helps co-ordinate motivation and movement; 3) to a reward learning system that boosts neurotransmitter chemical dopamine level as the reward.

Neurons with dopaminergic receptors are part of these last two brain pathways. The substantia nigra is a dopamine producing region. Given that dopamine plays a key role in bodily motor control, if its production declines the movement problems associated with Parkinson's disease can result. In contrast, if drugs like cocaine continually amplify dopamine's reward type effects, addiction can result. (Note addiction—which can be thought of in terms of a person's inability to stop doing certain things—has its own worldview theme, #33B) Other neurons in this part of the brain (specifically in the lateral habenula) are "reward-negative"—meaning they are activated by stimulii like unpleasant events, absence of reward or its unpredictability, punishment, etc.

The key brain path associated with movements you normally make without thinking links the brain stem, basal ganglia and the adjoining limbic system. The thalamus and hypothalamus are part of the limbic system. (Figure #5) The former functions to direct information to other brain locations for processing; the latter keeps various body status indicators (like body temperature, blood pressure, etc.) optimally adjusted to the environment and maintains homeostasis. It works with the nearby pituitary gland to do this and, critically, provide a connection between the body's nervous system and its endocrine system.

The almond-sized hypothalamus receives sensory input from various parts of the body and neural input from the brain stem. It is regulated by neurotransmitters like dopamine and serotonin and can promote or inhibit the pituitary gland's release of up to nine different hormones—most notably oxytocin. Hormones are chemicals released into the blood stream and carried by the circulatory system to various target organs.

Both the nervous system and endocrine system are information signaling systems—the former employs neurotransmitters for sending signals, the latter uses hormones. In contrast to rapid breakdown of neurotransmitters and very fast nervous system response, hormones hang around much longer and responses they initiate are both slower and longer-lasting. Besides hypothalamus and pituitary gland, the endocrine system includes the adrenal gland. This is responsible for freeing up glucose for energy and releasing hormones such as blood pressure raising cortisol (more in males than females), and adrenalin in response to stress.

Adrenalin is famously connected to the "fight or flight" response. It is produced in response to a powerful emotional signal—fear—sent out by the amydgala. Before adremalin primes the body for a fight, the nervous system has already responded dramatically. The amydgala's production of excess norepinephrine and dopamine neurotransmitters floods receptors and opens channels. This disconnects links between neurons in prefrontal lobes and effectively turns off conscious thinking. Control is ceded to an older automatic limbic brain regulated nervous system. The details of this have been described[5] in terms of "allowing emotionality and impulsivity to take over". In other words: thinking gives way to feeling and doing.

Thinking, Left / Right Brain, Reason / Faith

Taking charge of much "thinking" is the left hemisphere of the cortex. It is specialized for understanding verbal communication, speaking, reading and writing, along with analytical reasoning, abstract and critical thinking. In contrast, the right brain is active during physical activity, creative pursuits, non-verbal communications, dreams, assessing spatial relationships, aesthetic judgments, face/pattern recognition, and in making intuitive/ wholistic leaps. It's hypothesized that the LB processes information sequentially, "bit by bit" in linear, ordered fashion, while the RB stores and retrieves whole patterns, in "all at once" fashion.

One should realize that the human brain is very complex, and the above picture of the left brain/right brain distinction too simplistic—for starters, different neural connections are undoubtedly behind many LB/RB functional differences—but it provides the general idea. Two other responses to environmental stimuli provide quite a contrast to analytical reasoning, which

benefits from years of learning and from the evolutionarily much more recent fine-tuning of the left side of the cerebral cortex: instinctual behavior and intuition.

Instinctual behavior is genetically determined and hard-wired. It functions independently of previous experience, learning, or memory, and has a long (lower brain) evolutionary history that connects us with our animal ancestors. Intuition is immediate insight that occurs without inference, reason or (some would say even) conscious awareness. Some psychologists describe it as a response to subtle cues and stimuli received unconsciously. Others view it as an almost mystical process, a type of faith-based leap characteristic of how the right brain operates.

In assigning "T" values of TFJD codes to worldview themes, we need to assess the extent to which the theme is based on reason or on faith. We associate reason with a rational belief system: one supported by facts and concepts, ultimately linked to observation and experience, which fit together in a coherent way as part of a useful, logical framework. In contrast, faith—defined as the firm belief, complete confidence and trust in something for which there is no proof—is often associated with intuition and religion. It's linked more to feelings/emotions than thinking. For example, the last three values of the TFJD codes for #9A Religious Fundamentalism and #10 Secular Humanism worldview themes are identical: 321 (see Figure #2). But their "T" scores, 1 (the lowest) for Fundamentalism and 3 (highest) for Secular Humanism, are quite different—reflecting the results of a Reason / Faith assessment. (Note it's a choice in Figure #1.)

Note the left hand column of Figure #2 contains three themes where not only T is the same (=1) but J values (=2) and D values (=1) are also the same. Those themes are #11A Fatalism, #14B Reincarnation, and #9A Fundamentalism. Note these three differ in "Feelings" scores. So we can say the Fundamentalism theme involves more feelings than Reincarnation which had more than Fatalism. A similar conclusion can be drawn for the Figure #2 right hand column (T=3) themes of #5A Scientific Materialism, #42 Ethical Orientation, and #10 Secular Humanism.

As we transition from considering thinking to feeling, we pause and consider songs and music.

C. Your Brain: Songs, Rewards and Feelings
Music, Emotions, and the Brain

I have a list of words that I know from experience are a challenge to define. Among others, the list includes love, family, science, consciousness, emotions —and music. Just as I like definitions of science that use the word method, I like definitions of music that have the word emotion. So rather than "music involves organizing sounds to elicit an aesthetic response," I prefer "music is a form of intentional emotional manipulation."

This statement is from the *Wikipedia* article for "Pre-historic Music." It goes on to speculate that, from this perspective, music wasn't possible "until the onset of intentionality— the ability to reflect about the past and the future." Rather than focus on when humans developed this capability and the music/consciousness relationship, I want to save that discussion for part IIIb. Instead, here let's talk about the emotions music can trigger and corresponding changes in the brain.

Music can produce powerful emotions, and powerful emotions can produce music. The 1993 film *Philadelphia* provides a stunning portrayal of this in a scene in which Tom Hanks' character explains how the *La Mamma Morta* aria in the *Andrea Chénier* 1896 French opera makes him feel. Certainly some of the most basic human expression of strong feelings is triggered by the despair a mother feels when her baby is missing! Her painful wails aren't music —but they are sounds that communicate emotion and can rouse others to act. Many studying the origin of language look to the mother-infant relationship for clues. The *Wikipedia* "Pre-historic Music" article notes communication between mothers and infants "involves melodic, rhythmic and movement patterns as well as the communication of intention and meaning, and in this sense is similar to music." Parents who've sung to comfort distraught infants and help them sleep know how they often respond to lullabies.

The contrast between a mother's anguished screams and soothing lullabies provides an example of expression of feelings relevant to a pair of meta themes (Figure #1) used to rank feelings components of worldview themes. They are "chaotic, problematic" vs. "calm, restrained, responsible." A person thought of as "Passionately Impulsive" (theme #18A) and one described as "Dispassionate" (theme #18B) certainly have different ways of expressing emotion!

Research suggests that emotions associated with music stimulate parts of the brain like other emotionally charged stimuli. In particular, after measuring electroencephalogram (EEG) activity, Schmidt and Trainor report[1], "Subjects exhibited greater relative left frontal EEG activity to joy and happy musical excerpts and greater relative right frontal EEG activity to fear and sad musical excerpts." Similarly unpleasant melodies also activate the posterior cingulate cortex—a part of the brain many studies have linked to emotional pain and conflict (see Figure #6).

The amygdala (Figure #5) also has a key role in the emotional processing of music. In a 2007 study[2] of a rare patient whose brain damage was confined to the amygdala, a team of University of Montreal/ University of Iowa researchers reported the patient "was selectively impaired in the recognition of scary and sad music. In contrast, her recognition of happy music was normal."

For over a hundred years, doctors have realized that victims of a stroke centered in the left side of the brain often lose the ability to speak but retain a singing capability. Those—like Arizona Congresswoman shooting victim Gabrielle Giffords—whose left brain speech centers have been injured have sometimes resorted to communicating by singing! So there: music has some practical survival value!

I say this as if to answer a question, most notably posed by Charles Darwin in his 1871 book *Descent of Man*. We paraphrase this as, "What good is music —what evolutionary survival value does it have?" I've answered as I did for two reasons: 1) I want to reinforce the idea that music is primarily stored in our right brains. How this is done is interesting: it seems that music memory encoding in the auditory cortex is done by neurons organized according to musical tone frequency. 2) I want to set the stage for a response to Darwin's question based on 21st century neuroscience.

What I say may be surprising given what Harvard professor Steven Pinker said in a 1997 book[3]: basically that music has no survival value! Referring to it as "auditory cheesecake…crafted to tickle…our mental faculties," he wrote that if it were to suddenly disappear "the rest of our lifestyle would be virtually unchanged."

People getting pleasure from music has a long history. Some claim it goes back 40,000 years when people first made flutes by putting holes in bones. In the last two decades neuroscientists have studied what happens in brains during emotionally grabbing musical passages—those that send chills down your spine or bring joyful tears to your eyes. Their brain scans have noted changes in cerebral blood flow in frontal cortex and limbic system areas associated with emotion, like the amydgala and the basal ganglia—particularly its nucleus accumbens which plays a key role in the reward circuit (previously mentioned) involving our responses to stimuli associated with various emotions. As you might guess, they found dopamine release associated with emotionally moving music. But there's more…

As neuroscientists Zatorre and Salimpoor describe it in a *New York Times* article[4] "Why Music Makes Our Brain Sing," "What may be most interesting here is *when* this neurotransmitter is released: not only when the music rises to a peak emotional moment, but also several seconds before, during what we might call the anticipation phase. The idea that reward is partly anticipation (or the prediction of a desired outcome) has a long history in neuroscience. Making good predictions about the outcome of one's actions would seem to be essential in the context of survival, after all. And dopamine neurons, both in humans and other animals, play a role in recording which of our predictions turn out to be correct."

Worldviews, Emotions, and Brain Mechanisms

We've already linked worldviews with making predictions and feedback. In *The Worldview Literacy Book* I wrote, "Your mental development begins with building a conceptual framework on which a worldview is slowly constructed. Growing up involves acquiring experience and skills, learning how to fit into the world, and selectively refining your understanding of how it works. Ideally, by adulthood, you've made good choices and are comfortable with your worldview."

Elsewhere I've discussed the fit between your mental conception of the world and how the world really is. And about gauging how good this fit is— and by inference the practical value of your world-

view —by measuring how good the predictions it makes turn out to be.

And, in a chapter entitled "Imagining a Theory of Everything for Adaptive Systems" in the Springer Science volume *The Origin(s) of Design in Nature*[5], about societal worldviews I wrote, "I like the thought of competing worldviews. Seems to me the competition will be decided on the basis of which model best represents reality as measured by the ability to make useful predictions over the time frame of interest. And how well the conceptional system representation E_S fits the real environment representation E. The winner will be the worldview that minimizes the E_S-E difference over the relevant path in conceptual space…A next step is translating that difference into energy, or prediction error information counterpart."

Both of these paragraphs about worldviews are lacking in that they are set firmly in the thinking realm. But life is more than that: feelings are critically important! We can emphasize that partly using Pinker's words to provide a definition for another of those tough to define words: emotions. We define emotions as "Ancient survival mechanisms to protect us from danger that have evolved to also include (as he puts it) 'mechanisms that set the brain's highest level goals.' "

The work of Zatorre, Salimpoor and others is beginning to get at how reward circuits in the brain operate as part of those mechanisms. Their finding of dopamine release, in both the anticipation and peak emotional pleasure phases of listening to music, suggests the importance of predictions made by our mental models being validated. And inspired by the music context in which their findings are set, I like to think that pleasurable feelings (like security, validation and joy) derived from familiar tones, rhythm, and music have helped guide the last 40,000 years of human brain evolution. Guided it in a way that has significantly added to the ability of our species to survive! (For more, including speculation as to how this might have happened, see Part If.)

It has long been recognized that basic emotions like fear, anger, parental love, and perhaps others such as happiness, sadness, and disgust, not only have survival value, but can function without consciousness. As mentioned, raw primary emotions can trigger fight, flight, or appeasement without conscious decision to do so. More complex emotions arise only after processing by the conscious mind. These involve direct connection between the cortex and amygdala, and an indirect connection / feedback loop between these, the hypothalamus and the rest of the body.

We elaborate on this by considering a frequent condition: a person feels dissatisfied. Something is lacking. There is a desire for/want of something. This can be basic— involving nothing more than being hungry. Rita Carter, in her book[6] *Mapping the Mind*, describes it. "A stimulus from outside (the sight of food, say) or from the body (falling glucose levels) is registered by the limbic system which creates an urge which registers consciously as desire. The cortex instructs the body to act in whatever way is necessary to achieve the desire. The activity sends messages back to the limbic system which releases opiod-like neurotransmitters which raise circulating dopamine levels and create a feeling of satisfaction."

Since that was written, the role of dopamine has become better understood. Writing in the August 2012 issue of *Scientific American*, neuroscientists Kringelbach and Berridge cite evidence that wanting and liking are controlled by different brain mechanisms. Like Zatorre and Salimpoor, they don't strongly connect dopamine with the actual sensation of pleasure but to something else. Their research connects it to want, to desire, and to the same reward brain circuit involving the nucleus accumbens we've noted.

In contrast, they associate liking something with activity in "hedonic hotspots." They describe how two other neurotransmitters, enkephalion and anandamide, form a "pleasure-boosting loop of liking". The article ends by recalling that long ago Aristotle split feeling happy into "hedonia" or pleasure, and "eudaimonia," a sense of meaning. They lament that while scientists have made some progress in understanding the former, the latter is more of a puzzle. They hope future "discoveries will help people unite pleasure and purpose."

Patrick McNamara, Boston University neuroscientist, is investigating something that fits in this category: the origin of the pleasure that religiously oriented people get from either "a sense of transcendence or the pleasure of doing good." Based on studying Parkinson patients, he concludes[7] such religiosity is "spurred by the quest for unexpected reward." Dopamine figures prominently in his findings. He explains the plight of "left onset disease" patients who lost interest in religion, previously very important to them, as follows. "The dopamine receptors responsible for that transcendent, outsize sense of reward were dysfunctional on the right side of their brains."

How people have found purpose or put meaning into life can be viewed from a human cultural evolution perspective. Just as life propagates based on a genetic code carried in genes, we postulate that human culture is passed on via memes. These are units of cultural information such as ideas, rituals, behaviors, stories, songs, etc. that propagate from mind to mind guiding human cultural evolution.

How do memes differ from concepts? Some say there's no difference, and therefore there was no need for Richard Dawkins to introduce them[8] in 1976. Others would defend their introduction by pointing out that just as there is fierce competition in a survival of the fittest sense between genes, so too are there winners and losers among memes. The winners are associated with bits of culture that you like—things that enrich your life and infect your brain so that you want to enrich other lives with it by passing it on. Like your favorite song with an infectious melody accompanying some good lyrics. Perhaps successful memes are more closely linked to brain circuits associated with rewarding strong feelings than successful concepts? Those are more connected with success at making sense out of the world in the thinking realm. (We return to memes in Part IIIc.)

Finally before moving from feelings to joining, consider two things. First, a note regarding the third personality factor (see Part Ia): neuroticism. This is often related to feeling upset, distressed, anxious and the frequency with which this occurs. Second, the camp in affective (emotions/feelings-based) neuroscience occupied by locationists believes that particular emotions (like joy, fear sadness, anger, etc.) are biologically basic, can't be broken into components, and are linked to specific brain structures. Constructionists, in the other camp, see emotions as emerging from more basic components (such as neurons) when different neural systems interact. A similar divide in cognitive (mental process-based) neuroscience is between symbolists and connectionists.

D. Your Brain: Social Behavior/Joining
Explaining Human Success: Two Hypotheses

"Why has our species been so extraordinarily successful?" The short answer involves the fourth (see Part Ia) of our personality factors: agreeableness. Carver and Connor-Smith connect this with "a broad social perspective." The longer answer directs attention to the "social brain hypothesis." Formulated by University of Oxford psychologist Robin Dunbar in the 1980s, it notes a strong correlation among species between brain neocortex and size of the species' typical social group. And that bigger brains favor bigger social groups.

This widely accepted idea has been elaborated on.[1] In doing so many have cited the work of University of St. Andrews neuroscientist Richard Byrne. He pointed to the cognitive challenge early primates (monkeys, baboons, apes, chimpanzees, orangutans, humans, etc.) faced within groups in balancing co-operation and competition. Typically considered in a foraging for food setting, he argued that increasingly complex human social relationships aided their understanding of cause and effect relationships so critical to developing primitive tools and the beginning of our (most would say) wildly successful technology.

In 2012, a team headed by University of Zurich primatologist Carel van Schaik formulated the "cultural intelligence hypothesis."[2] It seemingly bridges the gap between Dunbar and Byrne's ideas. It stresses, as van Schaik puts it, "ecological skills learned through social learning processes, whereas the social brain hypothesis mainly or exclusively focuses on social skills." Given that social learning involves a (systems thinking inspired) learning cycle feedback loop of connecting—deciding—doing—reflecting—connecting, happening within a group, clearly this hypothesis is built on weaving together thinking, joining, and doing behaviors.

Feelings: Love, Hormones, Ethnocentrism

How do feelings—which are closely linked to both joining and doing behavior—fit into all this? Take one of the most powerful:love (as in "generosity, love" one of the Figure #1 meta-theme choices). Consider the first joining moment for most of us, with our mother. Given its role in this, oxytocin has variously been called "the bonding hormone," "the love drug," "the cuddle chemical," etc. Oxytocin, and also vasopressin, are released in humans by the pituitary gland during breastfeeding, childbirth labor, sexual and other activities. Lab studies indicate these chemicals are important to prosocial / joining behaviors—especially as related to pair bonding and reproduction. Closely related in chemical structure, it's been suggested that oxytocin represents an evolutionary long ago mutation of the older vasopressin hormone.

Vasopressin most notably functions in the human body to help it retain water and regulate blood pressure by constricting blood vessels. It often presents itself in two forms (either AVP or LVP) depending on whether it's bonded to amino acids arginine or lysine. Like oxytocin, vasopressin can function as both hormone and neurotransmitter. In this latter role, besides playing a part in social behavior, pair bonding and sexual motivation, it can help women cope with maternal stresses. Given its seeming ability to help cognitive function by aiding memory formation, it has been widely used as a "smart drug."

How oxytocin functions clearly links it to the feelings and emotional "rewards" brain circuits previously discussed. As a team of neuroscientists led by Carsten De Dreu recently reported[3], "...oxytocin's targets are wide-spread and include the hippocampus and the amygdala. Oxytocin interacts with dopaminergic, reward-processing circuits in the nucleus accumbens shell..." Extending the work of a team led by M. Kosfeld, which published a report in *Nature* in 2005 titled "Oxytocin increases trust in humans," DeDreu's team connects this chemical with other feelings and behaviors—not all of them positive.

The abstract of this report summarizes their findings as follows. "Human ethnocentrism—the tendency to view one's group as centrally important and superior to other groups—creates intergroup bias that fuels prejudice, xenophobia, and intergroup violence. Grounded in the idea that ethnocentrism also facilitates within-group trust, cooperation, and coordination, we conjecture that ethnocentrism may be modulated by brain oxytocin, a peptide shown to promote cooperation among in-group members. In double-blind, placebo-controlled designs, males self-administered oxytocin or placebo and privately performed computer-guided tasks to gauge different manifestations of ethnocentric in-group favoritism as well as out-group derogation... Results show that oxytocin creates intergroup bias because oxytocin motivates in-group favoritism and, to a lesser extent, out-group derogation...and suggest that oxytocin has a role in the emergence of intergroup conflict and violence."

This last sentence suggests the dark side of oxytocin is darker than what might be concluded from this research report's title "Oxytocin Promotes Human Ethnocentrism." I think of ethnocentrism in terms of someone using the social standards of his or her own culture or ethnic group as the basis for evaluating the social practices, customs, beliefs, etc. of another culture– and doing so in the belief that those standards are superior to those of other cultures. "The Man Who Would Be King" song I've written for theme #22B "Imperialism" (in part II) is about a British 19th century ethnocentrist who is portrayed as a good guy. This is consistent with the benevolent aspect of paternal "I know what's best for you" that I associate with ethnocentrism. So for me, linking oxytocin with ethnocentrism doesn't have the dark connotations that linking it with promoting "out-group derogation" and "intergroup conflict and violence" has. Nonetheless, accepting this finding provides a neurological basis for what I see as a fundamental divide in human nature.

Explaining Human Nature: Religion, Oxytocin

Simply put, the divide is between competition and co-operation. More completely it's between competitive, greedy behavior that can intolerantly involve inflicting pain on the weak at the bottom of some hierarchy, and the type of co-operative, altruistic, generous behavior seemingly advocated by all of the world's religions (see theme #16: "The Golden Rule/Village Ethic of Mutual Help.")

This key joining behavior divide has meta-themes of "Individualism"[4] and "Collectivism"[5] (Fig. #1) behind it. Other meta-themes important to joining, "Hierarchical Rigidity" and "Egalitarian Progressivism," will be discussed as this section ends. Note it's difficult separating out feelings here! The meta-themes "Intolerant Pain" and "Generosity and Love" are behind many themes with strong feelings behind them. Rather than trying to separate joining from feelings here, after

noting the plan to return to the role of oxytocin in all this later, let's first explore our suspicion that religion bolsters feelings promoting joining behavior, based on the prevalence of "Obey the Golden Rule," "Love Thy Neighbor," "Turn the Other Cheek" and similar advice in the preaching of major religions. Consider both Judeo-Christian and Islamic religious tradition and texts.

One can argue that the Christian *Bible's New Testament* and the words attributed to Jesus generally do promote "Generosity and Love." Even biologist and outspoken author of *The God Delusion*[6] Richard Dawkins once wrote an article entitled "Atheists for Jesus." Such an argument is more difficult to make for the Christian *Bible Old Testament* and Jewish *Torah* on which it's based.

The second chapter of Dawkins' book begins a counterargument as follows: "The God of the *Old Testament* is arguably the most unpleasant character in all fiction: jealous and proud of it; a petty, unjust, unforgiving control-freak; a vindictive, bloodthirsty ethnic cleanser..." He continues in the seventh chapter, devoting a dozen pages to picking apart the *Old Testament* God beginning with the story of Noah. He writes, "The moral of the story of Noah is appalling. God took a dim view of humans, so he (with the exception of one family) drowned the lot of them including children and also, for good measure, the rest of the (presumably blameless) animals as well." He continues, noting, "The ethnic cleansing begun in the time of Moses is brought to bloody fruition in the book of *Joshua*, a text remarkable for the bloodthirsty massacres it records and the xenophobic relish with which it does so."

What makes people do this? From stories in the *Bible* (or verses in the *Qu'ran*, see the next page), much of this ancient killing is done by those carrying out God's (or Allah's) orders. Likewise untold modern deaths can be traced to followers blindly obeying the wishes of an authority they put their faith in. An alternative answer is equally troubling: something in human nature is behind this. While perhaps that something can be connected with oxytocin promoting "in-group favoritism" and "out-group derogation" there are many other genetic, neurological, hormonal, psychological, and cultural factors to consider.

Some of these (like genetic factors) predispose

individuals to certain behaviors. Others help reinforce natural inclinations and trigger actual manifestation of the behavior. Cultural factors, such as people following religious dictates, can turn either natural but unrealized inclinations, or what otherwise might be unconscious acts, into deliberate actions. Sacred text passages like chapter 48, verse 29 of the *Qu'ran* explicitly teach it: "Mohammed is God's apostle. Those who follow him are harsh to the unbelievers but merciful to one another" meaning Intolerant Pain not Generosity and Love!

Before leaving oxytocin behind, consider a feelings—joining topic involving (previously discussed) emotions associated with music. Jaak Panksepp, the man who coined the term affective neuroscience and got the attention of the popular press with experiments designed to study laughter in non-human animals, is the focus of a June 2011 *Psychology Today* article "Why Music Moves Us," by Jeanette Bicknell. Or specifically why certain songs send "chills down your spine".

She writes, the "chills may emerge from brain dynamics associated with the perception of social loss, specifically with separation calls… cries by young animals that inform parents of the whereabouts of offspring that have become lost. The 'coldness' of chills may provide increased motivation for social reunion in the parents." The brain dynamics she refers to include a drop in oxytocin in response to vocal signals (either in distress calls or similar tension-building parts of songs)—an effect documented in the lab for women more than men. Associated with mother's decreased oxytocin level is a decrease in her body temperature—conditions that reunion with the lost baby rectifies.

Oxytocin based explanations of human behavior straddle both sides of the fence in a long-running controversy since this chemical functions as both a hormone and a neurotransmitter. The issue is treatment for those with mental problems. There are two schools of thought: one wanting to correct a chemical hormone imbalance problem, the other looking for faulty neural circuits involved. MIT neuroscientist Kay Tye has been studying one such circuit. Her research[7] may help improve treatment of mental problems involving impaired social interaction and anxiety.

Anxiety, Learning: Imitation vs. Innovation

Tye's research has been with the BLA-vHPC circuit in mice. She found that activating it in the subregion of the amygdala (see Figure #5), using blue light, led to increased anxiety. "Resident-intruder home-cage" testing linked increased anxiety to decreased likelihood of initiating social interaction and increased time self-grooming. Likewise she correlated turning off this circuit with increased social interaction in the form of "sniffing, nuzzling and closely following the novel stranger and less time exploring their own familiar cage"—all indicative of less anxiety.

In contrast to a raw primary emotion like fear, anxiety is more of a mood. It involves conscious processing and information exchange in the brain. As the experiments with mice suggest, anxious individuals are less likely to initiate social interactions, robbing them of problem solving advantages social learning can convey. Where novel circumstances require making decisions, and doing what they are comfortable with isn't an option, they are likely to imitate, not innovate.

Even without anxiety, there is a natural tendency to imitate both physical and social behavior. As Yale's John Bargh puts it, "Imitation fosters a social mindset without the need for providing an explicit road sign that instructs people what to do next."[8] Appreciating this, a starting point for considering one's worldview and behavior is worldview theme #34 "Valuing Traditions and Status Quo." (Note this theme's TFJD code is "2222," each of the four factors a neutral "2.")

It's typically valued by individuals comfortable with their place in the society they grow up in—even those near the bottom of some social order. The latter may be timidly willing to accept the "Hierarchical Rigidity" meta-theme (Figure #1), and its adhering to rules, conforming culturally, and submitting to an authority at the top of a typically centralized power structure organization. If that authority is feared, anxious individuals are more likely to accept inferior, unequal status, conform and be less likely to socially interact in a way that promotes social learning and innovation.

In contrast the "Egalitarian Progressivism" meta-theme is about valuing equality, belief that all human beings should have similar rights, opportunities and privileges, and with progress involving gradual social, political, and economic reform. The worldview theme #35B "Working for Change" is TFJD coded "3333" for being energized on multiple levels—especially doing.

E. Your Brain: Reflexive and Reflective Doing
Movement, Reflexive Doing, Habits, Instinct

I think of extroversion, the fifth personality factor (Part Ia), as built around a strong sense of sociability (joining), and a dominating sense of finding means to act, acting (doing), and moving. Movement is initiated by neural impulses in our brains' motor cortex which travel down through our spinal cords to muscles. The motor cortex sits in the sensing part of our cortex, as does the supplementary motor area (where movements are planned.) A pre-motor cortex at the edge helps prepare for and, both sensorially and spatially, guide movement. An older region, the cerebellum, integrates visual, auditory and other signals it receives from the reticular formation in the (still older) brain stem in helping to co-ordinate movement. The reticular formation, slow to develop in infants, also enables our maintaining attention.

We do things in response to stimuli or when sufficiently motivated. Instinctual behavior represents our pre-programmed response to environmental stimuli. In simple cases, it is genetically determined, hard-wired and independent of previous experience, acquired learning, or memory. Other less reflexive behavior is learned and may require motivation in the form of rewards. As previously mentioned, the neurotransmitter dopamine plays a key role in both brain reward circuits and in motor control function.

Reflexive doing involves behavior that happens in automatic response to environmental stimuli. The conscious mind is unaware of it. In contrast, reflective doing involves conscious deliberation, and thinking. These guide choices and decisions we make—all of which reinforce a sense of free will we employ in running our lives. Many behaviors can be classed as reflexive or reflective .

Sleep fits in the former category, when conscious thinking is turned off—apparently to allow memory consolidation that reinforces and prunes neural connections. We also behave reflexively in response to the extreme fear of emergencies. Then our nervous system turns off conscious thinking in the cerebral cortex and cedes control of our body to a more automatic, primitive unconscious limbic brain. And of course much of what we do in our daily lives is of an automatic/reflexive nature. With such behavior we draw on skills we've mastered unconsciously that become stored in our non-declarative memory as knowledge we have about doing things. Daily habits might go here.

But we must be careful. Perhaps the behaviors we call habits didn't start off as reflexive, they may have only become so after careful reflection and much practice. In "Good Habits, Bad Habits" a June 2014 *Scientific American* article, neuroscientists Ann Graybiel and Kyle Smith identify a "special habits circuit" centered in the basal ganglia. There neural activity associated with behavior that eventually becomes "acting without thinking" habits is encoded in chunks reminiscent of how the brain registers memories. But they also note "when it seems we are acting automatically, part of our brain is dutifully monitoring our behavior." Accordingly they report a region of the neocortex "has to be online for the habit to be enacted" and is under its continual control. Their research is promising. As they put it, "If we can fully understand how habits are made and broken we can better understand our idiosyncratic behaviors and hope to train them." Or get them back under our reflective, conscious control.

Our mental interaction with the environment...
...and making reflexive/reflective distinctions is complicated by poor understanding of consciousness. And by arguments raised by neuroscientists and philosophers who question whether we really possess free will! Certainly instinctual behavior is reflexive—dating from millions of years ago when our ancestors were essentially animals. But at some point in both human evolution and development of infants into children, doing is no longer just reflexive with the dawn of consciousness.

My conception of consciousness begins with equating it with my mind, centering it in my head just behind my eyes, and accepting that "The mind is what the brain does." I'd say consciousness includes possessing sentience or knowing "what it's like" to be someone because you are that someone. From there it extends to include what most of us feel exists inside us: a chief executive in charge of mind and body. This follows from feeling that one's mind gives free will to choose between actions and direct one's future.

We refer to this chief executive when using "I" in saying something like "I did this." With it, we are able to abstractly separate ourselves from the rest of existence. This means we can become a character in stories we tell or mental narratives we construct. The latter can be set in an imagined future, a capability that greatly increases the scope of our planning. Consciousness may unexpectedly emerge when the complexity of brains and the intelligence the neural connection coding embodies reaches a certain level. With this comes a wholistic sense of meaning for what otherwise might be a confusion of existence based on lots of sensory inputs, perceptions, feelings, etc. With this comes the beginning of a worldview.

For me, consciousness is more than awareness: it requires language in some form, some executive brain function, a certain amount of learning ability and technological awareness. The latter needs an ability to think abstractly—being able to conceive of yourself as a system S that operates within a bigger system: the surrounding real environment E. As Julian Jaynes (see Part If) puts it[1], "It is by the generated structure of consciousness that we understand the world." With consciousness comes the realization that the more we learn about our environment, the more feedback we get by interacting with it, the greater will be our capability to change it and make it more to our liking.

This brings us to the first pair of meta- themes (Figure #1, last row) for use in gauging doing aspects of worldview themes: the extent to which they are human system S centered vs. environment E nature centered. In assigning scores themes involving mostly mental, human mind centered activity score 1, whereas those that involve the most interaction with surrounding environment score 3. For example, the right hand column of Figure #2 contains three themes where not only T is the same (=3), but F values (=1) and J values (=1) are also the same. Those themes are #18B Dispassionate, #30 Intellectual Freedom, and #46A Technological Fix Mentality. Note these three differ in doing scores. We say the Tech Fix theme involves more doing than Intellectual Freedom, which had more than Dispassionate.

Of the eighty-one worldview themes, we noted #35B Working for Change (TFJD coded "3333") as being most energized on multiple levels. The feelings behind the doing here include both being dissatisfied with how some aspect of the world is, and being strongly motivated to change it. I'd say this first involves feeling what Paul Hawken (in

his book's title) called "blessed unrest" and then moving to summoning the "courage to change the things I can…" as "The Serenity Prayer" puts it.[2]

Its least energized opposite is TFJD coded "1111": #7A Mysticism. The state referred to is of perfect contentment—something most of us last experienced before we left our mother's womb! A state where our feeling of belonging to environment E is so complete, sense of difference or alienation so absent, that we don't separate our own system S from E. We have no feeling of the need to "do" or change something. Technological readiness /awareness is absent in this cosmic consciousness type state—as is self consciousness.

Absent too is conscious deliberation—something that many connect with free will. Some like author and neuroscientist Sam Harris argue we delude ourselves into thinking we have free will and are really "biochemical puppets." Certainly one can cite numerous examples of people behaving like that (i.e. after taking drugs that make them behave like robots or become pathological gamblers, or how a developing brain tumor triggers an interest in child pornography, etc.). But after recognizing times when we behave reflexively and are slaves to biochemistry, one can make still make a strong free will argument.

Nobel Laureate Francis Crick has suggested our sense of free will is centered in the anterior cingulate cortex (Figure #6). This area seems specialized to look for things that are wrong. It responds to stimuli that signal conflict and monitors for conflicts that actually or potentially cause errors. Brain scans (fMRI) reveal that it lights up when we exercise volition or consciously choose a particular action.

Figure #6

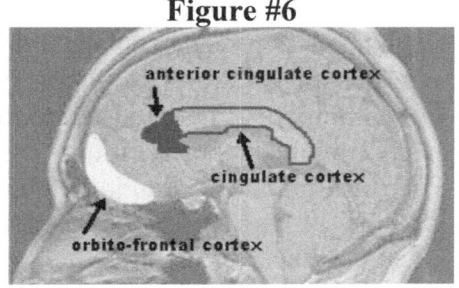

Deciding to Act or Not Act, Depression, Ethics

The orbito-frontal cortex is also believed to play an important role in decision-making with respect to assessing emotionally based urges as to potential rewards/punishments and helping us defer instant gratification in favor of long-term advantage. Its exceptional activity during (brain scans of) high energy good times, and relative inactivity during depression, connects it with "doing" or a "not doing" depressed state. The latter state can involve the anterior cingulate cortex latching onto sad feelings associated with "what's wrong." Nerve fibers that connect these areas, outer neocortex, and inner limbic region provide a link to the negative emotions often associated with the amygdala.

Recent University of British Columbia research[3] also links a small, evolutionarily ancient brain area, the lateral habenula, to decision-making. This area, tied to depression and avoidance behavior, receives input from the nucleus accubens, thalamus, hypothalamus, and hippocampus. Its output inhibits dopamine neurons in the substantia nigra.

Depression is linked to levels of three neuro-transmitters: serotonin, dopamine, and norepinephrine. Depression and low levels of serotonin, popularly associated with upbeat feelings, have long been treated with Prozac. Serotonin abnormalities may also be behind obsessive compulsive disorder (OCD). This involves irrationally repetitively doing tasks like washing hands, chewing food rituals, hoarding, etc.

We're noted dopamine's role in the reward brain circuit involving the nucleus accumbens, and connected it with addiction (a person's inability to stop doing certain things.) On the plus side: dopamine promotes alertness, whereas chemically related norepinephrine helps us maintain concentration. Like oxytocin, it is also a hormone. As a neurotransmitter, emotionally charged events trigger its release, and, with protein synthesis in the amygdala, long-term memory formation.

As noted, general memory formation typically involves large numbers of neurons acting together. A first step involves potentiation, in which neurons fire together and, aided by neurotransmitter glutamate, forge a bond that makes them more likely to fire together again and again. In recent years it has become apparent that memory and concept formation involve neural networks and hierarchical organization. And that a particular type of neuron is specialized for promoting learning by imitation: the mirror neuron. Discovered in 1996 in pre-motor regions of mon-

key brains, they encode the intentions of others. Finding them, and realizing the key role they've played in the evolution of communicative skills, led some neuroscientists to elevate the importance of brain motor system regions.

Others, while intrigued by mirror neurons, play down correlating of specific brain locations and structures with particular functions (often based on fMRI imaging). Many feel new discoveries will show overlapping activity at various locations that drive brain function. Rather than location, they focus on connections via neural network wiring.

Consider the Figure #1 last pair of meta-themes, which represent the ends of a continuum. At one extreme is doing things seemingly without concern for constraints or limits; at the other, being very aware of limitations and thus carefully weighing actions, based on right/wrong concepts. In short, this meta-theme involves ethical considerations that involve thinking before acting ("not doing.") Theme #42 Ethical Orientation falls into this category. I contrast it with other themes that also involve limiting or restraining actions, but involve less thinking: #14A Moralistic God, #17B Gratitude & Forgiveness, and #29A The Self Restrained Person. Here feelings and joining are factors behind the extent to which doing happens.

Our primitive hunter ancestors had an ethical existence based on "kill or be killed." Certainly this fostered communication, co-operation, social learning, and posed technological problem solving challenges. In an April 2014 *Scientific American* article, Kate Wong praises a volcanic glass shard cutting tip made by humans 279,000 years ago for "its conceptualization, manufacture and use."

Did they possess consciousness? Thought of as an emergent property of a complex system, consciousness may require a meta system transition that either happens or doesn't? Or perhaps there are degrees of consciousness? Connectionalists, who model mental processes with interconnected networks of simpler units (neurons) may prefer the former; symbolists (or computationalists), who understand mental activity with symbols, structures (based on underlying brain structure) and syntax rules for manipulating them, may prefer the latter. Even though their minds most probably did not work like modern minds, it nonetheless seems safe to conceive of these primitive early humans as thinking, feeling, joining and doing creatures!

F. Your Brain: When Muses Lived Inside!

In her 1940 book *Mythology*, Edith Hamilton wrote, "The very earliest musicians were the gods." She recounts how Athena invented the flute, how Apollo used the lyre to make captivating melodies, and how Zeus and Mnemosynes (words: memory and memes) had daughters who were Muses (words: music and museum). Of them Hesiod, 8th century BCE author of *Theogony*, wrote, "They are all of one mind, their hearts are set upon song and their spirit is free from care. He is happy whom the Muses love." These goddesses / water nymphs inspired him.

What was the pre-historic mind like? "When the world was young and people had a connection with the earth," Hamilton writes, "little distinction had as yet been made between the real and the unreal. The imagination was vividly alive and not checked by the reason, so that anyone in the woods might see through the trees a fleeing nymph…" Princeton professor, and author of the 1976 book *The Origin of Consciousness in the Breakdown of the Bicameral Mind*, Julian Jaynes took issue with some of this. "Bicameral men did not imagine," he wrote, "they experienced." He warns readers of the first pages of Hesiod's classic to "realize that all of it was probably seen and heard in hallucination, just as can happen today in schizophrenia or under certain drugs."

Jaynes asserts that a bicameral mentality existed before modern consciousness fully emerged. Those possessing it could not introspect and heard voices just as some schizophrenics do today. The voices told them what to do given new circumstances or times of stress. These voices, believed to be voices of gods, had their origin in the voices of parents, long dead relatives, leaders, kings, or other authority figures. Jaynes suggested that all humans once possessed this right brain mentality. Only with developing language did the left brain cerebral cortex gradually became specialized. Supposedly the transition to modern consciousness was mostly complete by 1000 BCE or so.

The earliest epic poems from this era were not originally written down, they were sung. Many of the authors were blind. The *Illiad* and the *Odyssey* say the Muses inspired these bards. Hesiod wrote the Muses came to him while he was alone, tending his sheep and "breathed into me a divine voice to celebrate things that shall be." Hesiod's con-

sciousness may have been modern, given Gisela Richter[1] describing him as the first poet who "regards himself as a topic, an individual with a distinctive role to play." As Jaynes documents, even modern humans to some degree still possess remnants of this ancient mentality, often manifesting itself when voices are heard or hallucinations experienced during times of stress or loneliness.

Centuries after Hesiod, the Muses continued to inspire people. Plato (in *Ion* sec 534) wrote "All good poets, epic as well as lyric, composed their beautiful poems not by art, but because they are inspired and possessed…there is no invention in him until he has been inspired and is out of his senses and the mind is no longer in him." Jaynes argues that by then fully bicameral minds were rare, so crazy people (like Plato notes) stood out.

Jaynes' critics had trouble conceiving of how human consciousness could so fundamentally change over such an evolutionary short time (roughly spanning the 2000 to 1000 BCE era.) Many argued from a genetic change preserved by natural selection viewpoint. While suggesting mechanisms to speed up the process—such as parents killing children who didn't fit in, society killing witches or those deemed crazy, etc— Jaynes also stressed the brain's plasticity.

Decades later, after lots of studies—including one documenting how blind people use the right visual cortex to instead understand rapid speech, facilitated by a right brain "specialized for processing low frequency information, which is typical of speech"—his neural plasticity argument looks stronger. Brain configuration and operation aren't dictated by rigid genetic blueprint says MIT neuroscientist Marina Bedny. "It's a self-building tool-kit. The building process is profoundly influenced by experiences you have during your development."[2] The process is a connecting the neurons one. As neuroscientists Yuste and Church write[3], "One intriguing theory postulates that the many neurons involved in the activity of a circuit develop particular sequences of firing known as attractors that may represent emergent brain states—a thought, a memory or a decision …"

While I like how consciousness works explanations that employ modern chaos theory, where ancients used Muses, I confess that I too invoked them for inspiration as I wrote songs for Part II.

Worldview Theme #1A: Humbly Unsure

Worldview Theme Summary: **for more:** www.projectworldview.org/wvtheme1.htm

When it comes to knowing what is right, what is best, what is the true nature of things, or having answers to life's important questions, I feel rather inadequate. While others most assuredly promote their beliefs with black and white certainty, I am silent and see shades of gray. I can't forget the complexity of the world or the smallness and ignorance of any one person. I'm not sure enough of anything to lay it on everyone else. I trust not in high principles, but in small experiences.

SONG

"The Doubt" by Stephen P. Cook
to be sung to the tune of "The Weight" by Berry, Stipe, Buck, Mill / The Band

Made it here Sunday morning[1]
But a war rages inside
To many questions I've no answers
And my beliefs often collide
Oh my God can you show me
Where I can find certainty[2]?
He looked at me and held my hand
And said "Seek humility!"[3]

Honk if you love Jesus[4]
Don't if you're unsure[5]
Honk if you love Jesus
Oh, Oh, Oh
I've got the doubt back in me

Humble Mother Teresa[6]
Helped the poor for seventy years
A candidate for sainthood
Her soul was full of fears
Jesus God Mary where are you
Inside I feel a lack there of
She touched me and whispered
"Find me in your love"

Honk if you love Jesus
Don't if you're unsure
Honk if you love Jesus
Oh, Oh, Oh
I've got the doubt back in me

I seek love[7] and belonging
To be part of a greater whole
I'm a small imperfect creature[8]
But have trouble playing that role
How can I find peace
Lose myself, become truly free?
From within comes an answer:
Don't preach, don't judge, just be

Honk if you love Jesus
Don't if you're unsure
Honk if you love Jesus
Oh, Oh, Oh
I've got the doubt back in me[9]

SONG—NOTES / COMMENTS   (this song is part of the author's personal story)

1—This song is dedicated to seekers who typically spend Sunday mornings in church, especially to children in Sunday school—which the author recalls regularly attending (from age three) and often being confused!

2—Think certainty is to be found in science and math? Given physicists' uncertainty principle, how chaos theory limits predictions, inherent uncertainty in measurement, and Gödel's theorem from math, think again!

3—All of us are born demanding attention and being admonished with commands in the form of black and white simple certainties: "Do this…Don't do that…!" As we grow up we slowly realize that everything does not revolve around us: we are a small part of a complex whole, one depicted with many shades of gray!

4—One of the first songs the author sang, proclaims, "Jesus loves me this I know, for the Bible tells me so!" This song's "Jesus" need not refer to a manifestation of God. Consider a heart metaphor: If "Jesus" represents the best inside every heart, "Satan" is the worst. (Conrad's *The Heart of Darkness*, and Emerson's "common heart" in "The Over-Soul" can be viewed similarly.)

5—With apologies to a Unitarian Universalist (UU) bumper sticker proclaiming: "Honk if You are Not Sure!"

6—Mother Teresa (1910-1997) experienced a "dark night of the soul" which lasted for many years.

7—"Real love is caring about the happiness of another person without any thought of what we might get for ourselves." Greg Baer

8—One might even say, "To be human, is to be imperfect!"   9—This song metaphorically figures in this book's ending.

Comment: This theme's open-minded, non-judgmental, tentative mindset girds you against mental stress that others might suffer from contradictory beliefs they hold or beliefs which might otherwise threaten their worldview. This striving for internal consistency is behind the discomfort cognitive dissonance can produce.

Worldview Theme—TFJD CODE: 2211 **VI=16** **Original Tune Era:** 1960s   **RS Top 500 List:** Yes

Worldview Theme #1B: Skepticism

Worldview Theme Summary:　　　　　　　for more: : www.projectworldview.org/wvtheme1.htm

I believe that knowledge is generally accompanied by some degree of uncertainty and doubt. I like where doubting can lead: to questioning, debating, reconsidering, testing, new knowledge, and eventually to the truth. I am suspicious of faith-based beliefs. In deciding what to believe, I prefer reason and critical thinking to emotion and wishful thinking. In putting down "true believers" and treating them with contempt I lack humility and can be arrogant.

SONG

"The House of Skepticism" by Stephen P. Cook

to be sung to the tune of "The House of the Rising Sun" traditional, Alan Price / The Animals

There is a part of my worldview
I call it skepticism
If you wanna meet this part of me
Just tell me 'Christ Has Risen'[1]

I've been trained in science[2]
Its methods fill my head
But it's common sense that tells me:
When you're dead, you're dead

I like reproducible results[3]
Without them I will doubt
So the faith-based claims you make my friend
For me don't have much clout

Doubting leads to questioning
Questioning to debate
But until we leave our biases behind
Finding the truth must wait

Hypotheses should be tested
Predictions verified
I'll put my faith in these my friend
Non-testable ones I'll deride

I don't much care for dogma[4]
Or conflict with reason and fact
So if you cite this authority my friend
I won't let you relax

There is a part of my worldview
I call it skepticism
If yours is built on faith alone
Please escape that prison

SONG—NOTES / COMMENTS

1—While this refers to a key belief of the Christian religion, the theme of the resurrection of the dead is common throughout many religions, including Christian, Islamic, Jewish, and Zoroastrian. Indeed, believing in a future time when the dead will be brought back to life—and we will be reunited with deceased loved ones—provides an important source of hope for faithful believers throughout the world.

2— Science is difficult to define. Here's one definition: a methodical effort, based on learning from feedback as one observes and probes, to provide a map or conceptual framework for understanding reality

3—Reproducible results are obtained by careful adherence to, and documentation of, experimental or other procedures so others can repeat the work and verify it. Obtaining them is a goal of scientific investigation.

4—Dogma refers to beliefs that are firmly held based on the authority of others, but are actually incompatible with existing facts or based on faulty premises or reasoning. For the record, the author categorically denies he knowingly promotes dogma. That, he believes, has led to much catastrophe. While he will doggedly defend the right of others to dispense dogma, and has no doubt they honestly believe it will catalyze something worth catalyzing, dog gone it, he refuses to do so! …So OK, say it, "What's the matter? Cat got your tongue?" (Something to ponder while in a chemistry lab in search of reproducible results: if cations migrate to negative electrodes, where do dog ions go? Working hypothesis: to the dog house?)

Comment: In an emotionally immature pre-emptive response you can protect yourself from attacks on your own lack of understanding or accomplishment by skeptically attacking what others have achieved. Emotionally arming yourself like this makes you emotionally unavailable for connecting with others regarding whatever the skepticism is directed against and is unhealthy. On the other hand if the skepticism is directed toward something which the skeptic has fully investigated, understands and feels threatened by (even in a cognitive dissonance sense—see theme #1A) the skeptical response is a protective, healthy one.

Worldview Theme—TFJD CODE: 3312 **VI=18 Original Tune Era:** 1960s　　**RS Top 500 List:** Yes

Worldview Theme #2A: The True Believer

Worldview Theme Summary: for more: www.projectworldview.org/wvtheme2.htm

My faith in what I believe is free from doubt. I understand what it is to be a Believer. I like to think of myself as devoted to noble causes. I too can overcome obstacles through courage, persistence, and Shining Purity. I define who I am, magnify my identity, and recognize my enemies through my crusades. (Note: True believers have an "excess of certitude.")

SONG
"Something I Truly Believe" by Stephen P. Cook
to be sung to the tune of "Something" by George Harrison / The Beatles

Somehow some words inspire me
In a dark moment like no other
Somehow they energize and lift me
I'll follow where they lead
I'll suffer, I will bleed

Something I truly believe
Now fills my heart[1] like no other
Something in this cause I'd die for[2]
Away from this I won't bend
Put objections away my friend

I'm telling you my faith[3] is strong
That I belong, I belong[4]
This logic[5] you've been sold
Leaves me cold, leaves me cold

Somewhere this righteous path heads
Through darkness and I think toward home[6]
Somewhere the guiding light leads
Away from that I'm not bound
I'm not seeking[7], I have found

Each day my commitment grows
That I know, that I know
In this battle we'll win out
Have no doubt, have no doubt

Someday we'll have set things right[8]
That feeling is what keeps me going
Someday we'll bask in the sun's light[9]
I can feel it now my friend
We'll triumph in the end!

SONG—NOTES / COMMENTS

1—"This fills my heart!" really mean something like "I feel this very deeply!" And the simple notion that thinking is done by the brain and feelings are from the heart is, of course, wrong! While the frontal lobes of the brain are where thinking, conceptualizing and planning are centered, the brain's limbic system and cortex, and their nervous system/neurotransmitter (brain chemical) connections throughout the body all have a role in emotions. Humans are supposedly rational creatures, but few doubt emotion often trumps reason!

2—Hundreds of millions of people have fought and died over differences in what they believe!

3—Faith refers to firm belief with complete confidence and trust in something for which there is no proof.

4— A feeling of belonging is critical to our devotion to some cause. Being part of a crowd of others who believe what we believe (a "band of brothers") gives us confidence. Given all the wars fought over beliefs, strength in numbers has more than psychological value: one's very survival can depend on it!

5— Logically justifying beliefs that depend on many facts (indisputably true information) involves 1) establishing and scrutinizing the standards or criteria by which the statement is true, 2) having evidence or data to support the above conclusion, and 3) evaluating the certainty with which the belief is established.

6—For some, dying may be a way of coming full circle or coming home.

7—Seekers vs. Believers–in *The Seekers* Daniel Boorstin writes, "We are all Seekers. We all want to know why. Man is the asking animal. And while the finding, the belief that we have found the Answer can separate us and make us forget our humanity, it is the seeking that continues to bring us together..."

8—"Set things right" = "the way things oughta be" —these are words used to identify what we value.

9—The reward envisioned varies. For the 9/11 perpetrators, it was those virgins they'd find in Heaven!

Comment: this theme has value as emotional armor. Losing yourself in idealistically fighting for a noble cause is a way to put off reckoning with unpleasant grim realities about yourself and your situation. Depending upon the fights you engage in (if any) and the extent to which they are emotionally charged, as a true believer you potentially risk suffering disappointments, personal attacks, or outright assault by those trying to shake your worldview / emotionally disarm you. This can result in your acquiring emotional baggage. More emotionally positive: what you strongly believe can give wonderful purpose and meaning to your life.

Worldview Theme—TFJD CODE: 1331 **VI=243** **Original Tune Era:** 1970s   **RS Top 500 List:** Yes

Worldview Theme #2B: I Know What's Best for You

Worldview Theme Summary: for more: www.projectworldview.org/wvtheme2.htm

I feel I have found "the answer" (what to believe, how to behave, the best way to do something, etc.) I feel obligated to share what I've found with you, so you can benefit. As I do this, please bear with me if it seems my evangelizing, persuading, etc. disrespects or devalues your beliefs, behaviors, or feelings—I have your best interests in mind.

SONG
"She Knows Best" by Stephen P. Cook
to be sung to the tune of "The Streets of Laredo" a traditional American cowboy ballad

As I walk down
The streets of Socorro[1]
And around the track
In Socorro today
Nearby a poor woman
Carries much baggage[2]
And a chip on her shoulder[3]
That won't go away

Hear this, she tells me:
I know what's best
The best for you
As we journey through life
She's smarter, works harder
Hard-headed, not soft spoken
My way or the highway
Says this woman my wife

Respect me, I beg her
Please don't devalue
My experience, my wisdom
My asking why
With mighty miss full bright[4]
I'm not even half right
Helpful words I welcome
To disdain say goodbye[5]

She's not a bad person
I fear I still love her
Love that is reckless
Unwise it must die
Please mighty miss full bright
Just run your own life
I'll resume running mine
With a painful goodbye

SONG—NOTES / COMMENTS   (this song is part of the author's personal story)

1—This refers to Socorro, New Mexico. This is an autobiographical song relating to the 2012—2013 period in the author's life. He came up with many song lyrics while running around the track there at Clarke Field.

2—According to the *Wikipedia* entry for "emotional baggage": "As a metaphorical image, it is that of carrying all the disappointments, wrongs, and trauma of the past around with one in a heavy load."

3—According to the *Wikipedia* entry for "chip on shoulder," this refers to holding a grudge or grievance that readily provokes disputation.

4—Reportedly when USA President Lyndon B. Johnson didn't like the position of the distinguished senator from Arkansas, and frequent critic of administration Vietnam War policy, William J. Fulbright, Johnson would refer to the senator as "half bright." In another context, the senator's name became connected with academic foreign exchanges and "Fulbright Scholars."

5—Sometimes other people who seem to feel "I know what's best for you!" really do have your best interests in mind and are honestly trying to help you. But given the real world of aggressive sales people, hidden persuaders, and everyone seemingly looking out for his or her own self-interest, it could be that those helpful, other-oriented folks freely offering their advice are in the minority compared to the more obnoxious ones. If one of them gives you an unsolicited phone call, you can simply hang up. Generalizing this strategy, seems that simply getting away from such folks is a good plan!

Comment: this theme can have value as emotional armor. From an emotionally immature "the best defense is a good offense" perspective, people who have doubts about their own beliefs and the path in life they've chosen can deflect others from probing this shaky foundation by being strong advocates. And wanting to take charge and steer someone else in a particular direction can help overcome feelings of being powerless in changing the reality of their own life. More emotionally positive: if you're a parent—or more generally someone who takes a genuine abiding interest in helping someone you care about—taking a tough love approach (see theme #39A) can ultimately be rewarding. Of course accepting the challenge to help your child or someone else, and embracing "I know what's best for you," can also fail miserably and cause pain.

Worldview Theme—TFJD CODE: 2312 **VI**=72 **Original Tune Era:** 1800s   **RS Top 500 List:** No

Worldview Theme #3: Focused Vision

Worldview Theme Summary: for more: www.projectworldview.org/wvtheme3.htm

I am focused on the here and now—and me in particular: my immediate personal concerns and crises. After that, my surroundings—home, workplace, etc—and people important to me—family, friends, loved ones, those with authority over me, those whom I have authority over, etc—get my attention. I am typically busy and focused on putting things in order or finishing a task. Often I pay more attention to lower level, immediate details rather than to higher level (or long term) relationships or goals. (Note: While specifics vary, generally there's little concern for the wider world, the past or future. Extreme cases can involve obsession with personal problems, pain and suffering, with a person or pet, with some thing or some pursuit—including job, hobby, avocation, etc—or with getting details right (perfectionism)).

SONG
"If I Grieve Completely" by Stephen P. Cook
to be sung to the tune of "She Smiled Sweetly" by Mick Jagger and Keith Richards / The Rolling Stones

Why do these tears fill my eyes again?[1]
There's pain, it hurts, there's a hole in my life
You were my best friend and also my wife

If I grieve completely
Pain and suffer discreetly
Let go bittersweetly
My life can go on

How to find closure, bring an end?
Wall off the pain, compartmentalize[2]
Respect this wall, I won't hear the cries

Wall off hurt completely
Confine thoughts concretely
Live humbly and meekly
My life can go on

Beyond surviving to thriving?
Prepare the soil, focus on here and now
Plant tasks in a list and through it I'll plow[3]

Remove anxiety completely
Order my mind uniquely
Bask in the sun so sweetly
My life will go on
On and on and on
My life will go on

SONG—NOTES / COMMENTS   (this song is part of the author's personal story)

1—This is an autobiographical song relating to the summer/fall 2013 period in the author's life.

2—This is perhaps the emotional equivalent of a general problem solving strategy: if facing the big overriding problem is simply a too difficult and intimidating task, then an oft employed way to proceed is to break it, into several smaller more manageable problems, and work on them one at a time.

3—Concentrating on small, mundane tasks or generally losing oneself in work can be a welcome alternative to thinking about bigger personal problems or big picture type concerns. A danger associated with narrowing one's viewpoint is becoming out of touch with the reality of a situation. One way of bumbling into that would be adopting childish wishing thinking in which ignoring problems seemingly makes them go away. This simplistic, fairy tale, magical, childhood fantasy way of dealing with problems is to be contrasted with the planning/hard work/needing to perform repeated trials before success situation that adults solving real problems more typically are faced with. Appreciating all that, one should nonetheless realize there can be times when keeping emotions under control requires purposely narrowing one's focus.

Comment: this theme has value as emotional armor. The song gets at how compartmentalizing can shield you from pain (walling it off!). This is part of a maladaptive coping mechanism called dissociation. It may work in the short run, but won't get at root causes or help you break painful associations. More emotionally positive: "focused attention" meditation provides an extreme application of one aspect of this theme. The cover of the November, 2014 issue of *Scientific American* advertises that "the neuroscience of meditation" shows that such practice "changes the brain, boosting focus and easing stress."

Worldview Theme—TFJD CODE: 2223 **VI=** 96 **Original Tune Era:** 1960s   **RS Top 500 List:** No

Worldview Theme #4: Global Vision

Worldview Theme Summary: **for more**: www.projectworldview.org/wvtheme4.htm

In contrast to narrow worldviews—ones tightly confined to the center of a space vs. time plot and closed to much—my worldview extends in space and time and can be broadly inclusive. It has room for statements like "Your body contains atoms once inside ancient stars." I appreciate cosmic distances, geologic time, evolution, natural cycles and the connectedness of things. I know that, increasingly, global interdependencies link me to people and events in remote places that affect living things and the environment. I realize that the past can provide insights into dealing with today's problems, and that the future consequences of what we do must be considered before we act. Sometimes, in focusing on higher level (or long term) relationships or goals, I miss lower level details.

SONG

"Evolution Row" by Stephen P. Cook

to be sung to the tune of "Desolation Row" by Bob Dylan

I like to start with the big bang[1]
And chronicle a great story
The billons of years it took to make
Minds to contemplate the glory

Of the connectedness of it all
And struggle to figure it out
Piecing together a puzzle
So it fits without any doubt

Consider how one man suffered
In his great quest to know
A human highlights film we watch
Here on evolution row.

His telescope revealed its wonders
But churchmen refused to look
The foundations of a worldview
His discoveries badly shook

He said Earth moved round the Sun
Churchmen said it stayed put
With God their side had power
They could turn people to soot

They tried to silence him
But it moves said Galileo
He ended up in prison
Here on evolution row

If curiosity lets you go there
I know you'll eventually see
The universe is awesome
As is how it came to be

Your body contains atoms
Once inside ancient stars
And rocks now found on Earth
Once rested peacefully on Mars

Slow change or God's instant creation
The fittest survive, what do we know?
That scientists side with Darwin
Here on evolution row

You say God provides life's vital spark
I speak of reduction oxidation potential[2]
I cite electronegativity[3] differences
You're positive about God and reverential

You say mindless random process
Can't gift us with the human eye
From the foot to top of mount improbable[4]
God's the explanation that can fly

But slowly climbing the gentle slope
Accumulating change started long ago
And we value geologic time
Here on evolution row

SONG—NOTES / COMMENTS

1—Theory that the observable universe began with everything in an incredibly compact, hot, dense state, after which an event (the Big Bang) occurred that began the universe's currently observed expansion.

2, 3—These terms relate to atoms losing or gaining electrons and the attraction an atom has for an electron.

4—*Climbing Mount Improbable* is the title of a book about evolution by biologist Richard Dawkins.

Comment: Carver and Connor-Smith (see Part Ia note) link "breadth of perspective" with personality factors of agreeableness and conscientiousness, and suggest the latter often implies "broad time perspective."

Worldview Theme—TFJD CODE: 3131   **VI**= 3   **Original Tune Era:** 1960s   **RS Top 500 List:** Yes

Worldview Theme 5A: Scientific Materialism

Worldview Theme Summary:　　　　　　　　**for more:** www.projectworldview.org/wvtheme5.htm

I believe that knowledge based on something other than observation and reason is invalid, and that it's not necessary to postulate that the universe, its life/humans had a Creator. Their existence can be explained by forces acting on matter and random chance. So the universe has no purpose or notion of good and evil, other than the meaning and value that we give it. Life involves only physical and chemical processes, not some vital spirit. Some day scientists will create it in the lab.

SONG

"Observe and Reason With Me" by Stephen P. Cook
to be sung to the tune of "Dream a Little Dream of Me" by Brown, Sutton, Bennett / The Mamas and Papas

Night time stars offer some clue
Day time sky is beautifully blue
In seeking knowledge of whatever you see
Observe and reason with me

Hot gas and nuclear fusion[1]
Makes stars shine—that's science's conclusion
And Rayleigh scattering[2] I'm telling you
Explains why the sky is blue!

To understand what Earth's about, dear
Take geologic time[3]
Mindless forces, not God's hand, steer
Continents in their prime-iimmee!

Say goodbye to superstition
And kiss off your own intuition[4]
And from huckster quacks[5] please flee
Observe and reason with me

To understand what life's about, dear
Embrace DNA[6]
Mindless forces[7], not God's hand[8] steer
Molecules at play--aaaaaaaaaaaaaaaaa!

Say goodbye to God delusion[9]
Kiss off this childish confusion
And from mystic quacks[10] please flee
Observe and reason with me[11]

SONG—NOTES / COMMENTS

1—Inside stars, where temperatures reach many millions of degrees and pressure is staggering, bare hydrogen nuclei are squeezed together to form helium in nuclear fusion reactions which liberate energy.

2—A physical law by which shorter wavelength blue light is scattered more than longer wavelength red.

3 — The Earth is 4.5 billion years old. Around a dozen large tectonic plates (some carrying continents) move relative to each other on its surface. Except during earthquakes when they may lurch forward suddenly, they move at about the same rate your fingernails grow: about one inch per year. So it takes millions of years for this movement to produce noticeable changes.

4— Intuition can be described as immediate insight that occurs without conscious awareness. Some think of it as a mystical process; others see it as a response to very subtle cues and stimuli received unconsciously.

5—Huckster quacks: those peddling pseudoscience—something that seemingly has a scientific basis, but closer examiniation shows does not—and making money from it. With money at stake, data contradicting what they're selling is often ignored.

6— DNA or deoxyribonucleic acid, the gene bearing double helix molecule, is the primary hereditary molecule. It's made up of millions or billions of pairs of linked subunits (called nucleotides) that, along the length of the molecule, can be specified using letters (only possible designations of each individual link: AT, TA, CG, GC) in composing a long genetic code sequence.

7— Forces are pushes or pulls (repulsion or attraction) of physical/chemical origin that matter experiences due to its proximity to other matter. The strength of these forces depend on different variables and can be computed by using the relevant equations.

8— God's hand is a metaphor (vitalist/spiritual view) along with Him providing vital spark or breathing life into inanimate matter.

9—*The God Delusion* is the title of a book by biologist and atheist Richard Dawkins.

10—Skeptics dismiss New Age mystic efforts to connect quantum physics with human consciousness, etc, and see those folks as urging others to believe in magic. (Note: the efforts of respected physicists like Roger Penrose are not so easily dismissed!)

11—Building the scientific conceptual framework by which our species collectively understands the universe, and our place in it, is perhaps the ultimate in learning from feedback exploration. Where will it lead? Perhaps, in the words of T.S. Eliot, "the end of all our exploring will be to arrive where we started and know the place for the first time."

Comment: Unless it is studying them, science generally seeks to separate itself from emotions. Scientists taking data or evaluating hypotheses are taught to behave like machines and leave any (sometimes emotionally based) biases behind. Anything in a paper submitted to a leading scientific journal that implies you reject this theme #5A will generally bring rejection. Thus many scientists are faced with separating (or reconciling) their cold scientist side from (or with) their warm, emotional, spiritual side. This can be a challenge!

Worldview Theme—TFJD CODE: 3121　VI=2　Original Tune Era: 1960s　　**RS Top 500 List:** No

Worldview Theme #5B: Vitalism
Worldview Theme Summary: **for more:** www.projectworldview.org/wvtheme5.htm
I believe living things are holistically endowed with something special, which can be variously referred to as spirit, life force, soul, organizing principle, etc. Life is something more than the sum of its parts—not something scientists will create in the lab. (Note: In China the life force is linked with ch'i (Qi), in India with prana or kundalini. Most religions involve belief in spiritual beings: in living things with souls, disembodied spirits, ghosts, angels, that natural objects are conscious (animism), etc.

SONG
"I'm Not Alone" by Stephen P. Cook
to be sung to the tune of "With God on Our Side" by Bob Dylan

You say life's no mystery: it's proteins and DNA
And there's no Creator, just random forces at play
Life has no purpose[1], I know you hypothesize
And if God is out there, why does He hide?

How life did begin[2] —your theories can't explain
Nor complex living structures, evolution it strains[3]
And what is consciousness[4]? You haven't a clue
You miss what holds it together: God is the glue.

Your mechanistic atheism—makes me see red
I will pray for your soul before going to bed
To find meaning in emptiness, surely you've tried
But I'm not alone: with the Holy Spirit inside

In India it's called prana, in China it's ch'i[5]
Whatever you call it, this energy's in me
My soul and astral body[6], my spirit is alive
I'm not alone: with God's[7] spark I thrive

Without vital life force my body won't tread
When it gives up the ghost, then it'll be dead
But my spirit will soar up into the sky
Merging with God, tears of joy it will cry[8]

SONG—NOTES / COMMENTS
1—The term associated with belief in design or purpose inherent in everything, and that events unfold toward some divinely specified ultimate end or to fulfill some purpose, is called teleology.
2—There is general agreement among scientists that life began on Earth around 3.8 billion years ago.
3—Seemingly the classic evolutionary natural selection mechanism needs help from complexity theory, epigenetic inheritance, and perhaps quantum mechanics.
4—Consciousness has many definitions: 1) as a process not a thing, traditionally thought to reside in the soul and identified with self awareness, 2) an inward sensibility or knowledge of one's own existence, sensations, thoughts, etc–and comprising the sum total of mental processes occurring at any moment, 3) the non-algorithmic, judgment-forming ability to separate truth from falsity, beauty from ugliness, etc, 4) what merely passively accompanies a sufficiently elaborate control system (based on algorithms)–but doesn't do anything, 5) self knowledge (including the ability to recognize one's self in a mirror), 6) sentience (knowing "what is it like" to be someone), and 7) others based on information, quantum physics processes, etc.
5— Ch'i (or Qi)–an ancient term from China referring to the vital breath or energy that animates the Cosmos. The goal of acupuncture is to stimulate the flow of ch'i through the human body.
6—Astral body refers to a duplicate of a person's physical body, but one that is nonphysical in nature. It is what supposedly leaves the body in out of body experiences.
7—See note 8 for the previous theme (#5A).
8—This refers to the ecstasy of mystical experience some have described.

Comment: this theme has value as emotional armor. Armed with a belief that souls leave the body upon death and (even more unusually) in ghosts, both of which suggest that part of us can survive death, your fear of death perhaps lessens. Likewise the pain of losing loved ones to death can be lessened if you believe their spirits are alive and nearby (or even in some distant Heaven where you can someday be reunited.) Likewise, if you believe you've got a "guardian angel" looking out for you, may feel better protected against unknown bad things that might befall you.

Worldview Theme—TFJD CODE: 1131 **VI=27 Original Tune Era:** 1960s   **RS Top 500 List:** No

Worldview Theme #6: Scientific Method

Worldview Theme Summary: **for more:** www.projectworldview.org/wvtheme6.htm

I value solving problems by scientific methods: gathering data, constructing hypotheses to fit the data, testing, refining, and publishing for others to verify. Scientists work to insure that bad experimental design, faulty controls, selection effects, bias, prejudice, errors, etc. are not part of their investigations. A complex problem may require reduction to many simpler ones (reductionism) and sorting out multiple causes/effects. I believe scientific methods work better than anything else when it comes to making good predictions and solving problems. If there were something else that worked better, I'd be for it! I don't like pseudosciences, magic, etc. for two reasons: 1) they don't work; 2) they often involve claims that can't be tested. Scientific statements can be tested and conceivably shown to be false.

SONG

"Learn From Feedback, Mack" by Stephen P. Cook

to be sung to the tune of "Hit the Road, Jack" by Percy Mayfield / Ray Charles

This problem this problem, it won't go away
But solving it without data, there's no way
Once you've got data that's good
Then you know what to do, you should

That's right!
Use the Method, Mack
Learn from feedback[1], feedback, feedback, feedback,
Use the Method, Mack

Controls[2] good controls, investigations need these
No nonsense for data, you want it to please
Once you've got data that's good
Then you know what to do, you should

That's right!
Use the Method, Mack
Learn from feedback, feedback, feedback, feedback,
Use the Method, Mack

Hypothesis[3] hypothesis, you gotta have one
Fit the data to it, that's how it done
If you find your hypothesis no good
Then form another one, you should

Test it out, Scout
Remove doubt, don't pout, don't pout, don't pout,
Test it out, Scout

Predictions good predictions, those you wanna make
If your hypothesis fits the data, it's a piece of cake
If you think your hypothesis is good
Then you know what to do, you should

Test it out, Scout
Remove doubt, don't pout, don't pout, don't pout,
Test it out, Scout

Problem solved not solved, before others get a look
Reproducible results—they make science cook
If others think your results are good
Then you know what to do, you should

Publish, help others learn, Mack
Learn more, learn more, learn more, learn more
Learn from feedback, Mack…
What'd you say?
Learn from feedback, Mack
I don't understand
Learn from feedback, Mack
Now I'm getting it
Learn from feedback, Mack

SONG—NOTES / COMMENTS

1—Feedback in general refers to information about the state of a system (output) that is returned or fed back to the system input to adjust, regulate, or modify its behavior. Scientists learn about systems they study via a feedback process. (See note 11 theme #5A)

2—A control group refers to a group of subjects who do not receive the experimental treatment of interest. Results for this group will be compared with those for the experimental group, which were treated.

3—A hypothesis is an educated conjecture or statement offered as a tentative explanation of data relevant to the problem being considered. It must testable—perhaps a mathematical relationship representing data or some other model is to be tested.

Comment: Applying this theme to finding solutions to everyday problems associated with stress can be used in what's called problem-focused coping, based on taking steps to remove, minimize or evade the stress.

Worldview Theme—TFJD CODE: 3122 **VI=4** **Original Tune Era:** 1960s   **RS Top 500 List:** Yes

Worldview Theme: #7A Mysticism

Worldview Theme Summary: for more: www.projectworldview.org/wvtheme7.htm

While things and events appear to be separate in space and time, I believe the perception of discrete objects and the passage of time are illusions. My words fail to describe the Oneness of everything and the connectedness that I am conscious of. Through this connection comes knowledge not available via normal cognition or human senses, which perceive explicate manifestations of implicate Oneness as dynamic interplay of opposites. By finding balance and losing ego one perceives more: many feel grasped by a power not their own, a few claim experiencing mystical union with God!

SONG

"Words Get in the Way" by Stephen P. Cook
to be sung to the tune of "The Games People Play" by Joe South

How words get in the way
Piece by piece we have our say
Mighty tough to put away
And get your head free
We see the world part by part[1]
Not as a whole work of art
Naming things gave it a start
Describing reality[2]

Then we had to step outside
Being apart, Oneness died
With words we hit our stride
They've served us well
They helped us make maps[3]
Put on our thinking caps
Meet goals, take victory laps
Compile stories to tell

With words we relive the past
Chart events from first to last
Time begins with a blast
To eternal reality
Your ego's like a bright sun
It dims if words you shun
Glimpse the Eternal One[4]
If you get your head free

If ego baggage you sell
And give into nature's will
If in the now you can dwell
You'll find the Over Soul
If with words you don't fight
Subject and object unite
In wise silence[5] take delight
Meet the soul of the whole

What if you really tried
Banish thoughts, from them hide
Trade apart for back inside
Feel the power of now[6]
Sail sea of joy far from port[7]
To the Mind of God pay court
To describe it words fall short
I'll use only one…wow!

SONG—NOTES / COMMENTS

1—This line appears in Ralph Waldo Emerson's essay *The Over-Soul*.
2—Reality can be defined as the totality of all things, structures (actual and conceptual), events (past and present) and phenomena, whether observable or not. It is what a worldview attempts to describe or map.
3—Conceptual maps
4—A phrase the author likes to think Einstein used (although what he wrote is translated from German "the old One").
5—Emerson's phrase
6—*The Power of Now* is the title of a book by Eckert Tolle.
7—This line honors two 1960s' songs with mystical overtones: the Stevie Winwood / Blind Faith song "Sea of Joy," and the Gary Brooker / Keith Reid / Procol Harum song "A Salty Dog."

Comment: feeling this ultimate connectedness can perhaps provide some emotional armor vs. the pain of alienation / loneliness. (See the related discussion in part IIIa, on the first page of that section.)

Worldview Theme—TFJD CODE: 1111 VI=9 Original Tune Era: 1960s   RS Top 500 List: No

Worldview Theme #7B: Magic

Worldview Theme Summary: **for more:** www.projectworldview.org/wvtheme7.htm

I believe some people are so in tune with reality or the universe—and the universe so sympathetic to them—that they are able to exercise power and control over it that defies explanation using either common sense or scientific conceptual framework. Beyond creation of illusion, I'd say the magic's origin varies. It may come from special knowledge, use of means such as incantations, amulets, ritual, etc, possession of paranormal gifts, ability to alter consciousness, communication with spirits, etc. While some may link the latter to religious worship, generally magic is more focused. The applied spirituality of shamans, who attempt to heal by restoring a person's balance with nature, provides one example.

SONG

"Alter Consciousness" by Stephen P. Cook
to be sung to the tune of "The Camptown Races"[1] by Stephen Foster

We count as children toss the ball	With ritual he makes a curse
Fool us! Fool us!	Vodoo![4] Vodoo!
We miss the gorilla's curtain call[2]	His rival's health soon be worse
Fool us your way!	Make Vodoo pay!
Magicians use misdirection	He sticks pins in a doll
Fool us! Fool us!	Vodoo! Vodoo!
We buy into their illusion	For his rival he plans a fall
Fool us your way!	Make Vodoo pay!
Alter consciousness	Alter consciousness
Mind plays a new role	Mind plays a new role
Was feeling aimless or hopeless	Was feeling aimless or hopeless
Now I've got some control	Now I've got some control
She sought the healer in her grief	Therapists use art to heal
Shaman![3] Shaman!	Sand tray![5] Sand tray!
For her soul get pain relief	Imagined worlds can reveal
Watch Shaman play!	With sand tray play!
To spirit world he makes his plea	Closing left brain opens new door
Shaman! Shaman!	Sand tray! Sand tray!
He heals with ceremony	Your inner wisdom to explore
Watch Shaman play!	With sand tray play!
Alter consciousness	Alter consciousness
Mind plays a new role	Mind plays a new role
Was feeling aimless or hopeless	Was feeling aimless or hopeless
Now I've got some control	Now I've got some control

SONG—NOTES / COMMENTS

1—This song was similarly used (as the basis for another song) in the plot of the book *Work Song* by Ivan Doig.
2—Refers to a famous video where a gorilla walks (unseen by many!) through a scene illustrating "inattention blindness."
3— Shamans attempt to heal by restoring a person's balance with nature. They believe in connectedness of all things and use knowledge of the local environment, altered states of consciousness, rituals, magic, etc.
4—Voodoo refers to Haitian religion/magic or related Louisiana, USA folkways where practitioners placate and serve spirits.
5—Sandplay therapy is a way to use art done in sand trays to heal and resolve conflict.

Comment: the possibility of gaining control of an otherwise hopeless situation provides emotional armor. A less productive use of this theme would be to engage in wishful thinking and not confront the reality of the situation you face. Such emotion-focused coping does nothing to get at the root cause of the stress.

Worldview Theme—TFJD CODE: 1233 **VI=324 Original Tune Era:** 1800s   **RS Top 500 List:** No

Worldview Theme #8A: Monotheism

Worldview Theme Summary: for more: www.projectworldview.org/wvtheme8.htm

I believe in one God who is the Creator of the universe and source of the vital spark that energizes life. God is conceived of, prayed to, and worshipped in diverse ways. Some believe God does not interfere with the workings of the universe (deism), others imagine a moralistic God dispensing justice. Some conceive of God as an Intelligent Designer who acted with a purpose. Some give God human, perhaps male, attributes (anthropomorphism), others worship a female Goddess (Gaia). In sacred texts of many religions God is celebrated. Such words, I believe, are to be valued for what they inspire, not as divine words subject to literal interpretation.

SONG
"Spark! Creative Source of All" by Stephen P. Cook
to be sung to the tune of "Hark the Herald Angels Sing" by Charles Wesley

Spark![1] Creative source of all[2]
Universe moves to your call
New day dawns on planet Earth
Glorious life has its birth
Web of life all in its place
Blessed by your mighty grace[3]
Throughout we see your design
In flowers, in stars that shine
Spark! Creative source of all
Universe moves to your call

Deists[4] see you their own way
Hands off, your approach they say
Laws in place it all works
With no miracles[5], no quirks
Without purpose this shaker
Works like a blind watchmaker[6]

Smart designers[7] disagree
With their teleology[8]
Spark! Creative source of all
Universe moves to your call

Have you clear human attributes
Or murky mystic cosmic roots?
Hail judgmental father
Or loving kind holy mother?
Do you provide holy word
Or speak in ways not heard?
One God we believe in you
In all of us you shine through
Spark! Creative source of all
Universe moves to your call

SONG—NOTES / COMMENTS

1—Spark, as in vital spark, refers to a technique for supposedly bringing inanimate matter to life made famous in Mary Shelley's *Frankenstein* (written early 19th century) when vitalism (theme #5B) was popular.

2— "Source of all" replaces "Lord of all" for Unitarian Universalists (UUs) singing "For the Beauty of the Earth."

3— Grace: a person's belief–sometimes difficult to sustain given hardships or evidence to the contrary–that God, nature or reality is ultimately on his or her side and will occasionally gift one with unwarranted help.

4— Deism–a monotheistic belief in God, who is believed to not interfere with the workings of the universe which proceed according to natural laws, combined with rejection of formal, organized religion.

5—Miracle can be defined as an act of God or some supernatural being that violates the laws of physics.

6—*The Blind Watchmaker* is the title of a book by biologist Richard Dawkins.

7— Refers to intelligent design: the belief that certain features of the universe and of living things are best explained by an intelligent cause, not an undirected process such as natural selection.

8—Teleology refers to the notion that there is a design or purpose inherent in everything, and that events unfold toward some divinely specified ultimate end or that everything strives to fulfill some purpose.

Comment: this theme has value as emotional armor. This can take many forms—note 3 above suggests one. Depending on your conception of God, see other comments. Example: if you have a non-personal conception of a God you merge with in mystical experiences, see the theme #7A comment. From a ***Project Worldview*** perspective you can imagine God actually behind the counter as you go into the Monotheism shop in The Reality Marketplace, as does one account[1]. When asked what's for sale, God says "Everything your heart desires." The shopper, who perhaps conceives of an omnipotent God in terms of love, wants to order love, peace of mind, happiness, etc. for everyone. But God stops her, "We don't sell fruits here. Only seeds."

Worldview Theme—TFJD CODE: 1231 VI=108 Original Tune Era: 1800s   RS Top 500 List: No

Worldview Theme #8B: Belief in a Personal God

Worldview Theme Summary: for more: www.projectworldview.org/wvtheme8.htm

I believe God is concerned with human beings personally. I conceive of God as a personal being (perhaps like a father) with a personality. I value communicating with God through introspection and praying. I believe God listens to our prayers, watches over us, and sometimes interferes with the workings of the universe. I believe that, given His personal interest in the world and its people, He will intervene on behalf of worshippers (performing miracles or whatever) or to punish those who are ungodly or disobey. Some conceive of God in terms of forgiveness and love, others in terms of vengeful, judgmental punishment.

SONG

"A Better Day" by Stephen P. Cook
to be sung to the tune of "Higher Ground" by Green, Agee, and Dorff / Barbra Streisand

I recall when My life turned Running scared Bridges burned Shame and death for me over the edge You made me stop and make a pledge	I once felt Alone, separate[3] With no spirit No hand to hold Lifeless concrete all around me Like an empty tomb: damned cold[4]
Calculating cynicism[1] I traded for faith and trust Facing life with humility[2] Not privileged upper crust	Finding You my salvation Greatly nurturing my soul Where sun finds cracked pavement We know flowers will soon grow
So oh my God How I live for You Be my guide Goodness shining through Keep me safe To You I pray Lead us to A better day	So oh my God How I live for You Be my guide Goodness shining through Keep me safe To You I pray Lead us to A better day

SONG—NOTES / COMMENTS

1—This recalls Pope John Paul II's "cynical society of consumerism" remark in his 1984 Christmas message from Rome.

2—Humility, or being humble, to Alan Morinis involves "limiting oneself to an appropriate amount of space while leaving room for others." In relating to others a humble orientation proclaims, "I don't have all the answers and I want your contribution."

3—Alone and separate is one way of describing feeling estranged or alienated. It is the opposite of belonging. If love involves what belongs together being together, then hate involves bringing about or enforcing their separation.

4—To some this may invoke the opposite of the traditional fires of Hell: a cold modern psychological state associated with spiritual death, pain, loss, and the ultimate alienation.

Comment: this theme has value as emotional armor. Just as fearful or bruised children turn to parents for security, reassurance, or comfort, millions of adults depend on a personal relationship with God, often conceived of as a parent. *Project Worldview* themes related to building a conception of God, or one of disbelief, include #1A, #1B, #2A, #5A, #5B, #7A, #7B, #8A, #8B, #9A, #9B, #10, #11A, #11B, #14A, and #14B. Got a "chip on your shoulder" and don't believe in a God who answers prayers? Perhaps you've spent your reality cash too soon, "before you have seen everything?" What you may not have seen is yourself scared out of your mind, totally alone, where it seems nothing short of a miracle will save you. When the chips are down, will you go quietly into the night, or will your whole being—with emotion you can not imagine—desperately cry for divine help? "There are no atheists in foxholes" is one of those complete sentences with its own *Wikipedia* entry; "Do not go gentle into that good night" from poet Dylan Thomas is another.

Worldview Theme—TFJD CODE: 1232 **VI**=216 **Original Tune Era:** 1990s   **RS Top 500 List:** No

Worldview Theme #9A: Religious Fundamentalism

Worldview Theme Summary: **for more:** www.projectworldview.org/wvtheme9.htm

As an orthodox follower of the ……………..(insert name of religion) religion, I believe that human behavior should not deviate from that called for in my religion's sacred text. This I see as the unerring word of God. I hold it to be literally true, and believe that it provides an absolute basis for morality. I believe that God can and has personally intervened in lives of people in ways consistent with stories in this sacred text.

SONG

"O Holy Book" by Stephen P. Cook

to be sung to the tune of "O Holy Night" by P.C. deRoquemaure

O holy book
Your words are ever steering
Our lives toward right
Away from wrong.
We find your truth
And words always calming
Our fearful hearts
When nights are long

We hear your plan
At us, your words they shout
"Obey my commands!
You can! Yes, you can!"
O great truth[1]
Of that, there's no doubt[2]
O book divine
The book that has your plan
O book, O holy book
O book divine
O book, O holy book
O book divine

O holy book
Testament to our faith[3]
Your words
Greatly simplify our lives
No need to worry
We do as you sayeth
Obeying your commands
Righteous[4] and wise

With joy we recite
We thrill to story
Of miracle
Compassion, and justice
We fall on our knees
Praising the glory
Of your creation
And will so righteous
O book, O holy book
O book divine
O book, O holy book
O book divine!

SONG—NOTES / COMMENTS

1—Literal truth. Note one who believes in the literal interpretation of a holy book like the *Bible* does not necessarily believe in its inerrancy—but in practice the beliefs often are either both held or not held.

2—The *Qu'ran* with "This Book, there is no doubt in it" (*Qu'ran* 2:2) even proclaims it is free from doubt.

3—Faith can be defined as having firm belief, complete confidence and trust in something for which there is no proof, often associated with religion and typically linked more to the one's feelings/emotions than one's rational/analytical side. Some give the concept deeper meaning. Christian philosopher Paul Tillich connected it with "ultimate concern" as in to what should one's life should be devoted. In his book *Stages of Faith*, James Fowler views finding faith as ultimately finding "an overarching, integrating and grounding trust in a center of value and power sufficiently worthy to give our lives unity and meaning."

4— Righteousness is a moralistic, theological term, important in Christianity, Judaism, and Islam, that refers to the quality of acting in accordance with moral law or divine plan, and thus being free of sin and harboring no guilt. Thus, in the *Bible's Old Testament* the guiltless are said to be righteous, the guilty are judged.

Comment: this theme can promote carrying emotional baggage, but also has value as emotional armor. For example, the Gideons promote turning to the *Bible*, for "comfort in the time of loneliness…and sorrow," "relief in the time of suffering," "protection in the time of danger," and "courage in the time of fear." Many Muslim worldviews are fortified with belief that reading and preaching the *Qu'ran* can bring divine rewards.

Worldview Theme—TFJD CODE: 1321 VI=162 Original Tune Era: 1800s   RS Top 500 List: No

Worldview Theme #9B: Apocalypticism

Worldview Theme Summary: **for more:** www.projectworldview.org/wvtheme9.htm
I believe that the end of the world, or some catastrophic event after which life won't be the same, is near. While my belief has a hopeful origin—God's victory (led by the return of a beloved religious leader/prophet) and the final triumph of good over evil— I realize there are other possibilities. The end of the world could come with the Devil's victory over God, some manmade global catastrophe—perhaps all out nuclear war or irreversible environmental disaster, or cosmic catastrophe in the form of events happening in space or objects arriving from there.

SONG

"Left Behind" by Stephen P. Cook

to be sung to the tune of "Paint It Black" by Mick Jagger and Keith Richards / The Rolling Stones

The End Time[1] is right now: Fate all sealed and signed I'm no believer pal, I've been left behind[2]	I'm jolted by the crash, my eyes burned and blind Firestorm then ash, all that's left behind
I hear the trumpet sound, see sunrise in the west[3] No Godly to be found, sinful scum all the rest	The End Time is right now: Fate all sealed and signed I'm no believer pal: My ashes left behind
I've lost all thoughts of love: Warm days soft and kind Here it's all push and shove, memories left behind	
	Innocence has ended, long strayed off the path Consequence intended: Slammed by God's full wrath
Innocence has ended, long strayed off the path Consequence intended: About to face God's wrath	[two verses of humming with music]
I search inside my heart: No goodness can I find I'm here with starving filth, I've been left behind	I can't believe I've been left, left behind Left with death, left with dark Animated life, bright sun: Gone from the sky!
I see bad darkness fall, painful sufferin' descends After bright Rapture's[4] call, too late to make amends	You know it's been left out, left out, left out: Left behind! Yeah!
I see shooting stars signal approaching doom[5] Cold prison without bars: Tribulation and gloom	[more humming with music]

SONG—NOTES / COMMENTS

1— End Times in Judeo-Christian tradition refer to a future period of great upheaval, trial and tribulation that precede the prophesized coming (or second coming) of the Messiah. Supposedly various omens will be seen confirming prophecy and ushering in this era (which some feel has already begun!)

2—*Left Behind* is the title of a series of books by Christian authors Tim LaHaye and Jerry Jenkins set in the End Times in which Christian true believers have been taken to Heaven leaving behind a chaotic world.

3—Blowing of the trumphet and sunrise in the west are Islamic End Times prophecies.

4—Rapture is Christian belief that refers to the final resurrection or resurrection of the righteous associated with Judgment Day (see book of *Revelation*); more recently it has come to mean being taken up to Heaven.

5—This line suggests looming cosmic catastrophe in the form of space debris striking the Earth.

Comment: this theme can provide emotional armor: fortifying you against current otherwise more troubling events with the belief they are predicted precursors of End Times. The extent to which it promotes carrying emotional baggage and inflicting new stress depends on when you believe the End will occur. If you feel the End will be very soon and act accordingly, what you neglect ➔ high volatility ➔ stressful consequences.

Worldview Theme—TFJD CODE: 1211   **VI=36**   **Original Tune Era:** 1960s   **RS Top 500 List:** Yes

Worldview Theme #10: Secular Humanism

Worldview Theme Summary: **for more:** www.projectworldview.org/wvtheme10.htm

I either don't believe in God (atheism), or don't know if God exists (agnosticism). Without faith in any divine reason for human existence or absolute moral code, I aim to discover or otherwise insert meaning, notions of good and evil, and universal values into my life. While I am troubled by ignorance and chaos, I tolerantly accept human imperfections, and pursue knowledge relevant to the human condition. I champion both the capacity for self realization through reason, and responsible living through brotherhood. Although I don't embrace a personal God, in asserting the dignity and worth of people, in helping them appreciate their place, I nonetheless maintain a hopeful and optimistic outlook on life.

SONG
"Rational World Dreaming" by Stephen P. Cook
to be sung to the tune of "California Dreaming" by John and Michelle Phillips / The Mamas and Papas

The God delusion's[1] gone
It's been swept away
Our childhood has ended[2]
With helpless yesterday
Life built on learning
In both work and play
Rational[3] world dreaming
Of this new brighter day

No holy books and Church[4]
No God or need to pray[5]
With ethical[6] caring
Love in new array
Life full of meaning
Put there our own way
Rational world dreaming
Of this new brighter day

Religion fueled hate
No longer on display
Faith based nonsense
Has no place today
Tolerance and sharing
Brotherhood[7] please come stay
Rational world dreaming
Of this new brighter day

Take responsibility
For your life today
Help others where you can
You got dues to pay
With reason and caring
Let us find our way
Rational world dreaming
Of this new brighter day
Rational world dreaming
Of this new brighter day
Rational world dreaming
Of this new brighter day

SONG—NOTES / COMMENTS
1—*The God Delusion* is the title of a book by biologist and atheist Richard Dawkins. It is also referred to in the last verse of the song "Observe and Reason With Me"—the theme #5A song which in a way sets the stage for this song. The original songs that both theme songs are based on were performed by the same group: the Mamas and Papas.

2—*Childhood's End* is the title of a book by science fiction writer Arthur C. Clarke.

3—Rationalism is a philosophical orientation that links finding ultimate truth to employing reasoning.

4—Holy books: many monotheistic religions view theirs (the *Bible*, *Qu'ran*, etc) as being the word of God, if not literally, then certainly providing a lesson/message inspired by God. Here is the potential source of intolerance where religious moralists find inspiration—and sometimes intolerant rigidity. Church is capitalized symbolizing the 1500+ year reign of the Catholic Church.

5—Prayer can be described as making a humble request of God—often preceded by praise, evidence of adoration, expression of gratitude, promises, etc—to annul the laws of the universe be on behalf of the one who utters the prayer. In general, praying is initiating communication with God, a Deity, higher power, etc.

6—Ethical means related to ethics, the study of right and wrong in matters of conduct.

7—Brotherhood refers to an idealized situation in which people treat each other in a highly considerate way as if they were members of the same family (brothers or sisters).

Comment: While scientists and those guided by reason not faith often embrace this theme, others may do so in an attempt to cast off emotional baggage they carry based on bad experiences they associate with religion.

Worldview Theme—TFJD CODE: 3321   **VI=18**   **Original Tune Era:** 1960s   **RS Top 500 List:** Yes

<table>
<tr><td colspan="2">

Worldview Theme #11A: Fatalism

</td></tr>
<tr><td colspan="2">

Worldview Theme Summary: **for more:** www.projectworldview.org/wvtheme11.htm

I believe that events are fixed in advance so that humans are powerless to change them, and that individuals don't control their own destinies. Whether you call it "God's plan" or "the will of God" — or call it determinism and involve factors beyond human control including natural laws, genetic endowment, the (predictable) response to environmental stimuli, etc. — like you I believe that our life's course is fixed as part of the larger scheme of things.

</td></tr>
</table>

SONG

"Fatalism" by Stephen P. Cook
to be sung to the tune of "Lodi" by John Fogerty/Credence Clearwater Revival

Many many years ago A notion in my head I was powerless—God's will I couldn't put it to bed I don't control my own life This was planted in my brain Oh Lord, got this fatalism And pain Often I hear people Meekly accept poverty[1] Saying don't question God's plan You know it's meant to be Hard work doesn't matter I'm resigned to my fate Oh Lord, got this fatalism Sad state	If I got reality cash[2] Whenever someone said to me This bad thing that happened, You know it was meant to be I'd get on that free will train Ride 'til my head got clear Oh Lord, got this fatalism Up here [vocalist smiles and to points to brain]

SONG—NOTES / COMMENTS

1—There appears to be a link between the prevalence of belief in fatalism and living in poverty. It has been suggested that some poor people become resigned to their poverty and feel that no matter what they do, since they were destined to be poor, they can't escape it. An important realization, of many who have worked with helping people get off government subsidized welfare programs, is that escaping welfare/poverty begins with taking personal responsibility. This is consistent with believing people have free will and that confronting the issue of whether to take personal responsibility is unavoidable. The crux of the problem: a poor person who is fatalistic may not relate very well to the concept of taking personal responsibility.

2— Reality cash is metaphorically what you spend in the Reality Marketplace–an imaginary place (made real on the *Project Worldview* website) where important ideas, beliefs, values, and worldview themes are bought/ sold. (see Part IIIb)

Comment: this theme can have value as emotional armor. Believing "things are meant to be" can absolve you of personal responsibility, and conceivably shield you from blame or the burden of guilt. More generally a belief that you're destined (or fated) to do something can provide an important sort of inspiration to keep going when stressful obstacles intrude that defeat less motivated people. The downside: believing that your destiny lies down a particular path can involve fantasy/wishful thinking that creates a gulf between your own experience and reality—a chasm that interferes with learning from feedback. (Also see the next comment, for theme #11B.)

Worldview Theme—TFJD CODE: 1121 **VI=18 Original Tune Era:** 1970s   **RS Top 500 List:** No

Worldview Theme #11B: Free Will

Worldview Theme Summary: for more: www.projectworldview.org/wvtheme11.htm

I believe that humans have the power to freely choose between alternatives, exercise rational control over their actions, and generally shape their destinies. (Note: Appreciation of quantum mechanics and chaos theory has led many scientists away from the notion that events always unfold in rigidly determined, predictable ways, as they once held.)

SONG
"Hymn #11: To Kill With Free Will" by Stephen P. Cook
to be sung to the tune of a medley of "Thick as a Brick" (first and last verses only)
and (all the rest) "Hymn #42" both by Ian Anderson / Jethro Tull

I really don't care to enter this fray
As to our free will I can't really say
I won't interfere if you want to pray
May even laugh as you children play
As you ponder the character of God [echo]
His choices should you applaud? [echo]
On Earth you continue to trod [echo]
And to kill with free will

Thank you God in Heaven
For giving me free will
Allowing me to freely choose
Who I'm gonna kill

But if God is love
And He's all powerful
Then He won't allow me
To bash in someone's skull

Thank you omnipotent God[1]
With your all knowing skill
You made the logical choice
Not to grant me free will

But what kind of God
Would condemn my soul to Hell
For behavior He pre-ordained
By not granting me free will?

Thank you omniscient God[2]
For giving me free will
You know what I'm gonna do
But still you let me kill

Yet if God is all knowing
But not all powerful
Then He can't stop me
From bashing in your skull

Thank you God in Heaven
For giving me free will
Allowing me to freely sin
And earn my place in Hell

Do we shape our own destinies
Or follow God's will on our knees?
I've watched you puzzle this out
Over logical fallacies seen you pout
You can't figure this character God [echo]
You can't seem to give Him the nod [echo]
Yet on Earth you continue to trod [echo]
And to sin with a grin.

SONG—NOTES / COMMENTS

1,2— Many conceive of God as all powerful (omnipotent) and all knowing (omniscient), with infinite knowledge and power. Invoking infinity can lead to difficulty and contradiction. Here's a relevant one, provided by cybernetic pioneer Norbert Wiener: "Can God make a stone so heavy that He cannot lift it? If He cannot, there is a limit to His power…if He can, this seems to constitute a limitation to His power too." Those who value free will have qualified God's omniscience by restricting it to knowing everything that can be known–excluding the free choices human agents will make in the future. Restricting God's knowledge in this regard can be avoided, but it comes at the expense of restricting His power: by assuming God knows everything that is to happen in the future, but lacks the power to do anything to alter that future.

Comment: Coping mechanisms of those valuing free will may differ from those used by fatalists. The former may prefer engagement coping, aimed at directly dealing with the stress; the latter may opt for disengagement /avoidance, where one is resigned to suffering and makes no effort to deal with the stress.

Worldview Theme—TFJD CODE: 2111 **VI=4 Original Tune Era:** 1970s **RS Top 500 List:** No

Worldview Theme #12: Artistic Orientation

Worldview Theme Summary: for more: www.projectworldview.org/wvtheme12.htm

As an artist, I aim to present my creation, not in isolation, but as part of an interconnected divine fabric. In sharing my vision/personal experience, I fix it forever in imposing a permanent, artificial structure on transient chaos from which it arose. My work should arouse feelings and maximize my audience's emotional commitment. I offer my creation to others, serving as their intermediary. Its birth can be traced to my isolation, suffering, ego suppression, then awakening, connecting—sometimes by analogizing—and above all, my empathizing. I hope that, in it, most perceive some of the harmony, vibrant mystery/grace that I have beheld. (Note: Some artistic creations are more narrowly focused! Many are born when passive looking ends and active observing begins. To some, all creative thinkers are artists!)

SONG

"Artist Suffering" by Stephen P. Cook
to be sung to the tune of "Tuesday Afternoon" by Justin Hayward / The Moody Blues

Artist suffering[1]
Here by myself all alone
Lose it, find the way
And make this creation my own
From my vision not stray

Dreamland, a nightmare
After much hurt, fear and pain
Again my dreams are sweet
After trauma comes gain
In my passion there's heat

I'm playing with my art[2]
Toying with my soul
Relaxing spurs me on
Helps if I let go

Celebrate creation[3]
With expressions of love
Acknowledge pain
Recognizing the value of
Human suffering
Human suffering

Muses[4] call to me
To share what I feel inside
To let it out through art
Bound no longer, I confide
In you, from my heart

Feel me, I touch you
My soul is bare in the raw
Can you feel my pain?
Released, I stand in awe
I let my art explain

SONG—NOTES / COMMENTS   (this song is part of the author's personal story)

1—Some artistic creations are more mechanics than expressing feeling. This song isn't about them. Like definitions of music that stress communicating or manipulating emotions (including pain turning to joy), it connects with a similar definition of art.

2—Art is one of those difficult to define terms, one whose definition depends on your point of view. Definitions of it can emphasize art as any of the following: expression, imitation, playful creativity, insight into reality, communicating feeling, etc. They can link it to beauty, pleasure, pain, empathy, and both idealizing common daily experience / escaping from it. It can be defined to include a wide range of creative works used to portray images and express feelings, including drawing, painting, sculpture, music, dance, theater, literature, architecture, etc. The author prefers thinking of art in terms of expressing / arousing feelings.

3— Creativity involves something new and worthy being created. It can involve creative thinking—thinking that happens without words or logic, and can involve images, intuition, emotions, and bodily feelings. Some feel certain types of creative expression are spurred by emotional trauma, stress, drugs, alcohol, etc.

4—Muses originally were nine sister goddesses in Greek mythology who were patrons of the arts. See part If for more.

Comment: this theme is associated with high emotional volatility and has been discussed in this context in the "Artistic Creativity—Risks and Rewards" section of Part IIIb. It suffices here to say if you've spent years both honing your skills and pursuing artistic endeavors, the toil and associated fallout may have left you carrying emotional baggage. But the emotional rewards can be great (ecstasy is a term sometimes used in describing feelings great music or art inspires!) and make it all worth it. If you survive the struggle—realize many do not, and succumb to mental health problems / addiction / suicide— a feeling of being both appreciated and connected can provide emotional armor vs. the pain of feeling unworthy, alone, alienated.

Worldview Theme—TFJD CODE: 1333 **VI=**729 **Original Tune Era:** 1960s   **RS Top 500 List:** No

Worldview Theme #13: Dancing With Systems	

Worldview Theme Summary: for more: www.projectworldview.org/wvtheme13.htm

I value solving problems using computer-aided modeling and systems thinking. Modeling complex systems involving living things can begin with reductionistic analysis, but our goal is a wholistic synthesis, which will require understanding properties that emerge in passing from lower to higher levels of organization. Modeling social systems should involve "dancing": humbly gathering data and learning, being mentally flexible, valuing information, being alert to how the system creates its behavior, and to feedback. Do all this—not to arrogantly control or predict the future—but to design a system that creates a desired future that we envision. Design mechanisms / policies that change with the state of the system. Factor in values, respect what's important, not just quantifiable. Expand time and thought horizons, and the boundary of caring. Go for the good of the whole.

SONG

"Dancing With Systems" by Stephen P. Cook
to be sung to the tune of "Under the Boardwalk" by Arthur Resnick & Kenny Young / The Drifters

When you're modeling something	Dancing with systems
Trying to give virtual life	Data jumping through hoops
Reduction analysis[1]	Dancing with systems
Cutting the whole with a knife	Mapping feedback loops
Dancing with systems	Dancing with systems
Model complexity	Flowchart branching like trees
Writing computer code	Dancing with systems
Where I wanna be	Toward a future we see[3]
	Dancing with systems, systems
Dancing with systems	
Data jumping through hoops	Modeling social systems
Dancing with systems	For the good of the whole
Mapping feedback loops	Deep understanding
Dancing with systems	From synthesis, that's our goal
Flowchart branching like trees	Dancing with systems
Dancing with systems	Showing engineers care
Emergent properties[2]	Respecting human values
Dancing with systems, systems	With algorithm[4] not prayer
Getting lower level function	Dancing with systems
Down pat is a must	Data jumping through hoops
So higher level output	Dancing with systems
Prediction you can trust[3]	Mapping feedback loops
Dancing with systems	Dancing with systems
Avoiding trash in, trash out	Flowchart branching like trees
Testing, refining, learning	Dancing with systems
Giving models more clout	Toward a future we see
	Dancing with systems, systems

SONG—NOTES / COMMENTS

1—Refers to breaking something complex into smaller, more manageable parts, and studying those. (The opposite of wholism.)
2—These can unexpectedly emerge —newly revealed—when higher levels of complexity are investigated.
3—In general, says Donella Meadows, "The future can't be predicted, but it can be envisioned and brought lovingly into being."
4— An algorithm is a problem solving procedure or method that is known to eventually give a solution.
Comment: This theme, unlike an engineering mentality that views society in terms of individuals acting like cogs in a machine, recognizes individuals have feelings. It's built on "dancing" not "rationally controlling."

Worldview Theme—TFJD CODE: 3223 **VI=24 Original Tune Era:** 1960s **RS Top 500 List:** Yes

Worldview Theme #14A: Moralistic God

Worldview Theme Summary: for more: www.projectworldview.org/wvtheme14.htm

I believe that every person is born with a soul condemned to suffer, but by behaving properly one's soul can be "saved." (Note: Christians, Muslims, and others believe that a moralistic God's favorable judgment can "save" someone. Upon death these souls spend a blissful eternity with God or Allah in heaven or paradise. Those souls with unpardonable sins spend an eternity in hell.)

SONG

"Moralistic God" by Stephen P. Cook
to be sung to the tune of "Lying Eyes" by Don Henley and Glenn Frey / The Eagles

Your guilty[1] conscience[2] often worries 'Bout where your soul will forever dwell Better get off this sinful[3] path you're on Or oh my God you'll end up there in hell	You were born a soul condemned to suffer[8] Behaving yourself you can be saved Start by having faith and repenting No sin's so great it can't be waived
Your not so restful sleep is full of nightmares Of hellfire's flames and how they burn How to escape tormenting bad dreams You just don't know quite where to turn	Find Jesus[9], the way to salvation[10] Protect your soul from suffering in hell What this church marquee sign is also saying Is "Hey, we have fire insurance to sell!"
Losing sleep your mind is still churning Like a pot of goat's head soup[4] on the stove You've sinned, broken God's commandments Your soul's like an emperor without clothes[5]	You can buy it every Sunday morning At the church up to heaven points its spire When God opens his Day of Judgment book You can avoid that awful lake of fire
Don't you hide from Moralistic God You can't escape from His jihad[6] Listen my friend if you've been ba—ad[7] You just can't hide from Moralistic God	Don't you hide from Moralistic God You can't escape from His jihad Listen my friend if you've been ba—ad You just can't hide from Moralistic God

SONG—NOTES / COMMENTS

1— Guilt is an emotional state produced by knowing that one has violated moral standards. If one accepts society's version of acceptable behavior, the punishment guilt produces is self-administered.

2— Conscience is a sense of what is morally right or wrong. When conscientious behavior and actual behavior diverge, guilt and feelings of remorse can result. Some connect it with "God's voice."

3—Sin refers to an act that violates moral law or offends God, breaking His laws, and producing alienation from Him. For some, guilt comes from one's conscience with notification that a sin has been committed.

4—*Goat's Head Soup*: a 1973 Rolling Stones' album, mentioned here to bring attention to goats and sheep.

5—Refers to the "The emperor has no clothes" story where a child sees and states what others overlook, and will not speak of.

6—Jihad is an Islamic term, linked to religious duty, which some connect with waging holy war.

7—Refers to a goat or sheep's way of negatively evaluating the worth of certain behavior. (It rhymes with God.)

8—Original sin appears to be a uniquely Christian belief. That tradition teaches that all people are saddled with this type of sin at birth due to the sinful choice made in the Garden of Eden.

9—Muslims can substitute "Allah" for "Jesus" here.

10—Salvation is the saving of one's soul from suffering and punishment that sins would otherwise justify, by forgiving their sins ➔redeeming their souls. This can happen by asking God for forgiveness, and backing the request with signs of repentance.

Comment: this theme promotes carrying emotional baggage (notes 1-3), but has value as emotional armor. Feeling "the next life" will be better and justice will finally be done can help people cope with their dissatisfaction with the life they're trapped in, pain from victimization, fear of death. The link between bad behavior ➔going to Hell and associated fear undoubtedly lives in neural connections inside billions of brains. The emotions associated with fearing God and equating God with love are as different as night and day. Many of those who instill such emotions may, like Machiavelli, find greater security in being feared than being loved.

Worldview Theme—TFJD CODE: 1212 VI=72 Original Tune Era: 1970s   RS Top 500 List: No

Worldview Theme #14B: Reincarnation

Worldview Theme Summary: for more: www.projectworldview.org/wvtheme14.htm

For me, like Hindus and some Buddhists, being saved means overcoming desire and self attachment, escaping a weary cycle of death/birth, then attaining Nirvana. I believe reincarnation, the rebirth of a soul in a new body, can provide for both life after death and cosmic justice. The latter results as a person's actions in one life produce karmic forces with ethical consequences in future lives.

SONG

"Reincarnation" by Stephen P. Cook
to be sung to the tune of "My Generation"[1] by Pete Townshend / The Who

Your body goes in the ground
You ride the Big Wheel round[2]
Your soul[3] leaves when you die
To return with a baby's cry

Reincarnation
This is reincarnation thank you

Death is not a tragedy
Your soul it will always be
Consciousness taking on new form
Law of Karma[4] not to scorn

Reincarnation
This is reincarnation thank you

All you do has consequence
Karma brings cosmic justice[5]
If something bad you do today
When reborn you may have to pay

Reincarnation
This is reincarnation thank you

You don't just go fade away
For a thousand lives you may play
I'm not trying for big consternation
I'm just thinking 'bout reincarnation

Reincarnation
This is reincarnation thank you

Going round again and again
Lives are full of suffering
The painful cycle can end
When all desire you transcend

Reincarnation
This is reincarnation thank you

Losing all pleasure and pain
Ego gone, Oneness to gain
Nirvana Moksha whatever[6]
Your soul dwells there forever

Reincarnation
This is reincarnation thank you
Thinking 'bout reincarnation
Thinking 'bout reincarnation
Thinking 'bout reincarnation
This is reincarnation thank you

SONG—NOTES / COMMENTS

1—Contemplation of this song's "Hope I die before I get old" line, and other lyrics suggests it has a living and dying theme.

2— Riding a Big Wheel is how a soul riding a cycle of death and rebirth might be roughly characterized.

3— To some the soul is "the vital spirit in all humans." Yet, according to Alex Lickerman, "no sect of Buddhism posits the existence of a non-corporeal 'soul'—an eternal, unchanging version of ourselves capable of living independently of a brain and a body." To Harvard's Richard Wolman, writing in *Thinking With Your Soul*, the soul represents "the essential whatness of a thing in the sense of its definitive meaning, the essential and enduring character of a body possessing the capacity for life."

4— Karma, says the Hindu *Bhagavad Gita*, "is the force of creation, wherefrom all things have their life." Some Buddhists feel karma is what gives us identity. A "Law of Karma" might be "What you give to the world, you receive back from the world."

5—Divine or cosmic justice refers to justice administered by God, either now, in judgment made after death, or by karmic forces.

6—This refers to a state of oneness with ultimate reality, of total liberation from human suffering, a state of consciousness beyond describing. Nirvana is a Buddhist concept—the equivalent in Hinduism is Moksha.

Comment: this theme has value as emotional armor. Feelings of dissatisfaction, hopelessness and pain of victimization can be mitigated with belief that "the next life" will be better and justice will finally be done.

Worldview Theme—TFJD CODE: 1221 **VI=72**   **Original Tune Era:** 1960s   **RS Top 500 List:** Yes

Worldview Theme #15: The Collective Cognitive Imperative

Worldview Theme Summary:	**for more:** www.projectworldview.org/wvtheme15.htm

If properly stimulated or sufficiently stressed, I can suspend analytical thinking, narrow my consciousness and passively transfer control of myself to some real or imagined authority. I put my faith and trust in, indeed I feel obligated and beholden to, this authority. (Note: The authority is associated with a culturally agreed on expectancy behind a belief system. The authority can be preacher, shaman, witch doctor, hypnotist, idol, voice from a speaker, TV image, drum, sacred book, magic charm, etc. This giving up control happens most often in settings where peer pressure to conform is strong, or involving rituals triggering trancelike behavior, and, in some cases, may involve auditory and / or visual hallucinations.)

SONG

"Come My Way" by Stephen P. Cook
to be sung to the tune of "Let It Be" by John Lennon & Paul McCartney / The Beatles

In the world of too much thinking
If you find yourself confused today
There's a simple answer
Come my way[1]

These people all around you here
They hang on every word I say
You can be one of them
Come and stay

Come my way
Come and stay
Don't delay
Or nay say
Trust in me my wisdom
Come my way

Lost lamb your good shepherd[2]
Won't let you go astray
Here in greener pastures
Children play

In a world of false messiahs[3]
Rejoice, you've found the way
The Chosen One leads you
Let us pray

Children play
Please obey
Don't delay
Or nay say
Trust in me my wisdom
Let us pray

We'll protect you and love you
Be there for you come what may
Honor God the Father
Dues to pay

If my words live inside you[4]
Then darkness will go away
Your faith greets the morning
A new day

Come my way
Please obey
Dues to pay
A new day
Trust in me my wisdom
Come my way

SONG—NOTES / COMMENTS

1—Highly suggestible people have been likened to dumb herd animals like sheep.
2—The good shepherd lays down his life for the sheep. This metaphor is used by Jesus and is in the *Bible's* 23rd Psalm.
3—False messiahs or false prophets are pretenders to being leaders chosen by God. The term, used by Jesus himself in warning his disciples, has a different meaning to Christians, Jews, and Muslims.
4—The internalizing of parental voices or commands of authority figures has an interesting history if one takes Julian Jaynes' ideas seriously. He believed that before modern consciousness was fully developed there was a different mentality based on auditory hallucinations called the bicameral mind. See Part If of this book.

Comment: This theme potentially offers an escape from what may be the painful, failed running of your life. With that escape seemingly comes ceding personal responsibility and positioning yourself so that you can no longer be hurt by those looking to assign blame. In that sense you have new emotional armor.

Worldview Theme—TFJD CODE: 1123 **VI=**54 **Original Tune Era:** 1960s   **RS Top 500 List:** Yes

Worldview Theme #16: The Golden Rule, Village Ethic of Mutual Help

Worldview Theme Summary: for more: www.projectworldview.org/wvtheme16.htm

I believe that all human beings are precious, special and worthy of treatment based on The Golden Rule: that is, treat others as you would want them to treat you. I don't lie, cheat, steal, discriminate, or arbitrarily restrict, because I don't want people doing this to me. If I see someone suffering, beyond empathizing / feeling their pain, I give them compassion. If I see someone in need, I practice a "village ethic of mutual help": I help them because someday I may similarly need help from someone. (Note: For many, the universal ethical principle known as the Golden Rule is the basis for a rational absolute morality. Some connect it with promoting good karma, others with "good cannot flow from evil.")

SONG
"Honoring the Golden Rule" by Stephen P. Cook
to be sung to the tune of "The Ghost of Tom Joad" by Bruce Springsteen

Bin Laden[1] loved the *Qu'ran*
Saw himself as a holy man
Somehow his faith got off track
To where there's no going back

Those he recruited for nine eleven
Told 'em martyrs go to heaven
What consequence has hate?
No peace, no good, no rest, grim fate

Hurt no one so none will hurt you
Mohammed[2] said, don't misconstrue
Didn't you learn at madrassa[3] school
'Bout honoring the Golden Rule?

Torquemada[4] a pious man
Was Christian zealot with a plan
To rid Spain of heresy
With deaf ear to many a plea

Somehow his faith got off track
Two thousand died on the rack

Tortured, sufferin' great pain
Can this be good? Please explain!

Treat others as you'd want to be
Said Jesus with great empathy[5]
Didn't you learn in Sunday School
'Bout honoring the Golden Rule?

At a table you sit in a dream
Food beckons but you want to scream
Despite long spoons at each seat[6]
With arms splinted how can you eat?

You stare straight ahead for awhile
Soon you've a friend with a smile
You feed each other—a good deal
It becomes a heavenly meal!

But in a related nightmare
At an enemy face you stare
Vengeful, his mouth you won't fill
You both end up starving in hell

SONG—NOTES / COMMENTS
1—Osama bin Laden (1957-2011), the founder of the Islamic terrorist group al-Qaeda
2— Mohammed (570-632), the great prophet and founder of Islam
3—The Arabic word for school, commonly referring to a fundamentalist Islamic religious school
4—Tomas de Torquemada (1420-1498), leader of the Spanish Inquisition
5— Empathy refers to "fellow feeling": imagining you're in the other person's shoes—experiencing their feelings, struggles, etc.
6—Based on *The Allegory of the Long Spoons*, which distinguishes people who go to heaven and those who end up in hell. It tells the story of a meal eaten with long spoons by people whose arms are restrained so that they must co-operate with the person sitting across the table. Those in hell won't and they starve!

Comment: this theme may have value as emotional armor. If you have a history of empathizing / helping others', and faith in cosmic justice, you might reasonably expect others will similarly aid you when you need it. This expectation might lessen your fear of facing the future, and the related anxiety. Many assume extending compassion automatically follows from empathy—but not necessarily. Example: a mother might be feeling her injured daughter's pain to such an extent that what her daughter gets is her anxiety, not compassion.

Worldview Theme—TFJD CODE: 2232 **VI=96 Original Tune Era:** 1990s   **RS Top 500 List:** No

Worldview Theme #17A: Bitterness & Vengeance

Worldview Theme Summary: **for more:** www.projectworldview.org/wvtheme17.htm

If my current state is less than desired, I often focus on what's wrong, feel bitter, angry, resentful, and look to assign blame. My response to feeling victimized is often to seek revenge and punish those responsible. (Note: Bringing religion into this, those worshiping a spiteful Old Testament God may opt for vengeance and "an eye for an eye, a tooth for a tooth.")

SONG

"When Justice is Finally Done" by Stephen P. Cook
to be sung to the tune of "When Johnny Comes Marching Home" by Patrick Gilmore

An eye for an eye, tooth for a tooth
Revenge! Revenge!
Smite your enemy, cutting guilt loose[1]
Revenge! Revenge!
Feeling victim is mighty bad stew
Rise up and hurt whoever hurt you
And you'll feel good when justice[2] is finally done!

You've been hurt, your life a waste
Revenge! Revenge!
Your honor trashed, don't lose face[3]
Revenge! Revenge!
The law's no help, so retaliate
Channel your anger, direct your hate
And we'll feel good when justice is finally done!

If you're Hamlet[4] in life's play
Revenge! Revenge!
You must make your father's killer pay
Revenge! Revenge!
A painful death, you'll plan it out
You'll enjoy the deed, you've no doubt
And we'll feel good when justice is finally done!

The Hebrew God said "Vengeance is mine!"[5]
Revenge! Revenge!
"You get what you deserve," Hindus sigh
Revenge! Revenge!
If the verdict is God's hellfires
Or what life's bad karma requires[6]
We'll all feel good when justice is finally done!

SONG—NOTES / COMMENTS

1—Or ignoring reservations you have about revenge based on the dictates of your conscience

2— Justice refers to implementing what is just, defined in various ways as being reasonable, proper, lawful, right, fair, deserved, merited, etc. For some, justice is intimately connected with fairness, a connection with three dimensions: equal treatment, the degree to which exercising freedom and liberty is to be allowed, and reward for contributing to the common good. There are many different types of justice, including cosmic (or divine) justice, distributive justice, restorative justice, retributive justice, transformative justice, etc.

3— The word honor can be linked to one's reputation, public esteem, keeping one's word, or ethics—or it can also be tied to vengeance. In this traditional sense, honor can be thought of as the desire to publicly avenge insults or right wrongs. It can be particularly valued in societies or subcultures that are otherwise beyond the reach of practically effective law enforcement. Even in modern settings with well-developed criminal justice systems, turning off the powerful lust for revenge emotion can be difficult if not impossible for many individuals. So the need to seek revenge is often linked to "saving face" and what the victim or family member feels needs to be done to recover from shame, humiliation, trashing of "honor", etc. Where poor people are involved consider what Mexican American Rafael Chacon (1833-1925) said, "I am poor. My only inheritance is my honor."

4—Hamlet, the main character in Shakespeare's 1601 play, agonizes over whether to seek revenge and kill.

5—Refers to Yahweh, the ancient Hebrew vindictive God of the *Bible's Old Testament*.

6—The Eastern notion of a law of karma, as in "If you give nothing but bad to the world that's what you'll receive back, if not in this life, then in the next" provides another route to cosmic or divine justice.

Comment: If you've been victimized, this theme can promote your acquiring still more unwanted emotional baggage—especially as your struggle for justice goes on and on (see note 4 of the theme #17B). But it also provides an action-based alternative to your continuing to wallow helplessly in the mud of injustice. And give you the focus, and drive the resolve to overcome some or all of the emotionally devastating feelings associated with victimization. In this way it provides armor to steel you against continually reliving the pain of hurt, loss, shame, etc. The contrast between themes #17A&#17B response to victimization is stunning: the former can often be hate driven, the latter by forgiving leniency that many see as foreign to human nature.

Worldview Theme—TFJD CODE: 1322 **VI**=324 **Original Tune Era:** 1800s   **RS Top 500 List:** No

Worldview Theme #17B: Gratitude and Forgiveness

Worldview Theme Summary: **for more:** www.projectworldview.org/wvtheme17.htm

If my current state is less than desired, I try to focus on what's right, feel grateful that I am alive, hopeful that my plight will improve, and become determined to make it so. When I'm feeling victimized, I try to make peace with what happened. When appropriate, I offer forgiveness, unload emotional baggage, and perhaps even make some good flow from evil. (Note: Bringing religion into this, those worshiping a loving New Testament God "turn the other cheek" and are lenient and forgiving.)

SONG
"Grateful" by Stephen P. Cook
to be sung to the tune of "My Girl" by Smokey Robinson and Ronald White / The Temptations

I've had trouble, been suffering pain[1]
When I'm down like that, dark clouds can dump rain
Tears now all spent
In my head this new mindset
Grateful, feeling so grateful[2]

Not blaming[3] you, I forgive and forget
Not backing resentment, not a good bet
Who's my sweet pet?
And why is life now no sweat?
Grateful, feeling so grateful

Expecting sunny days, my outlook bright
Running with a kind heart, traveling light[4]
I just won't let
Dark clouds make me cold and wet
Grateful, feeling so grateful

Less anxiety to get in my way
I'm grateful
With positive thoughts I now play[5]
I'm grateful
Feeling so, feeling so,
Feeling so grateful, yeah grateful
Life is good again and
I'm grateful

SONG—NOTES / COMMENTS   (this song is part of the author's personal story)

1—This semi-autobiographical song was written during an emotionally challenging period for the author: the late summer of 2013. Its inspiration (thank you, Muses!) came while he was running around a track in Socorro, New Mexico and it started to rain.

2—Increasingly, scientific studies link the subjective feelings of gratitude with increased well being: grateful people feeling less stress and anxiety, more in control of their lives, greater sense of purpose, more satisfaction with social relationships, greater self esteem, less depression, etc.

3—Blame is placed by a displeased angry person on another person, persons, or institution to communicate that they are believed to be responsible or at fault for the perceived (real or imagined) offense. Blame involves making a judgment, serving notice that another is being held accountable, and potentially seeking justice. Depending upon the intensity with which the person who has been offended pursues justice, this can lead in many directions: an apology which ends the matter, legal action, punishment by law, revenge, punishment by vigilantes, a cycle of violence, etc.

4—This refers to carrying less emotional baggage. In this regard, compare this worldview theme and song, with the previous ones': the "Bitterness & Vengeance" theme and the "When Justice is Finally Done" song. Simply the feeling conveyed by the songs alone presents a big contrast: the "heaviness" of the previous song with the relative lightness of this theme's song.

5—Since the 1952 publication of *The Power of Positive Thinking* by Norman Vincent Peale part of its basic message has won adherents: repeating good thoughts brings good things, while continually dwelling on negative thoughts can bring bad things. In short, people create their own reality by their thoughts.

Comment: this theme can lighten your emotional baggage load by casting off blame (see notes 3 & 4). An infusion of feelings of gratitude, positive thinking (see notes 2 & 5) can emotionally shield you from pain of reliving past trauma. The positive thinking can be part of a general strategy called "meaning-focused coping" in which you use your beliefs and values to instill meaning in a story you've constructed (to live in your head) about the good that came out of a stressful, painful event. Example: an economics student who values the "opportunity cost" concept is dumped by his girl friend. His mother comforts him by pointing out "when one door closes, another opens." Thinking about that, he realizes that as long as he chose to be with the former girl friend he missed out on finding a more awesome girl friend and incurred an opportunity cost.

Worldview Theme—TFJD CODE: 2221   VI=32   Original Tune Era: 1960s   RS Top 500 List: Yes

Worldview Theme #18A: Passionately Impulsive

Worldview Theme Summary: **for more:** www.projectworldview.org/wvtheme18.htm

I know that some people carefully, rationally weigh alternatives when they come to a fork in the road. I'm typically not like that. Often my needs seem urgent and my actions are guided by powerful feelings—fear, anger, jealousy, love, lust, frustration, intuition, sympathy, courage, possessiveness, insecurity, sociability, hostility, sorrow, etc. (Note: Rather than acting in goal-oriented, measured fashion, this person's actions are often based on primitive urges or childish reactions.)

SONG
"Oh My Darling Cheryl Ann" by Stephen P. Cook
to be sung to the tune of "Oh My Darling Clementine" (traditional)

Burbank for 'ya, California
In this conservative land
Dwelt a minor[1] sixty-niner[2]
And his sweetheart Cheryl Ann

Oh my Darling, Oh my Darling
Oh my Darling Cheryl Ann
You are lost and gone forever
Dreadful sorry, Cheryl Ann

Horny she was, it was scary
Making baby—no way, man!
He'd kiss her and resist her
So sorry, Cheryl Ann

Job she got: baby-sitting
Next door to where he dwelt
With sneaky, bed creaky
They could do the things they felt

One night he saw her signal
Gave in and jumped the wall
Naked in the master bedroom
They with passion had it all

Unexpected, clothes collected
Parents got back and he ran
Jumped the wall half naked
She faced them, Cheryl Ann

Job she lost: baby-sitting
Off to college was their lot
They were lusting and trusting
Soon to tie the marriage knot

She blew it, as a pre-med
Wayward passion killed their plan
She did it with an orderly
Too impulsive[3] Cheryl Ann

She got married to another
And the years how they passed
But she still needed baby
Or her marriage wouldn't last

In childbirth, a nightmare
Her husband held her hand
That sad day's grim toll did show
Baby lived, not Cheryl Ann[4]

Oh my Darling, Oh my Darling
Oh my Darling Cheryl Ann
You are lost and gone forever
Dreadful sorry, Cheryl Ann

SONG—NOTES / COMMENTS   (this song is part of the author's personal story)

1—An underage young adult
2—The author of this autobiographical song graduated from high school in 1969.
3—Many people do things impulsively: on a whim, without thinking or taking any time at all to consider the consequences. Typically youth are more prone to this type of behavior. Adults with a serious problem in this regard may suffer from Impulse Control Disorder. This condition is characterized by being unable to rein in impulses or resist temptation to engage in behavior known to be personally risky or harmful.
4—She died in 1986 at the age of thirty-five. Cheryl Ann lives on in the memories of those who loved her.

Comment: The impulsive unthinking actions this theme is associated with can cause pain ➔ emotional baggage (note 3). But sometimes they can bring joy, even ecstasy. Note the high emotional volatility index!

Worldview Theme—TFJD CODE: 1323 **VI=486** **Original Tune Era:** 1800s   **RS Top 500 List:** No

Worldview Theme #18B: Dispassionate

Worldview Theme Summary: **for more:** www.projectworldview.org/wvtheme18.htm

I am often stoically indifferent to pleasure or pain, and often unmoved by joy or grief. I typically make decisions after careful deliberation, free from passion, unaffected by emotions, and when necessary am able to resist instant gratification and wait. (Note: The differences between dispassionate and passionately impulsive people can be traced to differences in brain biochemistry.)

SONG
"Sail With Serenity" by Stephen P. Cook
to be sung to the tune of "After the Gold Rush" by Neil Young

I imagine leading a great armada
With much passion and heroic
Overcoming long odds in triumph
Famously judged by society's stick
But such stressful life in raging sea
Is not the one I'd pick
I'd rather chart my course alone
With little fanfare and much stoic[1]
I'd rather chart my course alone
With little fanfare and much stoic

Trying to calm my ship of state
As waves crash all around
Trying to steer with an even keel,
Often lost, sometimes found
Pieces of mind or peace of mind
When I'm lifted up then slammed down?[2]
Trying to hold it together
Here where there's no solid ground[3]
Trying to hold it together
Here where there's no solid ground

If I'm trusting enough to close my eyes
There's no way I can see
So I might overlook those rocks offshore
They can cause calamity
Even rapture in a sea of joy
Disturbs tranquility
I gotta cast off desire, go with the flow[4]
And sail with serenity
I gotta cast off desire, go with the flow
And sail with serenity

SONG—NOTES / COMMENTS   (this song is part of the author's personal story)

1— Stoic: one meaning of this term refers to someone who practices stoicism. In modern, popular conception this latter term means indifference to pleasure or pain, but its classical meaning connects with a whole philosophy. Ancient Greek and Roman stoics taught the importance of self-control, reason, and courage in maintaining clear judgment—especially during tumultuous times when one might otherwise succumb to destructive emotions. In general, stoics seek to maintain inner calm, have their lives flow smoothly and evenly. Like Buddhists, they believe that life is potentially full of suffering brought on by passions and desires. They believe that removing these—especially distress, fear, lust, delight—is the key to having freedom.

2—Slammed suggests a hard knock: that's life in The School of Hard Knocks!

3— No solid ground suggests a groping around to find a no firm footing or solid basis for one's actions given an environment with lots of hazards, uncertainty, doubt, etc.

4 —Some, like Joe Jaworski and Arthur Koestler, would argue when we "go with the flow" we begin to experience synchronicity

Comment: this theme has value as emotional armor. The song provides some idea as to why/how you might become a stoic (see note 1), calm down and disarm the emotional stress that can wreak such havoc in your life. If you have the expectation that life naturally and continually brings both mental and (for perhaps a majority of the world's population) physical suffering (note 1), this theme can help emotionally arm you against it. Unless you're genetically predisposed toward being dispassionate (like some autistic people?), cultivating this orientation in yourself may be challenging. Actively trying to desensitize yourself to certain expected and feared events may help in this regard. (The related coping mechanism is termed sensitization.) Note some jobs require a dispassionate orientation: policing a high crime area, working in a laboratory, etc.

Worldview Theme—TFJD CODE: 3111 VI=1 Original Tune Era: 1970s   RS Top 500 List: No

Worldview Theme #19A: Economic Individualism

Worldview Theme Summary: **for more:** www.projectworldview.org/wvtheme19.htm

I believe in free market capitalism where transactions involve individuals rationally making decisions based on economic self-interest. As the availability of resources, jobs, products and market conditions change, workers, employers, producers, buyers, sellers, etc. compete to maximize gain. Competition, whether for the most gain, best job, or whatever, promotes efficiency, stimulates people to work hard, innovate, and take chances. Laws and (limited!) government intervention should promote competition, protect property, serve individuals and small businesses—and corporations are people too! Since market system exchanges are voluntary, I believe the right to pursue self-interest is morally defensible.

SONG

"Free Markets" by Stephen P. Cook

to be sung to the tune of "Wild Horses" by Mick Jagger[1] and Keith Richards/ The Rolling Stones

Making money	So it hurts to see taxes
It's not hard to do	Take half of it all
One good idea	Free markets, they're what I prefer
Can bring lots to you	And less government, of that I'm sure
Innovate, take chances	
I always say	Governments meddle[6]
And work hard	From us they rob
If you wanna make hay	Needless regulation
Free markets[2], they're what I prefer	It destroys jobs
Free markets, economic ills they cure	Their subsidies[7] and tariffs
	Won't go away
In competition	A level field
I play to win	Where I wanna play
Seeking big profit[3]	Free markets, they're what I prefer
It's not a sin	And less government, of that I'm sure
In picking winners	
Seek out wisdom	Government bureaucrats
The market's good	They can be rough
At weeding out scum	Starting a new business
Free markets, they're what I prefer	It can be tough
Free markets, economic ills they cure	Social do-gooders
	Everywhere they lurk
It helps to have money	Welfare programs
To make even more[4]	Trash the will to work
Invest wisely	Free markets, we had them once
It's easy to score	Free markets, not more free lunch
You know I work hard	Free markets, where I wanna play
To raise capital[5]	Free markets, we'll have them some day

SONG—NOTES / COMMENTS

1—The author finds it ironic, given this song, that Mick once attended the London School of Economics!
2— A private, free-enterprise system based on consumers, a price system, and forces of supply and demand.
3— Profit is the revenue taken in minus the cost outlay associated with a business transaction.
4—This is the essence of capitalism and why generally its winners are those who start with more money.
5— Capital = the goods and resources (or their value) for production of other goods or to produce income.
6—This can involve outright ownership, purchases, production, taxation, transfer payments, regulation, etc.
7— Subsidy = government payment to producers or distributors in an industry that supposedly needs help.

Comment: Emotions like compassion, guilt, fear, etc. can adversely affect pursuing what this theme is about.

Worldview Theme—TFJD CODE: 2122 VI=16 Original Tune Era: 1970s   RS Top 500 List: Yes

Worldview Theme #19B: Corporate Capitalism

Worldview Theme Summary: for more: www.projectworldview.org/wvtheme19.htm

I see the dominant competitors in the modern capitalist economy as large profit-seeking corporations. Ultimately owned by individual shareholders who appoint a board of directors, such organizations are superior to individual owned small businesses in their limited liability, greater ability to obtain capital, lobby and shape government policy. While I am awed by their ability to harness the forces of production, satisfy consumers, and accumulate wealth, I wish corporate management more often pursued enlightened self-interest. Beyond seeking short-term profits for shareholders, they ought to be sensitive to the needs of all their stakeholders—including workers, the community at large, the environment, etc.

SONG

"From the Home of Corporate Giants" by Stephen P. Cook
to be sung to the tune of "From the Land of Sky Blue Water—Hamm's the Beer Refreshing"
words by Nelle Richard Eberhart, music by Charles Wakefield Cadman

From the home of corporate[1] giants [echo]
"Our monied corporations"[2]
Comes a business conscience
Now with corporate conscience

Born to rein in corporate power[3] [echo]
With self regulation
An ethical business movement
Now with corporate conscience

Embracing our democracy [echo]
Working for acceptance[4]
Good corporate citizens
Now with corporate conscience

Serving many stakeholders [echo]
Responsible actors
Good corporate citizens
Now with corporate conscience

Looking past short-term profits [echo]
With broader perspective
Good corporate citizens
Now with corporate conscience

Pro environment and caring [echo]
With people before profit[5]
Good corporate citizens
Now with corporate conscience

SONG—NOTES / COMMENTS

1— The corporation is the key organization unit of modern capitalist economies. They conduct business as a single legal entity, with rights &duties. Many argue corporations are not persons with moral responsibilities and cannot be criticized in moral terms.
2—Thomas Jefferson wrote, "I hope…we shall crush in its birth the aristocracy of our monied corporations." Over two hundred years later, someone described capitalism as follows, "A system that privatizes profits and nationalizes losses…" Was this a left wing radical? No, it was a columnist in *The Economist*. (See the "Buttonwood" column in the November 15 2014 print edition.)
3—Two concerns about corporate power involve a) corporate crime and b) the corporate state. The former recognizes that corporations and/or their employees sometimes break laws and use their power to ruin lives, endanger public safety, pollute the environment and these activities have a big negative impact on society. The latter recognizes that increasingly government and large corporations are run by the same people, so intermeshed that government and corporate goals/policy are the same.
4—Corporations are hardly democratic: their decision-making is typically dictated by short-term profit considerations and stock shareholder interests—not broader stakeholder or societal interests. A movement toward corporate social responsibility could begin to change that and give progressive corporations more legitimacy in the eyes of stakeholders. Even so, this movement will have a long way to go before qualifying as "economic democracy" —where decision-making is not in the hands of the corporate elite few, but rather vested more in workers through their management/ownership of productive enterprises.
5—The CVS Corp's early 2014 decision to quit selling tobacco products was praised using this phrase.

Comment: The song's "corporate conscience" reference suggests that if you fully embrace this theme you recognize that sensitivity to the needs of a wide range of stakeholders means also being sensitive to their quality of life—which includes emotional well being. Critics of this corporate state way of organizing economic activity charge that it represents a maladaptive coping strategy that, even with minor social responsibility tweaks, perpetuates inequality. (see comments: theme #48, theme #49B, #50B)

Worldview Theme—TFJD CODE: 3133 **VI=9 Original Tune Era:** 1950s **RS Top 500 List:** No

Worldview Theme #20A: Elitism

Worldview Theme Summary: **for more:** www.projectworldview.org/wvtheme20.htm

I have problems with democracy. I think most people are ill-prepared to decide what is best for society. Assemblies of such people are not to be trusted: I fear their collective strength. Society is best served by a select group of clear-sighted, capable leaders / experts. Highly educated, trained, and groomed to wield power, they should oversee maintenance of law & order, promote production of wealth, and guide the masses toward ends they deem to be appropriate. (Note: Elitists often identify with "capital"— rather than "labor," and with "capable leaders / experts" rather than the collective wisdom of common folks.)

SONG

"Among the Elite" by Stephen P. Cook

to be sung to the tune of "They Can't Take That Away From Me" by George Gershwin / Billie Holiday

With a homecoming queen Wearing tuxs and nice gloves In a fancy limousine Enjoying my place lifted up above	Society recognized me Giving me a trophy glow Now I feel it's right: My running this whole show
Phi Beta Kappa key[1] Being professor of Acclaimed Ph.D Enjoying my place lifted up above	Family coat of arms[3] House of Lords seat[4] Castle with modern charms Enjoying my place among the elite
Society recognized me Giving me a trophy glow Now I feel it's right: My running this whole show!	Fifth Avenue pad New York Stock exchange seat On *Forbes* List and glad[5] Enjoying my place among the elite
Earning stripes and bars Those medals on my chest General with four stars Enjoying my place here with the best	Society recognized me Giving me a trophy glow Now I feel it's right: My running this whole show!
Smartest guy you've met MacArthur genius quest[2] Nobel Prize Laureate Enjoying my place here with the best	Looking toward the day We're ruled by the best Experts with final say Putting meritocracy[6] to the test Putting meritocracy to the test

SONG—NOTES / COMMENTS

1—America's oldest, most prestigious and selective academic honors society

2—The MacArthur Foundation gives large $ grants for "exceptional merit and promise" in creative work.

3—These are distinguishing heraldic designs with significance in terms of tradition and aristocracy.

4—Britain's parliament house where membership is contingent on aristocratic credentials.

5— *Forbes*' magazine maintains various lists of the world's wealthiest individuals.

6— In a meritocracy people are promoted based on their merit, which generally refers to their education, expertise, qualifications, demonstrated ability to do the job, experience, etc. rather than who they know, their membership in some favored group, etc.

Comment: A cold, unemotional wish for competent people to make society function better may be one reason why some people value this theme. (Arrogance provides another.) It can promote carrying emotional baggage—especially if superficial superiority hides deep-seated inferiority. But feeling "special" can provide emotional armor against feeling worthless. The coping mechanisms implied here are maladaptive in that they reduce symptoms of one's suffering but don't get at the root cause of the distress (low self esteem?)

Worldview Theme—TFJD CODE: 3211   **VI=4**   **Original Tune Era:** 1940s   **RS Top 500 List:** No

Worldview Theme #20B Authoritarianism

Worldview Theme Summary: for more: www.projectworldview.org/wvtheme20.htm

If its regime rules wisely, I am willing to submit to the authority of the leader(s) of a non-democratic authoritarian socio-political system. While some may be able to meekly accept subjugation of individual rights, I would be more comfortable living under a system in which a social contract exists by which law and order can be maintained, and the duties and rights of citizens are spelled out. Whether the leader(s) is (are) from the aristocracy, single political party, military dictatorship, dogmatic religious organization, etc, I believe these people have legitimacy to the extent they have the consent of those they govern.

SONG
"Respect Our Authority, Our Party the CPC" by Stephen P. Cook
to be sung to the tune of "Big Brother" by David Bowie

You ask about Chairman Mao[1]
And why he's relevant now
Let's seek truth from hard facts
Truth lurks in what works, greet the rest with smirks

They built a Forbidden City[2]
A gate between rich and misery
We've produced enormous wealth[3]
They gave you Death's scream, us the Chinese Dream

Respect our authority
Our party, the CPC[4]eeeeeeeeeeeeeeeeee
A place to belong, together we're strong
We are New China, our patriot song
On the right track we'll fix what's wrong
We want you to join us, please join us

Our central market planning
With top down control[5], a good thing
Bottom up democracy's slow
In crisis we move fast, our problems don't last

Yes we have pollution
Inequality, corruption
With our single party state tools
We'll beat them back soon, as we shoot for the moon

Respect our authority
Our party, the CPCeeeeeeeeeeeeeeeeee
Make your commitment, inside our big tent
Come give your consent, help make change ferment
Promote sustainable development
We want you to join us, please join us

I took the oath you may have heard
I memorized it and repeated every word
Discipline…communism
Never betray the Party

A place to belong, together we're strong
We are New China, our patriot song
On the right track we'll fix what's wrong

Make your commitment, inside our big tent
Come give your consent, help make change ferment
Promote sustainable development

A place to belong, together we're strong
We are New China, our patriot song
On the right track we'll fix what's wrong
We want you to join us, please join us

SONG—NOTES / COMMENTS

1—Mao Zedong (1893-1976) founding father of modern China and its first chairman (1949-1976)
2—The location of Imperial China's ruling elite's palaces /administration for 500 years until the early 1900s
3—It is generally acknowledged that in three decades starting in the 1980s China created more wealth and lifted more people out of poverty than has any other nation in human history during a comparable time span.
4—The Chinese Communist Party
5—Top down governments with authoritarian rulers of centrally planned economies can act much more rapidly than cumbersome, democratic bottom up type governments. However, many people in authoritarian states may lament their relative lack of freedom.

Comment: beyond emotional armor, this theme may have survival value, depending on the nature of the authoritarian regime you are expected to meekly submit to. Whether the authority is a fascist dictator or domineering spouse, some people are more willing to submit / be blindly obedient than others. Psychologists debate whether this is best explained by genetic predisposition or by long-time conditioning.

Worldview Theme—TFJD CODE: 1112 VI=18 Original Tune Era: 1970s RS Top 500 List: No

Worldview Theme #21A: Populism

Worldview Theme Summary: for more: www.projectworldview.org/wvtheme21.htm

"The People—Yes!" This sums up my trust in the collective wisdom and resourcefulness of the people. "Together, We Are Strong!" This embodies my faith that—though they struggle to do so—they'll triumph over outside forces wanting to divide them, dominate their workplaces and wrest power from communities seeking to democratically control their own affairs. I recognize their hard work and promote their continuing education. Like Jefferson, I feel that common people are "the most honest and safe... depository of the public interests"

SONG

"The People Yes My Friend" by Stephen P. Cook
to be sung to the tune of "God Bless America" by Irving Berlin / Kate Smith

The People Yes[1] my friend
Here you belong[2]
Work beside us
Help guide us
Together we can right every wrong[3]

From the grassroots[4]
In the classrooms
In the boardrooms[5]
Hear our song

The People Yes my friend
Together strong[6]
The People Yes my friend
Here you belong

The People Yes my friend
Here place your trust
Watch as we learn
And discern
Seeing light in the night through the dust[7]

Fight deception,
Cynicism[8]
And corruption
Fight we must

The People Yes my friend
Struggle[9] we must
The People Yes my friend
Here place your trust

SONG—NOTES / COMMENTS

1—"The People, Yes!" most notably refers to the title of a 1936 book written by populist poet and writer Carl Sandburg. For many years it was also the message emblazoned on a sign one encountered upon entering the student community of Isla Vista, California next to the University of California campus. There, during the late 1960s and early 1970s, students, counterculture enthusiasts and activists drew national attention—most notably with protests over an oil spill in the Santa Barbara channel and a torching of a branch of the Bank of America during a Vietnam War related protest.

2—Feeling you belong is the opposite of alienated. Alienated people can be hopeless, resigned and cynical.

3— Populist movements can be movements for social justice—or in general social and political movements in which diverse groups bridge their differences and come together to work for change. Populism can also refer to use of appropriate, persuasive language in political appeals to common people.

4—The term grassroots suggests a "bottom up" movement to bring change.

5—The term boardrooms suggests corporate leaders are not necessarily part of the power elite enemy if they accept ordinary people as stakeholders as part of corporate social responsibility efforts.

6—This line recalls the "United we are strong!" line in the "Solidarity Forever" left wing populist anthem.

7—This refers to fighting those who fear transparency, "muddy the waters" or "baffle with bullshit."

8—Cynics don't make good populists since their dim view of human nature precludes needed trust.

9—Struggle is a word associated with populism and people power, as in appreciating their "heroic struggle." Throughout the world ordinary people, if they are willing to struggle, have the potential to claim political power given their numbers and oust self-serving elite who may otherwise rule.

Comment: this theme has value as emotional armor. The feeling of joining others magnifies your identity and offers strength protecting against feeling alone fears. And certainly feeling that you are working for change can counter feelings of hopelessness. Of the five personality factors (identified and briefly discussed in Part I), extraversion (which combines joining and acting) may the one best linked to populists.

Worldview Theme—TFJD CODE: 2331 **VI**=108 **Original Tune Era:** 1940s	**RS Top 500 List:** No

Worldview Theme #21B: Service to Others

Worldview Theme Summary: for more: www.projectworldview.org/wvtheme21.htm

I value and admire those who wish to serve others, either out of a sense of civic duty, a desire to give something back to the community, or simply because they care about people suffering and struggling and want to help. While not all of us can run for public office, work for a non profit community service organization, or volunteer to help the sick, deprived, uneducated, etc, we can show our support for dedicated public servants and groups that do. At times I have felt good about giving my own time and energy or charitable contribution to aid such efforts.

SONG
"Hey Help Us Out Pal" by Stephen P. Cook
to be sung to the tune of "Hey Look Me Over" by C. Leigh, Cy Coleman / Bing Crosby, Rosemary Clooney

Hey help us out pal, lend us a hand
Service to others, doing what you can
Help pound the pavement, help with the phone
Volunteer[1], feel good, change your life's tone

And your effort will help us give something back
It will lift those who need it, get them back on track
We'll all feel good inside, knowing that we tried
And in helping out we take pride!

Hey help us out pal, write us a check
Charity[2] can help lives that are a wreck
If you're grateful for what you've got
Show it and share with the have nots

And your gift will help us right life's wrongs
Cheering those sufferin' like favorite songs
We'll all feel good inside, knowing that we tried
And in helping out we take pride!

Hey help us out pal, in government
Some must carry the ball, all can't punt
Stand for election, apply for selection
Public servant[3], a noble profession

And your work can help us right what is wrong
Doing our part to make government strong
We'll all feel good inside, knowing that we tried
And in helping out we take pride!

Hey help us out pal, with leadership
Service to others, a meaningful trip
Leaders are servants[4], if they care to be
Great leaders know this, yeah it sets them free

Such leaders can help us right what is wrong
Doing our part to make society strong
We'll all feel good inside, knowing that we tried
And in helping out we take pride!

SONG—NOTES / COMMENTS

1—Volunteerism is the giving of one's time and energy to work on behalf of others, without any expectation of pay or real material gain. Many volunteer simply because helping others gives them a good feeling and they like the idea of their "giving back" something to society. Some volunteer both for that reason and to gain experience. As the 21st century began, over 40% of USA adults were engaged in some type of volunteer work, averaging around fifteen hours per month.

2— Charity and philanthropy generally refer to active efforts to promote good will and the quality of human lives. Philanthropy specifically refers to the giving of money, material goods, time, or energy to a charitable organization in support of specific goals or programs that help others or enrich lives. As the 21st century began, Americans altogether annually made nearly one-quarter of a trillion dollars in charitable contributions: over $800/person/year.

3— Becoming public servants: instead of selling their services in the private sector to the highest bidder, some people feel called to work in the public sector, perhaps even in an elected position, and to work for the government for lesser pay. There are various reasons why people might choose to do this. For some, such work is based on professional—and perhaps family—tradition in which one takes pride in unselfishly serving the public interest.

4— Servant leadership (after R. Greenleaf's 1970 essay) refers to leadership practices and philosophy. A servant leader disdains accumulation of power, seeking instead to empower others with total dedication to the group mission and meeting others' needs.

Comment: this theme has value as emotional armor given the real psychological benefits —including feel good reduced stress and increased self esteem (see theme #41)—associated with helping others. Working with those less fortunate than yourself can also enhance your feeling of gratitude (see theme #17B) for what you have, given your relative well being when compared to those you're helping. Of course, in providing that help, it's important not to adopt a condescending feeling of superiority!

Worldview Theme—TFJD CODE: 2332 **VI=216** **Original Tune Era:** 1960s **RS Top 500 List:** No

Worldview Theme #22A: Expansionism (Economic)

Worldview Theme Summary: for more: www.projectworldview.org/wvtheme22.htm

I believe that an economy is healthy when it's expanding, creating lots of new jobs, and there's good public / private sector co-operation. Investing in infrastructure and better access to information improves productivity and decision-making. Investing in human skills leads to new ideas, new technologies—and new markets. The benefits of growth and free trade will overcome poverty. While environmental problems are formidable, government and corporate planners—backed by scientific and technological expertise—are up to the challenge. They can fine tune the economy and deal with problems: no fundamental changes are needed.

SONG
"Economic Growth Will Lift Us All" by Stephen P. Cook
to be sung to the tune of "Stairway to Heaven" by James Patrick, Robert Plant / Led Zepplin

Economists are sure all that matters is growth
And economic growth[1] will lift us all
Their concurrency floats: rising tide lifts all boats
There's wisdom behind their declaration
Truu….uust: Economic growth will lift us all

There's a rule in the book, you can go take a look[2]
It's called the rule of seventy two
Divide seventy two by growth rate per year
To get doubling time of what's growing[3]

Oooooooooooooooooh I hear the thunder
Oooooooooooooooooh I hear the thunder
Clouds gather in the west
Proclaim those who know best
They're depending on it to keep raining
Soon pennies from heaven[4], like yeast used to leaven
Will lift all boats in steady rising

Oooooooooooooooooh I hear the thunder
Oooooooooooooooooh I hear the thunder
Of Noah flood type breakdown
Preach a few maverick clowns
And talk of limits and ethics
Their sustainability path: we'll all take a bath
Everyone will be equally poor

That misery from inequality, give it no thought now
Policy should focus on growth rate
Pollution we'll manage, corruption no damage
There's no need to change the course we're on
And I hear the thunder

Reward productivity[5] and new technology
Good investment advice to heed
And high growth emerging markets
Make them your targets
Economic development[6] we need

[tempo of background music picks up dramatically, as does intensity of lyrics to come…]

And so we use our crystal ball
To assess a world as rain falls
Let economic growth not stall
Four percent a year no trouble
In eighteen years output doubles
Thirty two times more in ninety years[7]
Our planet can't take it some fear[8]
Others see the promised land:
Poverty is gone, life is grand
[subdued and slow]
And economic growth will lift us all

SONG—NOTES / COMMENTS
1—As measured by the rate in % per year of a nation's growth of real gross domestic product per capita
2—See the *Wikipedia* article "Rule of 72" for example.
3—Example: An economy growing at a rate of 3% per year means that the economic output will roughly double in 72 / 3 = 24 yrs.
4—Title of 1950s song w/ lyrics "Every time it rains, it rains: pennies from heaven."
5— Productivity refers to production output per unit of input.
6— Economic development is about improving the quality of human life, especially in poor countries.
7— 90 yrs = 5 x 18 yrs = 5 doubling times 2— so five doublings means 2 x 2 x 2 x 2 x 2 = 32 times more
8— The concern is our planet's "carrying capacity" will be exceeded resulting in environmental collapse

Comment: Theme proponents argue economic growth ➔ good job ➔ material needs met ➔ physical well being ➔ emotional well being. Critics scoff that extreme focus on growth is a societal maladaptive coping strategy: a short term fix that avoids root causes of much stress: inequality, corruption, pollution, crowding.

Worldview Theme—TFJD CODE: 3123 VI=6 Original Tune Era: 1970s   **RS Top 500 List:** Yes

Worldview Theme #22B: Imperialism

Worldview Theme Summary: **for more:** www.projectworldview.org/wvtheme22.htm

I welcome more developed nations and their multinational corporate representatives extending their power and influence over less developed nations, and believe everyone can benefit. The former benefit from new markets for products, resource extraction, etc, the latter from economic development and exposure to the values and lifestyles of the developed world—which I view as superior to those they supplant. I view favorably the nation-building that sometimes accompanies military interventions, and may even accept territorial expansion of the more developed at the expense of less developed world. Certainly I have no problem as globalization spreads modern culture throughout the world.

SONG
"The Man Who Would Be King" by Stephen P. Cook
to be sung to the tune of "Pinball Wizard" by Pete Townshend / The Who

Born in British India[1]
Got English schooling
Grew up loving the empire
"God save the king!" he'd sing

Joseph Conrad[2] wrote of him
So did Mister Kipling[3]
Adventurer Jim Brooke[4]
The man who would be king!

Bought a massive warship
And sailed it to Kuching[5]
Helped the Malay ruler
Put down rebel uprising

The sultan kept his promise
Giving daughter for a fling
And making him rajah
The man who would be king!

He's an ethnocentrist[6]
There trying to do good
With an ethnocentrist's
Plan for their livelihood!

Does he really help them?
I can't say!
Does he do them good?

He puts a stop to pirates
And ends head-hunting
Stops intertribal warfare
Causes bad guys to take wing

He writes laws and brings justice
Slavery ends with freedom's ring
He's moderate, accepted
The man who would be king!

You'd think England would be his big fan
But some there made his life tougher—poor man!

Self serving foreign ruler?
That charge you can't bring!
He spent his own fortune
To help Malays do their thing

His nephew followed him
Decades more of ruling
Good Rajah of Sarawak
The man who would be king!

SONG—NOTES / COMMENTS
1—Throughout the 19th century until 1947, India was the crown jewel in the huge British Empire.
2—Joseph Conrad (1857-1924) novelist who wrote *Lord Jim*, inspired by the real life story of Jim Brooke.
3—Rudyard Kipling (1865-1936) British writer was put down for his cheerleader support of imperialism.
4— Jim Brooke (1803-1868) is the man whose exploits in the Malay Archipelago this song celebrates.
5—a city in Malaysia (once referred to as Sarawak) on the island of Borneo
6— Ethnocentrists believe their society's values and way of living are superior and use them for evaluating the social practices, customs, beliefs, etc. of other cultures, often failing to appreciate that culture.

Comment: Those who value this theme may possess an attitude associated with ethnocentrism: a condescending, "we know best" feeling of superiority of their cultures over the ones in the less developed world.

Worldview Theme—TFJD CODE: 3322 VI=36 Original Tune Era: 1960s RS Top 500 List: No

Worldview Theme #23A: Sustainability

Worldview Theme Summary: for more: www.projectworldview.org/wvtheme23.htm

Unrestrained growth threatens Earth's biosphere. I believe we need sustainable development: meeting present needs without compromising the future. Each generation should leave the next at least as much wealth per capita as it inherited, where wealth includes both manmade & natural capital. Economies should be based on people and environment friendly technologies, renewable energy use, and resource recycling. Their health should be gauged by indicators of sustainability and human well-being. To transition to future sustainability, we need education that promotes new values and a long-term, global perspective.

SONG

"The Earth Can Stand Tall" by Stephen P. Cook
to be sung to the tune of "Rolling in the Deep" by Adele, L.B. and Epworth, P.R. / Adele

There's a danger, growing every day
If we ignore it, our children will pay

Much of what we do: unsustainable
We can change our ways: think renewable[1]

We all need to leave fossil fuel[2] behind
Rising C O two, got us in a bind[3]

Solar energy, it's the way to go
Or else climate change[4] will soon cause us woe

Pollution thoughtless, it hurts all of us
Rein it in, recycle[5], do this or we fall
With nature we start, not man apart[6]
If we change our ways, the Earth can stand tall[7]

There's a danger, growing every day
If we ignore it, our children will pay

Much of what we do, and powers that be
Cause needless waste so think efficiency[8]

Work to stop leaks of water and energy
Tighten up, brighten up: use resources wisely

We all need to leave old mindsets behind
And teach children: treat Earth nice and kind

Corporate growth mindless hurts all of us
Grow sustainably, do this or we fall
Earth's life support, protect and comfort
If we change our ways, the Earth can stand tall

Earth's wilderness leaves me breathless
If we change our ways, the Earth can stand tall
Respect nature's wholeness: children we bless
If we use restraint, the Earth can stand tall
If we change our ways, the Earth can stand tall
The Earth can stand tall

SONG—NOTES / COMMENTS

1— Renewable resources are continually being replaced or replenished by natural processes ultimately driven by solar energy. Examples include direct solar, wind energy, biofuels, hydropower, wood, etc.

2— Fossil fuels are hydrocarbons (derived from ancient plants) stored in coal, oil, and natural gas that can be burned to release energy. Over 85% of global energy needs are met using this non-renewable resource.

3—CO_2=carbon dioxide is a waste product of burning fossil fuels. In the atmosphere it can trap radiation that otherwise would escape to space. The steadily rising atmospheric levels of CO_2 due to human activity have upset the planet's energy balance by enhancing the greenhouse effect resulting generally in global warming.

4—Climate change refers to regional / global changes in climate over the last few decades that scientists, with over 95% certainty, attribute to human activity. Their future projections predict both steadily increasing temperatures and changes / greater variability in regional weather patterns. If left unaddressed: disaster?

5—Instead of throwing away certain materials they can be taken to recycling centers to be sold and reused.

6—"Not Man Apart" is a phrase from poet Robinson Jeffers long used by the group Friends of the Earth.

7— Standing tall refers to maintaining integrity. See note 6 for theme #27.

8—Energy efficiency is the energy used divided by total energy input. An old incandescent light is 4% efficient, meaning 96% of input energy is wasted. Newer lights (LEDs) are 20% efficient or more.

Comment: Today's infants—typically baby boomer grandchildren who could still be alive in 2100—are often utilized by those who value this theme. They are used to make arguments, about steps that need to be taken now to insure a livable future environment, more emotionally compelling.

Worldview Theme—TFJD CODE: 3132   VI=6   Original Tune Era: 2000s   **RS Top 500 List: No**

Worldview Theme #23B: Enoughness

Worldview Theme Summary: for more: www.projectworldview.org/wvtheme23.htm
I like lifestyles that maximize well-being, while minimizing consumption and one's ecological footprint. I am a fan of reusing, recycling, voluntary simplicity, "small is beautiful," and appropriate technology—which has little or no significant environmental impact and takes advantage of what is relatively abundant (including human labor) where it is employed. I do not view economic growth as unequivocally good, nor do I agree "bigger is better." (Note: Some practice enoughness less for environmental, ethical, or spiritual reasons, and more out of necessity. For them it begins with a frugal orientation and involves lots of creatively "making do.")

SONG
"Living Life Simply" by Stephen P. Cook
to be sung to the tune of "Killing Me Softly" by Gimbell and Fox / Roberta Flack

I wanted to live the good life	Steering my life back to basics
With love shoot for the moon	Living sustainably
But building her dream house	Living life simply in my home
Ended with pain and gloom	Minimizing pollution
I didn't want luxury	Telling the world that I care
I wanted most her love	
	Let's teach all our children
Steering my life[1] back to basics	'Bout pain too great to bare
Living sustainably	If we don't respect limits
Living life simply[2] in my home	And make do with a fair share[5]
Minimizing consumption[3]	No one's greedy excess
Telling the world that I care	Should cause others great distress[6]
I'd say living the good life	Easing the pain with our lifestyles
Is grounding ourselves in love	Living sustainably
But with seven billion people[4]	Living life simply in our homes
There's lots of push and shove	Maximizing well being[7]
I don't want us sufferin'	Telling the world that we share
Nor trashing our small planet	

SONG—NOTES / COMMENTS   (this song is part of the author's personal story)
1—This is a semi-autobiographical song written during the late summer of 2013.
2—Voluntary simplicity is a simple, typically environmentally sound and ecologically grounded, non-consumerist lifestyle that people voluntarily choose, typically for ethical, environmental or spiritual reasons.
3—Done through paring needs to essentials, relying on one's labor to meet certain needs, reusing consumer products, recycling materials, trading inefficient technologies for more efficient ones, sharing, etc.
4—Seven billion: the human population in the spring of 2012—it grows by roughly 80 million per year.
5—Fair share will make some think of Ecosharing. This represents an environmental ethic for people to live by: their own impact on Earth's biosphere should be limited to no more than their fair ecoshare. An ecoshare is determined by assessment of human impact on the biosphere, computer models of its future condition, and necessary limits imposed by sustainability criteria.
6—A 2014 Oxfam report said the world's 85 richest people owned as much wealth as its 3.5 billion poorest!
7—This phrase will make some think of "small is beautiful" philosophy of "enoughness" popularized by E.F. Schumacher in the early 1970s. Appreciating both human needs and limitations, and appropriate use of technology, Schumacher questioned focusing on increasing GNP and economic growth. He argued, "The aim ought to be to obtain the maximum amount of well being with the minimum amount of consumption."

Comment: An "enoughness lifestyle" can be seen as a mechanism to cope with the numerous stresses associated with a modern affluent consumption based lifestyle. Example: a life based on having "less stuff" would help cope with stress created by needing more money / working longer hours / being in debt, —all to have and store more stuff …That's one area of stress. Others include: maintaining stuff and storing it, getting technology (associated with stuff) to work, guilt caused by all the time invested in getting / having stuff, etc.

Worldview Theme—TFJD CODE: 1132 **VI=54 Original Tune Era:** 1970s   **RS Top 500 List:** Yes

Worldview Theme #24: Struggling With a Basic Need: Sustenance

Worldview Theme Summary: **for more:** www.projectworldview.org/wvtheme24.htm

At times my life is dominated by a struggle to produce or provide basic necessities so my family and I can continue to survive. This tiring struggle often leaves me in a weakened state, but regularly I pause and ask, "Are my basic sustenance needs being satisfactorily met, and are prospects good that they will continue to be met in the future?" If the answer is no, then I must make changes. What I most fear is the day when I have no options, when I don't know what changes to make. Then I will worry that a slow, painful death lurks nearby. (Note: Sometimes, in their struggle to survive, poor people will not accord other people or the environment the respect that they would if their making a living were not so difficult.)

SONG

"The Long Night of Our Discontent" by Stephen P. Cook
to be sung to the tune of "The Night They Drove Old Dixie Down" by Robbie Robertson / The Band

Joe Have Not is my name
And my life's no gravy train
But when bad times came
I didn't look for someone to blame
We all really hunkered down
And worked hard to lose the frown
But it's tough not finding a job
And at night hearing my wife sob

The long night of our discontent
Fighting back our tears
The long night of our discontent
Overcoming our fears
Like no job…ob ob

Out scrounging food today
Trying to keep hunger at bay
Watching my children play
Thinking they're wasting away
Dumpster diving's cruel
They need to be going to school
Keeping faith, expecting no iron bowl[1]
To escape this dark night of the soul

The long night of our discontent
Fighting back our tears
The long night of our discontent
Overcoming our fears
Like hunger naws…aws aws

Hauling water's part of our scene
I just wish it was clean   We boil it to kill bad stuff

For baths there's never enough
The sanitation stink is thick
Yeah and many are sick
To the toilet down the street
Every night we drag our bare feet

The long night of our discontent
Fighting back our tears
The long night of our discontent
Overcoming our fears
Like cholera…rah rah

In this tar paper shack
The cold wind finds the cracks
A nice fire to warm my back
It's a dream not a fact
It takes money to buy fuel
Here poverty rules
I keep going when all hope seems gone
But ya know it's darkest before dawn

The long night of our discontent
Fighting back our tears
The long night of our discontent
Overcoming our fears
Like being cold cold cold

The long night of our discontent
Fighting back our tears
The long night of our discontent
Overcoming our fears
Like feeling old old old

SONG—NOTES / COMMENTS

1—This Chinese idiom refers to (the now abolished) guaranteed lifetime job with the state
Comment: this theme can promote carrying emotional baggage, but winning the struggle ➔ self reliance. Proactively accumulating resources during good times to use during bad times is a related coping strategy.

Worldview Theme—TFJD CODE: 1223 **VI=216** **Original Tune Era:** 1970s   **RS Top 500 List:** Yes

Worldview Theme #25: Anthropocentrism

Worldview Theme Summary: **for more:** www.projectworldview.org/wvtheme25.htm

I believe that the natural environment should be used, developed, and enjoyed— in short, nature should serve people. Creatively developing the land so that it's more to my liking, and fully utilizing its resources or otherwise benefiting from such activity, is part of being human —not something I should apologize for or feel guilty about. Doing this is not just morally defensible, it's human nature. So basically I think nature should serve people. Having dominion over the natural world, people should not hesitate to use it to meet their needs and enhance their comfort. (Note: Some will bring religion into this, arguing that God gave humans dominion over nature and created the world with their happiness in mind.)

SONG
"Wise Use" by Stephen P. Cook
to be sung to the tune of "Proud Mary" by John Fogerty / Credence Clearwater Revival

I like it here in the city
Concrete and buildings wherever I look
Monuments to progress, legacy, largesse
Dominion over[1] nature says the good book

Machines work to keep us free
Wise use[2] of technology[3]
Rolling, rolling, rolling over nature

No one would call me tree hugger
Forests are here for us to use
Paper from pulp, homes from wood
Cutting 'em down brings much good

Machines work to keep us free
Wise use of technology
Anthro, anthro, anthropocentrism[4]
Rolling, rolling, rolling over nature

Let's dam this free flowing river
Control floods, make electricity
Irrigation, recreation
Use it or lose it to the sea

Development sets us free
Wise use of technology
Controlling, controlling, controlling nature
Rolling, rolling, rolling over nature

SONG—NOTES / COMMENTS

1— "Dominion over" is a phrase from the *Bible's* book of *Genesis* used in God's instructions to man: "Be fruitful, and multiply, and replenish the earth, and subdue it: and have dominion over…every living thing." Supposedly the original Hebrew this was written in communicates a gentleness and familiarity that is less like subjugation and more like stewardship than the meaning communicated in the English translation above.

2— "Wise use" refers to a supposed common sense philosophy about how land should be developed. The movement with this name is led by people who feel that the government has no right dictating what private landowners can and can not do with their land. The movement, linked to the "Sagebrush Rebellion" in the western U.S. which also involves public land management concerns, grew out of increasing frustration with laws containing environmental restrictions, protecting endangered species, limiting development, etc.

3— Technology, which increasingly is linked by some to computer based tools and information, is more traditionally defined in various ways: 1) what humans do to gain control over nature in shaping the environment to their liking, 2) the sum total of special knowledge and the tools / means employed by people to provide goods and services for human sustenance and comfort, 3) knowledge relating to how available resources can be turned into goods and services.

4— Anthropocentrism refers to a human being centered viewpoint that sees humans as the most important thing in the universe, and assigns value to other things based on their usefulness to humans.

Comment: Emotionally charged content appears in the second sentence of this theme's description. Suppose you live where the forest surrounds you, seemingly going on forever—and you value this theme. You feel there's no need to apologize for, or feel guilty about, cutting trees to build shelter and to facilitate planting a garden, and to otherwise creatively develop your land to meet your family's needs. Since working to provide basic necessities/increased comfort using whatever technology is available is as old as the human species itself, how could it be wrong? Working like this each day and seeing the land slowly transform as your children grow is rewarding, it seems healthy—how could it be wrong? (see comment, theme #27.)

Worldview Theme—TFJD CODE: 2213   **VI=48**   **Original Tune Era:** 1960s   **RS Top 500 List:** Yes

Worldview Theme #26A: Consumerism

Worldview Theme Summary: for more: www.projectworldview.org/wvtheme26.htm

I value having the freedom to spend money and buy things. If I like what a product can do for me, like its image and the message associated with it—and I encounter these images / messages everywhere—I will buy it. If I am envious of something someone else has, I will work to get one for myself. When I tire of a possession, I discard it for something new. Often, I express who I am through what I buy. Often I find my needs can be met if I shop around, and I like to shop.

SONG

"What I Buy" by Stephen P. Cook
to be sung to the tune of "Sharp Dressed Man" by Beard, Hill and Gibbons / ZZ Top[1]

Arby's, Bud Light	Mac Pro, Nike
Gonna have a good time tonight	Buying top brands, that's for me
Chevron, Dodge Ram	Omni, Pepsi
Making payments[2] the best I can	What they see when they look at me
Shopping's American[3] like apple pie	Shopping's American like apple pie
Just expressing who I am through what I buy	Just expressing who I am through what I buy
E Trade, Fed Ex	QVC, REI
Never know what I'm doing next	Indoors, outdoors freedom to fly
GE, HP	Sitcom, TV
Filling my home with quality	Soap got your shirts white I envy[6]
Shopping's my religion[4], that's no lie	Shopping's my religion, that's no lie
Meeting important needs with what I buy	Meeting important needs with what I buy
I phone, J Lo	U Haul, Walmart
Shopping online's the way to go	I'm still shopping as an old fart
Kindle, Lego	Exxon, Zillow
On Amazon prices are low	Money's the life blood making it go
I can't stop shopping[5], that's no lie	I can't stop shopping, that's no lie
Hope to be shopping on the day I die	Hope to be shopping on the day I die

SONG—NOTES / COMMENTS

1—On the day in the early 1990s the author closed the sale of his property in the Arkansas Ozarks his realtor directed his attention to ZZ Top band members driving off to property nearby they'd just purchased.

2—Making payments or buying on credit spread to millions of consumers with the invention of buying things on "the installment plan" in the early 20th century. A greater push came years later with plastic credit cards given their ease of use and convenience.

3—After the national tragedy of September 11, 2001, many feel USA President George W. Bush seemed to suggest you could not only help the country recover by shopping, but that it was your patriotic duty!

4— On the topic of shopping as a religion, various books have argued that consumerism is a culture that increasingly meets or replaces religious needs of affluent Western shoppers. The Christmas holiday season, and the parallels between religious and consumerist aspects, is typically a key part of such arguments.

5—Cynics charge that many have succumbed to pervasive advertising messages and adopted a consumerist lifestyle based on wanting, valuing, and continually spending money on things that they don't really need.

6—The Rolling Stones' 1965 classic "Satisfaction" poked fun at advertisers: "how white my shirts can be."

Comment: this theme has value as emotional armor. Many people go shopping when emotionally upset! And, according to Northwestern University researchers D. Rucker and A. Galinsky, "people use consumer purchases to compensate for psychological states of insecurity" including feeling powerless.

Worldview Theme—TFJD CODE: 2123   VI=24   Original Tune Era: 1980s   RS Top 500 List: No

Worldview Theme #26B: The More is Better Mentality

Worldview Theme Summary: for more: www.projectworldview.org/wvtheme26.htm

I often prefer things or experiences that are bigger, louder, longer, stronger, faster, with more power or more features. (Note: Often such a "more is better" mentality is part of a "knows no limits" mindset. Sometimes "macho" arrogance, excess, and waste are part of this—typically humble pleas for restraint are not!)

SONG
"Bigger is Better" by Stephen P. Cook
to be sung to the tune of "A Day in the Life" by John Lennon and Paul McCartney / The Beatles

At Burger King he'd have his way
Whoopers he preferred to Big Macs
Super size[1] drinks he bought a lot
Then he knew what he sought
Double super bacon cheese[2]
Macho fat and grease to please!
Yes bigger is better

The SUV[3] in his driveway
A tank that weighed four tons it sat
Trade it in he would get
Supercharged Corvette[4]
With six hundred horsepower
Fast, he'd be first not last!
Yes bigger is better

A dollar a ticket he'd pay
A chance to win the Mega Millions prize
Six hundred million dollar pot
With women he'd be hot
If his prayer[5] was blessed
With trophy wives he guessed!
Yes bigger is better

The lady[6] had her way I'd say
Bulldozed a twelve million dollar home
With a hundred million to rebuild
A castle she killed
I guess nine thousand square feet[7]
And eight bathrooms wasn't enough?
Yes bigger is better

SONG—NOTES / COMMENTS

1— "Our Super-sized Kids" is a phrase that has been used (most notably in a 2009 *Time* magazine cover story) to characterize a whole generation of Americans.

2—This monster burger from fast food chain Carl's Jr. also offers 1100 calories, 71 grams of fat and 1780 mg of sodium.

3—Large SUVs and pickup trucks certainly provide a sense of power and strength. Critics charge they waste lots of gas, pollute more, kill people when they crash into smaller cars, hog parking and road space, and have features (large cargo space, extra horsepower, four wheel drive, etc.) that people really don't use much.

4—This refers to the 2015 Chevy Corvette Z06 with 625 horsepower.

5—In arguing that pursuing money and a shopping based consumer lifestyle is a religion, buying a lottery ticket has been likened to saying a prayer.

6—Elin Nordegren's exploits after receiving a large settlement upon her divorce from golfer Tiger Woods are referred to here. After Tiger, thirty-three year old Elin was reportedly dating a fifty-five year old billionaire coal magnate.

7—This size dwarfs that of a regular McMansion, a slang term that refers to homes in the 3000 to 5000 ft^2 range and their sameness/homogenization. In the 1980—2010 period, while the average USA family size decreased by 16%, the average new USA home size increased (from 1700 ft^2 to 2350 ft^2) by 38%.

Comment: this theme has value as emotional armor. Feeling small and powerless can be countered by surrounding oneself with big and powerful things. See note 3. above. Such feelings of insecurity play out in consumer purchases related to male / female courtship. As young adults, the males often buy large "pickup" trucks, while some females opt for oversized padded bras. More mature very wealthy men, many of whom undoubtedly feel less insecure—given their wealth—than their younger, poor counterparts, nonetheless want to advertise to prospective young "trophy wives" the size and number of their super McMansion homes, and various specifications related to other status symbols they own.

Worldview Theme—TFJD CODE: 1213   **VI**=108   **Original Tune Era**: 1960s   **RS Top 500 List:** Yes

Worldview Theme #27: Belonging to Nature	

Worldview Theme Summary: **for more:** www.projectworldview.org/wvtheme27.htm

I believe that humans are part of nature, not its rulers. People should cherish, revere, and sometimes stand in awe of natural beauty, not despoil it or threaten the integrity of ecosystems. Nothing in nature should be considered good or bad. The interconnected unity of its parts and processes should be valued without regard to usefulness to people. (Note: Bringing religion into this, some feel that God's creation should not be compromised, that its beauty brings glory to the Creator. Some connect belonging to belief in the benevolence of God and the concept of grace, others with a groundedness that comes from working the soil. Natural pantheists identify God with a self-organizing, ever evolving Universe. Animists may talk of the god inhabiting a special place.)

SONG

"Amazing Place" by Stephen P. Cook
to be sung to the tune of "Amazing Grace" by John Newton / traditional

Amazing place, our Earth profound	Live lightly on the land and share
Its cycles, its ecology[1]	With all creatures great and small[5]
Tread softly on its fertile ground	Your lifestyle says that you care
Let its ecosystems[2] be	When through you nature stands tall[6]
Leave, not take, and you can belong[3]	Our species had a million years[7]
To biotic community[4]	Belonging to nature's scheme
Wilderness how sweet its song	Now standing apart the time nears
Life's dynamic harmony	To live a sustainable dream

SONG—NOTES / COMMENTS

1— Ecology is the study of living things and their interrelationship with each other and the environment.

2—An ecosystem is a self-sustaining, interacting community of animals, plants, and their environment. Each living component has a continuing, dynamic relationship with the others. If numbers of species A fall, numbers of species B, which preys upon A, will similarly fall. With less predation of A its numbers begin climbing, and likewise numbers of species B recover as well. While matter cycles through such systems, with solar input, energy moves in one-way (linear) fashion through the associated food chain.

3—Daniel Quinn's 1992 classic book *Ishmael* tells the human story in terms of "takers" and leavers" and provides insight into what "belonging to nature" means.

4—Critically important to such a community is its biological diversity and genetic variation. It can be gauged by counting the number of species the ecosystem contains. Preserving biodiversity can be important to the stability of the ecosystem, and may have practical benefits in that little studied or unknown species can be sources of new drugs for medical treatments, food crops, inspiration for engineering design, etc.

5—This line is from Cecil Frances Alexander's old Anglican hymn. Its first verse is: "All things bright and beautiful, All creatures great and small, All things wise and wonderful, The Lord God made them all."

6—"Stands Tall" here, as in the (theme #23A) song for Sustainability "The Earth Can Stand Tall," refers to existing with integrity. Its opposite is compromised, diminished—as in rain forests' being clear-cut, wilderness being mined, pollutants fouling water/air.

7— The evolutionary paths of gorillas, chimpanzees and humans split around ten million years ago. The first members of the genus "Homo" appeared around 2.5 million years ago, and our "Homo sapiens" species around 250,000 years ago.

Comment: this theme has value as emotional armor. Retreating to the beauty or loneliness of wilderness in times of emotional difficulty has a long history of giving those who do so renewed strength. **Response to the comment of theme #25:** this person either values freedom from limits (see Fig #1 Basic Choices in Part Ia) or, like an ignorant child, is unaware of the need for limits. The number of similarly ignorant people has reached billions; what their machines can do has reached awesome. Their collective activity raises a question "Why does society persist in destroying its habitat?" Paul Shepard ("Nature and Madness," in *Ecopsychology*) considers answers like "lack of information, faulty technique…greed," etc. before referring to "human psychopathology." He writes, "The West is a vast testimony to childhood botched to serve its own purposes, where history, masquerading as myth, authorizes men of action to alter the world to match their regressive moods of omnipotence and insecurity." Those who value limits / ethics see this collective action as wrong.

Worldview Theme—TFJD CODE: 2333 VI=324 Original Tune Era: 1800s   RS Top 500 List: No

Worldview Theme #28A: Hedonistic Orientation

Worldview Theme Summary:　　　　　　　　　**for more:** www.projectworldview.org/wvtheme28.htm

I live life to maximize my own pleasure and happiness, and minimize pain, suffering, and doing without. Accordingly, I seek lots of whatever brings me pleasure: food, drink, material things, consumer goods, interactions with friends, sexual gratification, music, sports, games, gambling, recreational drug use, etc. (Note: In embracing "eat, drink, and be merry, for tomorrow we die," some hedonists neglect their health.)

SONG
"I Want to Live" by Stephen P. Cook
to be sung to the tune of "Ain't We Got Fun" by Richard Whiting, Raymond Egan, Gus Kahn / Billy Jones

Every meal time, in between time
I like to eat
Jelly doughnuts, cheese and cold cuts
I like to eat
Sugar coasting[1], herbs and roasting
Make for tasty treat
Peking duck thighs, spicy Pad Thai
I like to eat

Each night or day, home or away
I like to drink
Good Scotch whiskey, makes me frisky
I like to drink
Give me fine wine, just right to dine
Let me relax not think
Turkey's raki, Japan's sake
I like to drink

In the meantime, in between time
Let's use pot
Reefer madness, prolong gladness
Let's use pot
Smoking sweet leaf, eating brownies
Munchies hot to trot
Just one more toke, silly old bloke
Let's use pot

In the summer, in the winter
I like to rock
Music blasting, iconoclasting[2]
I like to rock
Rock opens doors, lets me out[3]
Gives me the key to the lock
Free form dancing, playful prancing
I like to rock

In the morning, in the evening
Don't we make love?
Groping lusting, rhythmic thrusting
Don't we make love?
Earthy creatures reach for the sky
The heavens above[4]
Heads are spinning[5], sleep on linen
Don't we make love?

The rest of life, sunny and bright
I want to live
At my leisure, constant pleasure
I want to live
Live for today, cares go away
For bliss what I'd give
Maximize gain, minimize pain
I want to live

SONG—NOTES / COMMENTS
1—Sugar coating here would fit and make sense, but sugar coasting = on a sugar high is more playful!
2— Iconoclasting can be thought of as the challenging of societal conventions, widely held beliefs, etc.
3—David Bowie sings about this in his 1970s song "When You Rock and Roll With Me."
4—Both orgasmic pleasure and intense feeling of oneness that bonding in love-making provides can lead to the type of transcending experience that has been likened to mystical union with God, going to Heaven, etc.
5—Naturally high, we feel drugged—and we are. The neurochemicals (like oxytocin, serotonin, dopamine, etc) released in lovemaking are designed by evolution to immobilize us and improve the chances of conception / successful reproduction.

Comment: behavior associated with this theme has value as emotional armor. Many people comfort themselves when emotionally upset by indulging in treats. Whether this can truly be termed a (conscious) coping mechanism is unclear, since it may be an unconscious response that our brain—assisted by the enteric nervous system (ENS) in our gut—is instigating. After discussing (see Part Ic) the role of dopamine in reward circuits in the brain, we note here that ENR neurons are thought to release as much dopamine (and another signaling molecule serotonin) as those in the brain. It seems signals the gut sends the brain affect our moods.

Worldview Theme—TFJD CODE: 1313　**VI**=243　**Original Tune Era:** 1920s	**RS Top 500 List:** No

Worldview Theme #28B: Healthy Orientation

Worldview Theme Summary: for more: www.projectworldview.org/wvtheme28.htm

I've taken to heart the following advice: "You only get one body. How well you care for it—or don't care for it—makes a big difference in the length and quality of your life." (Note: Those who embrace this lesson—and opt for a healthy orientation—will need to take care of their body's immediate health needs and also educate themselves as to its continuing and long-term needs.)

SONG
"Good Health" by Stephen P. Cook
to be sung to the tune of "Your Song" by Bernie Taupin / Elton John

Growing up Dad[1] would say at times he saw fit
Son, you get one body—so take care of it!
Didn't think much on this 'til I got real sick
Then oh my God help me—get me well quick!

As adult I took charge and learned to say no
To smoking and junk food and give healthy a go
Healthy food, water, and air—they mean much to me
And from pollution and stress I want to be free

So hey there everybody, "I'm in good health"
A simple fact—but gimme it over great wealth
I don't do pain well, I don't do pain well:
So I live like I should
It's wonderful, life[2] is, when my body feels good!

So pardon my joy at eating tasty whole food
Like apples or broccoli[3] that brightens my mood
And after whole grain breakfast if I go and run
Forgive me again—with exercise I have fun[4]!

But my active lifestyle includes something more
As medicine advances, I work to keep score[5]
Adopting best practices and checking feedback
So my long-term health stays right on track

So hey there everybody, "I'm in good health"
A simple fact—but gimme it over great wealth
I don't do pain well, I don't do pain well:
So I live like I should
It's wonderful, life is, when my body feels good

SONG—NOTES / COMMENTS   (this song is part of the author's personal story)

1—This is a semi autobiographical song. The author's dad died in 2007 at nearly ninety two years old.

2—The classic 1946 movie *It's A Wonderful Life* gets at something that's critically important to the long-term maintenance of good health: having friends and people who care about you. Seems this is part of having a meaningful life—a reason to live. More generally doctors increasingly recognize the importance of the mind-body connection to good health. If the contents of one's mind are unhealthy (anxiety-ridden, negative, full of blame, etc) it can literally make the body sick, or interfere with healing. Similarly, psychological health, reducing stress, being upbeat, feeling loved, or having expectations can be linked to maintaining or regaining physical health. To underscore the importance of feeling loved / not being lonely, Dr. Dean Ornish writes, "I'm not aware of any other factor in medicine–not diet, not smoking, not exercise, not genetics, not drugs, not surgery–that has a greater impact on our quality of life, incidence of illness and premature death."

3—Despite President George H. W. Bush's putdown of it, broccoli is both tasty and a super health food!

4—Running can be a great time to think; other sports can be great fun precisely because to succeed at them requires totally abandoning all thinking and simply relying on the skills your body has learned.

5—For example, in the roughly five years between the writing of *The Worldview Literacy Book* and this book, research findings suggest a link between the progression of mind-robbing conditions like dementia / Alzheimer's disease and intake of sugar (specifically blood glucose level). Some, including the author, in response to books like *The Grain Brain*, have made dietary adjustments in carbohydrate consumption.

Comment: this theme has value as emotional armor. Fear of future illness can be replaced by the feeling that you're doing what you can to protect yourself from that as this song suggests. And from a psychological / physiological coping mechanism perspective, taking care of yourself with good nutrition, exercising, getting plenty of sleep, readies you for the next (often unexpected) time stress threatens, or you've suffering the pain of loss. Given mind / body connections, being emotionally distressed take can lead to physical illness or worse.

Worldview Theme—TFJD CODE: 3212 **VI**=8 **Original Tune Era:** 1970s   **RS Top 500 List:** Yes

Worldview Theme #29A: The Self-Restrained Person

Worldview Theme Summary: **for more:** www.projectworldview.org/wvtheme29.htm

Like many lives, my life involves self-denial and adherence to behavioral guidelines imbedded in my conscience. The origin of such guidelines, whether they stem from work schedule, marriage vow, legal, military, financial, health, family, environmental, ethical, or religious considerations, can differ. And commitments differ. Monks and nuns commit to a life of asceticism, others to a life of voluntary simplicity. For dieters, those battling addiction, athletes, those working a job they don't enjoy, self-restraint lasts until some goal is attained.

SONG
"Use Restraint" by Stephen P. Cook
to be sung to the tune of "You're So Vain" by Carly Simon

You've got this goal that's important to you	Someday you'll reach the promised land
And you wanna take your life there	And this dream keeps you going
It's gonna be rough what you'll have to give up	You'll step into the sun it's gonna be fun
But about this you really care	With proud accomplishment you'll be glowing
So you list behaviors that lead astray	But this moment will never really be
And those heading to your goal	Without hard work and sacrifice
Then you stamp out the former, promote the latter	'Til then you must delay gratification[3]
Stamp out the former, promote the latter and	Delay gratification and
Use Restraint	Use Restraint
Let your inner voice[1] guide you	Let your inner voice guide you
Use Restraint [echo] Restraint	Use Restraint [echo] Restraint
Do what reasoned prudence[2] tells you	Do what reasoned prudence tells you
Do it, Do it, Do it	Do it, Do it, Do it [4]

SONG—NOTES / COMMENTS   (this song is part of the author's personal story)

1—One's inner voice = one's conscience. While this is perhaps more readily connected to guiding behavior toward what is morally/ethically right not wrong, its potential to steer one toward actions that a) will produce more pleasure and happiness vs. more pain and suffering in the long run, b) will be praised rather than blamed, and c) potentially promise benefits if risks and potential liabilities can be dealt with, should not be overlooked! See also note 4 below.

2— Beginning with the ancient Greeks, exercising reasoned good judgment and self-discipline in governing one's life—that is, prudence—has been recognized as being an important virtue. (In fact it's been referred to as "The Mother of All Virtues"!)

3—Delaying gratification refers to the ability to postpone receiving some reward and control impulses pushing for instant gratification. Those possessing this ability are generally thought to be more emotionally mature than those lacking it.

4—The author dedicates this song to his own inner voice: the chairman of that board of directors in his head, affectionately known since 1980 as "The Growling Bear." The story of the actual bear's visit to his Ozark wilderness home is told on page 319 of his *Coming of Age in the Global Village* book. Months later the bear was named during a friend's visit. Without the internal discipline The Growling Bear provided, these songs / this book would not exist. Neither would many other accomplishments.

Comment: Those valuing this theme may have a temperament that's been called effortful control. According to Carver and Connor-Smith, this features "the ability to override impulses to act and the ability to make oneself undertake or persist in difficult, uninteresting, or unpleasant tasks." This theme has value as emotional armor in girding oneself for less pain in the long run (see note 1). As note 3 above describes, delaying gratification or reward may signal emotional maturity. This is an important component of self-control, which generally refers to exercising restraint over one's impulses, desires and emotions. University of Mannheim (Germany) psychology researchers Englert, Bertrams, and Dickhauser have investigated this in relation to various coping styles people have for dealing with stress. In a 2011 paper they write, "Higher levels of dispositional self-control capacity were associated with lower levels of anxiety and with positive coping style, so it may be useful to focus on self-control capacity in order to enable individuals to regulate their anxiety and to enhance individuals' coping skills."

Worldview Theme—TFJD CODE: 2112 **VI=8 Original Tune Era:** 1970s   **RS Top 500 List:** No

Worldview Theme #29B: The Threatening, Violent Person

Worldview Theme Summary: for more: www.projectworldview.org/wvtheme29.htm

I often am able to get what I want by intimidating and instilling fear in other people, by verbally and/or physically threatening them. Since this succeeds to the extent the threat is believable, I've got a reputation associated with verbal abuse and occasionally resorting to actual physical violence. (Note: Some who lack restraint use the old threat system, based on "Give it to me or I'll hurt you" or "Pay me and I'll quit bothering you." A more modern approach is to file or threaten a lawsuit. Of course abandoning restraint is often justifiable.)

SONG
"You Use Fear and I Pay" by Stephen P. Cook
to be sung to the tune of "You Give Love a Bad Name" by Bon Jovi, Child, and Sambora / Bon Jovi

Of wife beating you disapprove[1]
Why don't I think you're telling the truth?
The fact is you dominate me
Cajoling and controlling, I'm not free

Oh! You mean son of a gun [Yeah!]
Oh! Being bullied's no fun
I can't love you with what I've been through

Verbal abuse most every day
You use fear and I pay
[I pay]
You intimidate, I have no say
You use fear and I pay
[I pay]
Hey, you use fear and I pay

In the bedroom I can't say no
Can't run from you, got nowhere to go
The way you grab me when you're mad
Leaves me bruised and sore, hurtin' real bad

Oh! You mean son of a gun [Yeah!]
Oh! Being bullied's no fun
I can't love you with what I've been through

Threatening me most every day
You use fear and I pay
[I pay]

You intimidate, I have no say
You use fear and I pay
[I pay]
Hey, you use fear and I pay

I'm a bad mother, you proclaim
You say I'm taking drugs, that's to blame
Telling lies, you're not bothered one bit
You threaten divorce, taking the kids

Oh! You mean son of a gun [Yeah!]
Oh! Being bullied's no fun
I can't love you with what I've been through

Verbal abuse most every day
You use fear and I pay
[I pay]
You intimidate, I have no say
You use fear and I pay
[I pay]
Hey, you use fear and I pay

Threatening me most every day
You use fear and I pay
[I pay]
You intimidate, I have no say
You use fear and I pay
[I pay]
You use fear, You use fear   [I pay]

SONG—NOTES / COMMENTS

1—While this song tells a story from a battered wife's viewpoint, more generally it is about domestic violence. This occurs when one person in a relationship (or family) attempts to control or dominate— either physically or psychologically— the other (or another family member). This can range from continual emotionally abusive name-calling/putdowns to sexual/physical assault.

Comment: this theme has value as emotional armor. Armed with belief that you are feared and known to be someone not to be crossed, they have less reason to fear others and more to expect to get what you want. In looking for personality factors (five of them were introduced in Part Ia) behind threatening behavior, Carver & Connor-Smith write, "People low in agreeableness use displays of power to deal with social conflict."

Worldview Theme—TFJD CODE: 2313 **VI**=108 **Original Tune Era:** 1980s   **RS Top 500 List:** Yes

Worldview Theme #30: Intellectual Freedom

Worldview Theme Summary: for more: www.projectworldview.org/wvtheme30.htm

Free inquiry is an important freedom to have. I believe that the best way for humankind to extend knowledge and maximize understanding is by allowing individuals a maximum amount of liberty of thought, belief, questioning and inquiry. I particularly value having this liberty because, unlike many, I am especially curious. I'm driven to seek out and explore new territory in pursuing intellectual rewards. I get a thrill out of acquiring new knowledge, distinguishing between knowledge and speculation, probing the world of appearances for the underlying reality, making new connections, and applying my reasoning and analytical skills in refining and extending my worldview, that conceptual map that's my guide to finding the way through and making sense out of the confusion of existence.

SONG
"The Lifelong Learning Parade" by Stephen P. Cook
to be sung to the tune of a medley of "The Fool on the Hill" (left column) and "The Magical Mystery Tour"
by John Lennon and Paul McCartney / The Beatles

Week after week	Sign up, Sign up	The Lifelong Learning Parade
I sit here in class	For the Lifelong Learning Parade!	Will help find concepts to link
Listening, taking notes	Head right this way!	Concepts to link
All these facts I amass		Get you to think
	Sign up, Sign up	
Seems you often	For the Lifelong Learning Parade	Rewards?
Try to help me	Curious?[2]	Find them in books
You know I want to learn	Sign up for the Lifelong Learning Parade	Signup for the Lifelong Learning Parade
Though I seldom		Meaning?
Have the answer	Sign up	Discover how life cooks
	Join the explorations	Signup for the Lifelong Learning Parade
But what I want to know	Sign up for the Lifelong Learning Parade	
As I try to do my best	Curious?	The Lifelong Learning Parade
This difficult concept	Make meaningful connections	Can help you turn work into play
Will it be on the test?	Sign up for the Lifelong Learning Parade	And see shades of gray
		Find your own way
Year after year	The Lifelong Learning Parade	
I teach these same classes	Will help you cubbyhole facts	Values?
Lecturing, trying to reach	Keep track of facts	Decide how it oughta be
All you lads and lasses	Order the stack	Sign up for the Lifelong Learning Parade
		Baggage?
But what's most important	Curious?	Unload beliefs you don't need
When all is said and done	Inquire freely all you please	Sign up for the Lifelong Learning Parade
I have just one answer	Sign up for the Lifelong Learning Parade	
	Anxious?	The Lifelong Learning Parade
As a life long learner	Set your mind at ease	Will help you sort false and true
I've built this map inside me	Sign up for the Lifelong Learning Parade	Separate false and true
A conceptual framework[1]		Refine your worldview
Makes sense of reality		

SONG—NOTES / COMMENTS   (this song is part of the author's personal story)

1—This refers to an idealized way of making sense out of a complicated world, beginning in early childhood with recognizing similarities/differences between objects and building concepts. The process continues building conceptual schemes and fitting these together into a framework. Note: This song is semi-autobiographical and metaphorically figures in this book's ending.

2—Intellectual curiosity is the desire to use one's abilities to investigate, explore, and learn more about a particular part of intellectual terrain and do this often in extending one's conceptual map of reality.

Comment: Those who value this theme tend to be curious, imaginative, and creative—all of which suggest that engagement/problem focused coping that explores new perspectives may help them deal with stress.

Worldview Theme—TFJD CODE: 3112 VI=2 Original Tune Era: 1960s   RS Top 500 List: No / No

Worldview Theme #31: Education for Democracy

Worldview Theme Summary: **for more:** www.projectworldview.org/wvtheme31.htm

I believe that making free K—12 education in a state supported system available to everyone is critically important to democracy, since well educated citizens are, as Jefferson put it, "the ultimate guardians of their own liberty." Such education should provide all students with equal opportunity to find their place in society based on their own interests and ability. It should give them tools to learn more efficiently, help them learn to get along with others, better understand the human experience/accumulated knowledge, select their own moral and political values, and ultimately to select good government leaders. As society grows technologically and ethically more complex, voters are increasingly asked to make decisions involving such complexities. Education should also prepare students for doing this.

SONG

"Strengthen Democracy" by Stephen P. Cook
to be sung to the tune of "My Country 'Tis of Thee" / by Samuel Francis Smith / Thomas Arne

Strengthen democracy[1]
Safeguard our liberty[2]
Through public schools[3]

Independent thinking
From tough choices not shrinking
Social contract[4] inking
Let smart people rule

Ignorance has no place
Knowledge wins the race
For democracy

Schools provide the drills
To build much needed skills
In children they instill
A dream to live free

Lets work for common good[5]
And peace and brotherhood
Through public schools

Build our community
Home where we want to be
Good life for you and me
Let compassion rule

Big money you will fail
Our votes aren't for sale[6]
Banish corruption

Students who take good notes
Grow to cast better votes
High tide lifts all boats
Good education

SONG—NOTES / COMMENTS

1— Democracy is government by the people, controlled by majority vote of the people as a whole, as opposed to government controlled by a particular class, group, or individual. A democratic government where a constitution provides laws guaranteeing rights and liberties is known as a liberal democracy.

2—Many argue that making liberal democracy succeed is best done by promoting liberal education. The Association of American Colleges and Universities describes this as "education that empowers individuals with broad knowledge and transferable skills, and a stronger sense of values, ethics, and civic engagement ... characterized by challenging encounters with important issues" (in contrast to narrower fields of study).

3— Public schools can be distinguished from religious schools—the former are government-supported secular free schools that are financed by taxpayers; the latter are schools affiliated with some religion, which typically promote the religious beliefs of their sponsor, and charge students tuition.

4— A social contract is between the people and their rulers in which the duties and rights of each are defined and constrained. It says that rulers have legitimacy only if they have the consent of those they govern.

5— The common good can be defined narrowly as what is good for every member of the community; others broaden the community here to include all human beings, and their planetary home.

6—Cynics of the USA political/lobbying/campaign huge $ contribution influence peddling scene say "We have the best government money can buy!"

Comment: In "Democracy and the Evolution of Societal Intelligence," Tom Atlee defines the latter as "the ability of a whole society to learn and cope creatively with its environment." And identifies the challenge as learning "to become not only democratic but wisely democratic as individuals, as groups and as a society."

Worldview Theme—TFJD CODE: 2131 **VI**=12 **Original Tune Era:** 1800s   **RS Top 500 List:** No

Worldview Theme #32: Valuing Human Rights

Worldview Theme Summary: **for more:** www.projectworldview.org/wvtheme32.htm

I believe that all people are born equal in dignity and entitled to certain rights and freedoms. To everyone at birth, I would grant the following legal rights: life, liberty, equality before the law, legal recourse when rights have been violated, presumption of innocence until proven guilty, and the right to appeal conviction. Legally they would be protected from discrimination (by race, sex, color, nationality, language, sexual orientation), unwarranted invasion of privacy, arbitrary arrest, torture, inhuman treatment and servitude. I also would extend to them certain freedoms: of movement, of speech and creative expression (exempting what is hateful or hurtful to society), of assembly, to practice religion, to work (and to fair compensation for their work), and to choose a marriage partner.

SONG

"Human Rights" by Stephen P. Cook

to be sung to the tune of "Glory Days" by Jack Allsopp / Bruce Springsteen

Moralistic bigots say to gay lovers
We passed a law, you two can't marry
Rich white racists say to poor blacks
Try to vote, things will get scary
Mexican illegals picking our crops
Poisoned by pesticides—so what?
Cause trouble, we'll call immigration[1]
Or simply order your pay cut

Human Rights, we need to fight for them
Human Rights, if not now, then when?
Human Rights, Human Rights

Islamic extremists say to young girls
We don't want you going to school
If you take off your headscarf in public
We can beat you, it's there in the rules[2]
Wanna change your religion?[3] No way
Even if you accepted Islam as a child
It's blasphemy the penalty is death[4]
With stones the crowd will go wild

Human Rights, we need to fight for them
Human Rights, if not now, then when?
Human Rights, Human Rights

In mountains of Yemen, the shores of Tripoli
We target Islamic bad guys
With remote controlled drones, lasers lock on
We deliver bombs, quite a surprise
But I worry for every bad guy we kill
Many good innocent people die
Smart technology is stupid and criminal
If it brings injustice from the sky

Human Rights, we need to fight for them
Human Rights, if not now, then when?
Human Rights, Human Rights

I'm no terrorist just a simple civilian
Trying to make it in the USA
I value my privacy, I respect the law
And expect others to feel this way
It scares me thinking Big Brother is
Messing with my email, tapping my phone[5]
Today with computer, tomorrow with drones
I just wanna be left alone

Human Rights, we need to fight for them
Human Rights, if not now, then when?
Human Rights, Human Rights

SONG—NOTES / COMMENTS

1—Such a threat, perhaps made by growers in the California, might involve calling USA immigration authorities = INS = Immigration and Naturalization Service asking them to deport workers in the country illegally.
2—In Sudan, according to Amnesty International, this often happens, based on Sharia inspired law rule 152.
3—This is called apostasy, a crime under Sharia law most Islamic scholars feel deserves death or prison.
4—Pakistan has especially harsh blasphemy laws
5—Late 2013 revelations revealed that the USA National Security Agency (NSA) was illegally doing this.

Comment: Emotionally armed with this theme, you might expect others will respect your own rights and have less fear they won't. Of course how you cope with those who threaten your own or others human rights is another matter. In their *Protection Manual for Human Rights Defenders*, the Frontline Defenders group identify numerous coping strategies. The ones to use depend on type of threat, environment, resources, etc.

Worldview Theme—TFJD CODE: 2231 **VI=48 Original Tune Era:** 1970s **RS Top 500 List:** No

Worldview Theme #33A: Servitude

Worldview Theme Summary: **for more:** www.projectworldview.org/wvtheme33.htm
I have something in common with lots of other people, something I'm not pleased with: my freedom, and the control I can exercise over my life, is severely limited. While we are all rather powerless, the cause of this condition may be quite different: extreme poverty, massive debt, harsh environmental conditions, ignorance, prejudice against us, disability, the authority of some dominating individual who exploits us, dogmatic beliefs, imprisonment, restrictions imposed by an authoritarian government, etc.

SONG
"Sixteen Johns" by Stephen P. Cook
to be sung to the tune of "Sixteen Tons" by Merle Travis / Tennessee Ernie Ford

I do sixteen johns, not work I seek
As sex slave[1] in a typical week
A loving God wouldn't let this happen to me
He's all yours, I just wanna be free!

Was born in China, went to university[2]
Restless, I sought a job in the land of the free
Trained in accounting, English I speak
They said I'd start at a thousand a week

From that I'd pay back the smugglers' fee
For the fake passport, airfare, taking care of me
They'd front the money, it'd be a loan
Against this was pledged the family home

I do sixteen johns, not work I seek
As sex slave in a typical week
A loving God wouldn't let this happen to me
He's all yours, I just wanna be free!

Got to mid Manhattan, learned the big lie:
Prostitution, not accounting, I wanted to die!
My dreams of New York had all been sweet
Not this nightmare on thirty sixth street

I was gang raped, beaten, held with a gun
Starved and shut up where I couldn't see sun
Filmed naked, they humiliated me
If I fight back, they'll show my family

I do sixteen johns, not work I seek
As sex slave in a typical week
A loving God wouldn't let this happen to me
He's all yours, I just wanna be free!

One of twenty whores, I'm called Yummy Lee
For three years trapped in this slavery
The johns don't know, they think I get paid
Most wouldn't care: they just wanna get laid!

One day my friend was handcuffed by a john
Beaten, strangled, I found her nearly gone
Took her to a hospital, went to the law
Told 'em 'bout the pimps and bad guys I saw[3]

I do sixteen johns, not work I seek
As sex slave in a typical week
A loving God wouldn't let this happen to me
He's all yours, I just wanna be free!

SONG—NOTES / COMMENTS
1— Forced prostitution is a form of sexual slavery in which someone is forced into working as a prostitute. Poor women in developing countries are often required by extreme poverty to sell their bodies. Others are lured into the sex trade by false promises (say of a good job in a rich country) and are unable to escape.

2—This song is loosely based on the story "A Woman. A Prostitute. A Slave" about Yumi Li (a nickname) written by Nicholas D. Kristof and appearing in *The New York Times* on November 27, 2010.

3—After confronting the pimps and threatening to go public, they moved, and never mailed the video to Yumi's family. She got help from a NYC nonprofit devoted to helping victims of human trafficking.

Comment: living the reality associated with this theme can promote your carrying emotional baggage. Otherwise this theme may have value as emotional armor. Knowledge that your plight is not your fault—it's someone or something elses'—may help shield you from your own, and others', harsh judgment.

Worldview Theme—TFJD CODE: 1113   VI=27   Original Tune Era: 1950s   **RS Top 500 List:** No

Worldview Theme #33B: Addiction

Worldview Theme Summary: **for more:** www.projectworldview.org/wvtheme33.htm

I am one of those people imprisoned in another way—by my brain biochemistry: I can't stop doing certain things. (Note: Such people are addicted to certain substances and/or behaviors. These include addictions to tobacco, alcohol, illegal drugs, painkillers, caffeine, food, sex, sweets, soft drinks, gambling, shopping, etc.)

SONG

"Living Best We Can With Addiction" by Stephen P. Cook
to be sung to the tune of "Living for the City" by Stevie Wonder

A boy grows up smoking a pack a day
He tries to quit but finds there's just no way
Tobacco kills, puts many in early graves
One billion a century die from what they crave[1]
Living best they can, best they can with addiction[2]

Soda pops, he downs them just like candy
Sugar rush, caffeine buzz it comes in handy
'Bout health, schools could teach kids to care
But many help promote this nutrition nightmare[3]
Living best they can, best they can with addiction

Our boy's no sissy, he's friends with ol' Jim Beam[4]
It dulls his pain, has stifled many a scream
At school many mornings his mind in a funk
Trying to learn when hung over or drunk
Living best he can, best he can with addiction

Looking at girly pics with his friend Captain Jack[5]
Women become objects, gotta get 'em in the sack
Orgasmic pleasure—he just can't get enough
So he shoots up smack[6] if the going gets tough
Living best he can, best he can with addiction

Paying for expensive habits, making ends meet
He takes to stealing, selling drugs on the street
When deals go bad, to get away fast he runs
Away from crack dealers after him with guns
Living best he can, best he can with addiction

Emergency rooms, prison, life got hellish mean
It took many years but he finally did get clean
Today he helps young people find their way
To watching sunrise on a drug free new day[7]
Living best he can, best he can with distinction[8]

SONG—NOTES / COMMENTS

1—According to the UN's World Health Organization, 100 million people were killed by tobacco in the 20th century and as many as one billion are expected to die in the 21st century if current trends continue.

2— Addiction is a difficult to define term that generally connects with a person being out of control and unable to stop engaging in some activity known to be harmful but instead continuing to compulsively pursue it. Some addictions can be traced to the physiological and / or psychological dependence on particular chemical <u>substances</u>–such as drugs, alcohol, or foods–which produce a craving for the substance. Others are connected with certain <u>behaviors</u> that involve rewards–such as gambling, sex, and shopping. Both involve withdrawal symptoms–continued craving, anxiety, irritability, and depression– when the substance or opportunity to engage in the pleasurable behavior is unavailable. In either case, it seems that an addicted person's brain fails to successfully send a "stop" signal.

3—Many health professionals link sugary carbonated drink consumption with the epidemic of obesity.

4—A brand of Bourbon Whiskey, 80 to 86 proof = 40% to 43% alcohol, produced in Kentucky since 1795.

5—"Captain Jack" is the title of 1973 Billy Joel song about masturbation (although some say heroin).

6—Smack is another name for heroin.

7—Contrast this with people who light up a cigarette first thing every morning!

8—Distinction refers to differentiating oneself from others. Here someone is finally able to stand apart from all of those people addicted to drugs.

Comment: living this theme's reality can promote carrying emotional baggage. Otherwise this theme may have value as emotional armor. Armed with knowledge that your inability to stop doing things known to be harmful is not your fault—it's all due to your brain biochemistry—you may (to some extent) feel shielded from your own, and others', harsh judgment. Of course that probably won't help you quit. In general, disengagement / emotion-focused type coping strategies, in which you simply try to escape the distress/pain that stresses are causing, are not long-term solutions. With them, rather than directly confronting the stressor and getting to the root cause of the problem, you instead turn to drugs, alcohol, shopping, gambling, etc. These often create other (health, social, legal, financial, etc.) problems leading to additional stress, etc.

Worldview Theme—TFJD CODE: 1312 **VI=162** **Original Tune Era:** 1970s   **RS Top 500 List:** Yes

Worldview Theme #34: Valuing Traditions and Status Quo

Worldview Theme Summary: **for more:** www.projectworldview.org/wvtheme34.htm

I believe that the rules and customs of any long-lived society deserve respect. This glue, shaped by challenges of untold demands, holds society together. While those guided by self-interest may not like the limits on behavior that society imposes, accepting them is a responsible choice. (Note: Those who respect authority, law & order, and value the hard work/sacrifices of their ancestors will be comfortable with this theme. So will those who value the institution of marriage and traditional gender-based roles, according to which men, seen as tougher and more aggressive, are expected to financially support the family, while women, seen as more passive, gentle, and nurturing, are expected to care for children and be homemakers.)

SONG

"When Our Days on Earth Are Done" by Stephen P. Cook
sung to the tune of "Wild Montana Skies" by John Denver / performed by John Denver, Emmy Lou Harris

Into tradition and prejudice
The plain where I was born[1]
Learning to do what I was told
Not expressing any scorn
Respecting parents and elders
My true self not taking wing
A coddling mother shaped me
Sometimes she would sing

Dear God we pray, guide our family
Help us honor and better serve You
Staying strong and healthy
Help us be cheerful kind hard-working
Facing adversity not run
Then guide us home to Heaven
When our da----ays on Earth are don----ne

The times they were a changing[2]
Off to university I went
Held onto some of what I'd been given
But some of it got spent
Becoming a card-carrying hippie
Discounting tradition
Identifying with disturbance[2]
And consciousness revolution[2]

On the USA bicentennial
I finally spread my wings
And headed for Ozark wilderness
Doing a back to the land thing

Finding freedom hard work and discipline
Thinking I was pretty tough
And like that red tail hawk I'd see
I was sailing past the bluff[3]

After twice becoming a father
I started writing a book[4]
A coming of age story
And some foundations got shook
As new projects were launched
Some took flight and soared
Others crashed and burned
But seldom was I bored

Singing to my two young children
Mom's song was never heard
But singing it someday as Grandpa
Perhaps with changing a few words
Looking back on life's hard knocks
Some bowing to tradition
But after all life's disturbance Mom
I hear your rendition[5]

Dear God we pray, guide our family
Help us honor and better serve You
Staying strong and healthy
Help us be cheerful kind hard-working
Facing adversity not run
Then guide us home to Heaven
When our da----ays on Earth are don----ne

SONG—NOTES / COMMENTS   (this song is part of the author's personal story)

1—The author was born in 1951. This song is semi autobiographical.
2—Dylan protest songs, the Stones' "Street Fighting Man," Yale's Charles Reich's *The Greening of America*
3—And metaphorically free, flying high "above the plain of tradition and prejudice" (Kate Chopin's phrase)
4—*Coming of Age in the Global Village*, published in 1990
5—Or, like a disturbed extended spring's restoring force returning it to equilibrium, we return to traditions we were born into.

Comment: For many the path offered by this theme is the least resistance, least stressful one.

Worldview Theme—TFJD CODE: 2222 **VI=64 Original Tune Era:** 1980s   **RS Top 500 List:** No

Worldview Theme #35A: Self Reliant Nonconformity

Worldview Theme Summary: for more: www.projectworldview.org/wvtheme35.htm

I believe in myself: in my mind, in my skills, in the importance of the work I do, in what's inside my heart, in my sense of right and wrong, and in my ability to cope with whatever life throws at me. Increasingly, I rely on myself, on my own wisdom and effort, not on the authority of others, their help, or government help. I find that I no longer envy or imitate others, or blindly conform to custom or societal convention. (Note: Individual choice and societal choice often conflict. While a motto for the self reliant is "If it is to be, it's up to me," if non-conformists really want to change society, they must work with others.)

SONG

"Self Reliance Matters" by Stephen P. Cook

to be sung to the tune "Nothing Else Matters" by Cox, Battey S., Battey C., Palacios, Clark / Metallica

A good team right from the start[1]
Trusting in you with all my heart
Together 'til death do us part
Our love is what mattered

Life was ours, lived our own way
Codependent, sharing each day
Then she asked what others would say
Soon something else mattered

No, we can't do our own thing!
Why? My objection would sting
Conformity explains nothing[2]
Soon our love shattered

I want to be a teamplayer
Not a difficult naysayer
I gotta be me[3]

I won't lose me to find you[4]
What's inside me must come through
Believing in me, that rings true
Loving yourself matters

I want to be a teamplayer
Not a difficult naysayer
I gotta be me

The insecure[5] march in lock-step
Trusting myself, doing my prep
The drummer I hear he's got pep
Self reliance matters

Bring it on world, I can cope
But to custom I may say "Nope!"
New ideas they give us hope
Self reliance matters

I want to be a teamplayer
Not a difficult naysayer
I won't blindly conform
I won't blindly heap scorn
I gotta be me—yea—ah!

I may leave this world all alone
To asking for help, I'm not prone
When my time's up, I won't moan
Self reliance matters

SONG—NOTES / COMMENTS (this song is part of the author's personal story)

1— This is a semi-autobiographical song written in the fall of 2013.

2—In his famous 1841 essay *Self Reliance*, Ralph Waldo Emerson wrote, "Your genuine action will explain itself, and will explain your other genuine actions. Your conformity explains nothing."

3—"I've Gotta Be Me" is the title of a 1968 song made famous by Sammy Davis, Jr.

4—This line reinforces the sentiment expressed in the Sammy Davis, Jr. song. It refutes the opinion expressed in the 1971 song "Bargain" recorded by The Who: "I'd gladly lose me to find you."

5— Insecurity refers to a person's lacking confidence and assuredness, feeling uncertain and unsure–perhaps even unprotected and unsafe. Feelings of anxiety ➔ insecurity. Security is something that is associated much more with a course of action, path or road perceived to be "safe"—the well-traveled road of conformity alluded to in Robert Frost's poem *The Road Not Taken*.

Comment: feeling self reliant can provide emotional armor in overcoming fear. Practically speaking, what's behind that feeling may be most important in taking a generally adaptive or constructive coping approach to stress. If you've generally gone through life relying on yourself rather than others to find solutions, you've undoubtedly accumulated lots of problem-solving know how. Depending on the nature of the stress, you may turn to this. If it presents a different challenge, turning to others for help / emotional support may be needed.

Worldview Theme—TFJD CODE: 2113 VI=12 Original Tune Era: 1990s RS Top 500 List: No

---

Worldview Theme #35B: Working for Change

Worldview Theme Summary: for more: www.projectworldview.org/wvtheme35.htm
I am dissatisfied with things as they are: the status quo. Three factors—1) the degree of my dissatisfaction,
2) the amount of the perceived gap between how things should be and how they are, and 3) the extent to
which I believe in the need for and/or rightness (in a social justice sense) of the change I'm working for—all
determine the strength of my commitment. (Note: Activities the dissatisfied pursue can include raising
public awareness, political campaigning, lobbying, building social movements to reform the system from
within, filing lawsuits, organizing strikes, boycotts, civil disobedience, violent revolutionary/terrorist tactics,
etc.)

SONG
"Be Change" by Stephen P. Cook
to be sung to the tune of "Dream On" by Steven Tyler / Aerosmith

Every time someone considers me
Just what is it I want them to see?
I think I know-oooooooooooooo
Seems I want my life to show
Others the right way
Toward a better future someday-aaaaaaaaaaaa

Well.......ell—today so many think
So much sits on the brink[1]
Could be without your pledge
We find it falling over the edge

Every time I want something to be
What if making it so is up to me?
Here's what I'll do—ooooooooo
Work so hard, to recruit you

Work with me, work for the change
Work with passion the world to rearrange
Join with me: let us show 'em today
Let's bring the change to sweep the past away-aaaa

Work with me, work for the change
Work with passion the world to rearrange
Join with me: let us show 'em today
Let's bring the change to sweep the past away-aaaa

Be change, be change, be change
Be the change you want to see
Be change, be change, be change
Be the change you want to see
Be change
Be change
Be change
Be change
Be change
Be change
Be change Oh-ooooooooooooo

Work with me, work for the change
Work with passion the world to rearrange
Join with me: let us show 'em today
Let's bring change to sweep the past away

Work with me, work for the change
Work with passion the world to rearrange
Join with me: let us show 'em today
Let's bring change to sweep the past away-aaaa

SONG—NOTES / COMMENTS

1—On the brink implies something teetering on the edge. We can add to the metaphor with the term tipping point—certainly
something that's become part of concerns about climate change. This term can add a sense of urgency to the need to work for
change: perhaps one's small but timely effort can help tip the balance! In physical systems analysis of what it takes to irreversibly
trip the system into a new state is obviously much more straight forward than in social systems. There explaining something like
the so-called "hundredth monkey effect" —where new behavior supposedly spreads rapidly—is a challenge! In economic
situations a dominant player or technology triggering a tipping point can result in a "winner take all" result—something those
concerned about growing inequality in society worry that economic outcomes increasingly produce.

Comment: this theme has value as emotional armor in that it can help protect against feeling hopeless. The
feeling of joining others in working for change magnifies your identity and overcomes feeling alone fears.

Worldview Theme—TFJD CODE: 3333 **VI=81 Original Tune Era:** 1970s   **RS Top 500 List:** Yes

Worldview Theme #36A: Cynicism

Worldview Theme Summary: for more: www.projectworldview.org/wvtheme36.htm
Once I thought people could be trusted, had good intentions, were caring, decent, honorable—I now know better. Humans beings, I believe, are self serving and can't be trusted to do good. Those who profess to be altruistic are deluded, not seeing misguided self-interest for what it is. Most are lazy, mean, corrupt, and immoral—hypocrites, too stupid to see themselves as such. I was once more accepting and forgiving, now I am critical—sneering at, and finding fault with, much of what people do and say.

SONG

"Cynicism Grows" by Stephen P. Cook
to be sung to the tune of "Anything Goes" by Cole Porter / Frank Sinatra

The bad guy killers on nine eleven
Died dreaming of going to heaven
Almighty God knows
Cynicism grows!

Staying married 'til death do you part
Maybe, for a newly wed old fart
So will you propose?
Cynicism grows!

Corporate cats sit on trillions in cash[1]
And escape taxes[2] that dog my ass
Smelling like a rose
Cynicism grows!

The world's eighty five billionaires
Own more than three billion sucking air[3]
Few highs lots of lows
Cynicism grows!

Hunger brings a shoplifting spree
Now prison in the land of the free
Wearing new clothes
Cynicism grows!

Young black males often rule
More likely in prison than in school[4]
Raw deal jim crows
Cynicism grows!

What's growing faster than government spending?
Regulations—they're never ending!
Pages and pages of prose
Cynicism grows!

Those who know say burning coal is bad
And climate change can make us sad
We can't say whoa!
Cynicism grows!

Millions die in war's deadly fires
Who's to blame? Thieves[5] and liars!
Give peace a chance foes
Cynicism grows!

SONG—NOTES / COMMENTS

1—As of early 2014, estimates were $5 trillion to $7 trillion for US companies. Invested in putting people to work at $70,000/yr per job, the latter figure would fund ten million pretty good USA jobs for ten years!

2—According to a 2013 study by US PIRG, "By booking profits to subsidiaries registered in [offshore] tax havens, multinational corporations are able to avoid an estimated $90 billion in federal income taxes each year. These subsidiaries are often shell companies with few, if any employees, and engage in little to no real business activity."

3— A 2014 Oxfam report said the world's 85 richest people owned as much wealth as its 3.5 billion poorest!

4—Although frequently cited, this is an exaggeration. According to Howard University professor Ivory Toldson, as of April 2013, there are 1.4 million US black men in college and 840,000 black men in prison.

5—Many recent wars in Africa can be traced to kleptocracy–where government ruler (or rulers) loot the national treasury and extend personal wealth to the detriment of the people they are supposed to be serving.

Comment: this theme has value as emotional armor in protecting yourself from attacks on your own failings and hurt due to others' failings. Rather than assign blame, you accept that human nature is imperfect and emotionally move on. Unfortunately many cynics embrace something not so healthy: a pessimistic attitude that fully expects (and perhaps even encourages?) bad outcomes. Those lead to more stress and a tendency to withdraw, avoid, deny—rather than employing more engaged, adaptive or constructive coping strategies.

Worldview Theme—TFJD CODE: 3311 **VI=9 Original Tune Era:** 1930s	**RS Top 500 List:** No

Worldview Theme #36B: Conspiracism

Worldview Theme Summary: **for more:** www.projectworldview.org/wvtheme36.htm
My suspicions of other people's motives often extends to imagining the existence of a conspiracy: a few individuals with their own hidden agenda are conspiring to infiltrate key institutions, manipulate events and shape outcomes to their liking. (Note: This imagining can 1) devolve into paranoia, 2) lead to a simplistic black and white portrayal of something that's actually much more complex, and 3) uncover an actual conspiracy—although more typically no such thing exists! Some link their belief in a particular conspiracy to seemingly unrelated societal problems.)

SONG
"Ballad of a Fat Conspiracy" by Stephen P. Cook
to be sung to the tune of "Ballad of A Thin Man" by Bob Dylan

With corporate executives
I've shared many a drink
Minds tuned to profits
I know how they think
They've hatched evil plots
Their laundry really stinks
Their agenda hidden
Beyond scrutiny

But what has occurred
Based on what I've heard
Sounds like…conspiracy

They packed food with calories
And saturated fats
Sweetened with corn syrup
Tested on rats
With hydrogenated oils[1]
Additives and all that
Marketed heavily
And sold on TV

But what has occurred
Based on what I've heard
Sounds like…conspiracy

I really have no doubt
To make us big and stout
A campaign they did mount
With collusion[2] beyond our detection
Riding lawnmowers we expect
Exercise we neglect
Do you begin to suspect
Subliminal advertising manipulation[3]

You've seen the lard asses
And not liked their looks
Nor couch potatoes at restaurants
With deep fat fryer cooks
But have you ever linked them
To food industry corporate crooks?
Maybe you have
If you're paranoid[4] like me

So how our nation got fat
I've traced it to that
Corporate conspiracy

SONG—NOTES / COMMENTS
1—The merely hydrogenated oils apparently aren't as bad as the partially hydrogenated ones! Parts of this song should be taken with a grain of salt. If you haven't caught on, it's supposed to be funny!
2— Collusion refers to a secret agreement between businesses or firms that sets price and output in a way that decreases competition and increases profits.
3—Supposedly subliminal stimuli—beneath the threshold humans can consciously detect—can nonetheless affect the unconscious brain and influence behavior. In a study documenting this, "Hungry? Eat Popcorn!" was flashed for 1/3000 sec over motion pictures shown in a theater. During a six week test, popcorn sales rose 58%! (Ads using such messages are banned in Britain.)
4—Paranoia, in mild form, is characterized by excessive or irrational suspiciousness and distrust of others; in severe psychological disorder form it also involves delusions: of persecution, grandeur, jealousy, etc.

Comment: this theme can facilitate shifting blame away from yourself and provide emotional armor. Of the five personality types (part Ia), neurotics are more likely to embrace conspiracy theories. In their book *American Conspiracy Theories*, Uscinski and Parent cite lab experiments and write, "Inducing anxiety or loss of control triggers respondents to see nonexistent patterns and evoke conspiratorial explanations."

Worldview Theme—TFJD CODE: 2311 **VI=36** **Original Tune Era:** 1960s   **RS Top 500 List:** No

Worldview Theme #37A: Proud Identification

Worldview Theme Summary: for more: www.projectworldview.org/wvtheme37.htm

I take pride in being a(n) _____ (insert name of nationality, religious / ethnic group, tribe, etc). I very much identify with other members of this group, and sometimes favor them as I interact with people in general. I proudly display symbols of this affiliation and will fight or otherwise serve our cause in battles where our interests are at stake.

SONG

"Proud to be Anatolian…Armenian…Athenian" by Stephen P. Cook
to be sung to the tune of *Proud to be An American* by Lee Greenwood

It means so much to me:
The heritage where I belong
But it's complicated
My forebears didn't much get along
I'd say celebrating it requires three songs
And even those could not begin
To right all the wro—oongs

First I'm proud to be Anatolian[1],
Living in modern Turkey
Homeland of Indo-European
Language diversity[2]
It began at Catalhoyuk[3]
And was fought for at Galipoli[4]
And by our father Ataturk[5]
Turkey's nationality

And I'm proud to be an Armenian[6]
And hear you call me Hye[7]
In Yerevan[8] with Mount Ararat[9]
Or here seeking to glorify
Our past as the first nation
To adopt Christianity[10]
And after genocide[11] and occupation[12]
Today being free

And I'm proud to be an Athenian[13]
My mother used to say
Logos'[14] triumph over chaos
Gave us the Greek way
Men like Socrates and Plato
Inspired democracy
And building a world on reason
The key to being free

SONG—NOTES / COMMENTS

1—From Anatolia, the westernmost protrusion of Asia sometimes called Asia Minor.
2—The oldest written versions of this language family, spoken by three billion people today, are from here.
3—One of the first proto-cities, this Neolithic site is 9500 years old. It was once home to ~10,000 people.
4—This World War I battle site—where huge numbers of young men died in a protracted invasion battle—is not only important to Turkey's heritage, but also to Australians' and New Zealanders'.
5—Mustafa Kemal Ataturk (1881-1938) was modern Turkey's founder. Roughly speaking, what George Washington did for the United States, Ataturk did for Turkey (and perhaps then some!)
6—From Armenia, a small mountainous country east of Turkey.
7—In Armenian, this word describes one as an Armenian (just as USA citizens call themselves Americans.)
8—The capital of modern Armenia.
9—In the *Bible's Old Testament*, this is where Noah's ark came to rest. It lies on the border between Turkey and Armenia.
10—This happened in 301 AD, twenty or so years before Christianity became the Roman Empire's religion.
11—Over one million Armenians were killed in the 1915-1917 genocide: deliberate, systematic mass slaughter of an ethnic, political or cultural group. Turkey denies responsibility and claims the deaths were part of a civil war in the region (which was already engulfed in World War I).
12—Briefly independent from 1918 to 1920, Armenia was incorporated into the Soviet Union until 1991.
13—From Athens, the capital of modern Greece, and the birthplace of democracy in the fifth century BC.
14—To Aristotle (384-322 BC) logos meant "reasoned discourse" ➔ the idea of an orderly universe

Comment: this theme has value as emotional armor: 1) joining others offers strength protecting against feeling alone fears, 2) feeling part of a heritage offers continuity and protection from feeling isolated, alone. But behind this theme's "feel good" joining, as was discussed in Part Id, may be (oxytocin fueled) prejudice, outgroup derogation, ethnocentrism, etc. potentially leading to conflict and violence.

Worldview Theme—TFJD CODE: 1133 **VI=81** **Original Tune Era:** 1980s **RS Top 500 List:** No

Worldview Theme #37B: Global Citizen

Worldview Theme Summary: **for more:** www.projectworldview.org/wvtheme37.htm

I do not identify with any particular nationality, religious or ethnic group, but think of myself as a global citizen. (Note: In ethical decision-making considerations involving "people" and "place," global citizens identify all human beings with the former, and planet Earth with the latter. No one is excluded from this group's ethical concern tent—everyone is inside, all are family.)

SONG

"Imagine An Election" by Stephen P. Cook
to be sung to the tune of "Imagine" by John Lennon

Imagine an election
People everywhere vote
Us global citizens
We're all in the same boat

We travel all together
Sharing Spaceship Ear--th[1]

Three issues on the ballot
I'll explain them now
Each has a keyword
And a little know-how

We travel all together
Sharing Spaceship Ear--th

First choice is Peace yes or no?
Responsibly defend[2]
No aggression allowed
All out war could be our end[3]

Imagine we the people
Voting here today--ay

Next choice Freedom yes or no?
With responsibility[4]
Yes for human rights[5]
No for tyranny

Imagine we the people
Voting here today--ay

Last choice Ecoshares[6] yes or no?
Give and take ethically
Vote no, short term greed wins
Yes, long term stability

Imagine we the people
Voting here today--ay

You and I know what they'd choose
Peace, Freedom, and Ecoshares
So let's have this election
And the world will show it cares

SONG—NOTES / COMMENTS

1—A term popularized in the 1960s. It suggests that we live on a small, fragile planet with limited resources so we need to get along, treat each other fairly, and not allow our pollution to degrade life support systems.

2—Voting "Yes" here commits one to peace and non-aggression, but defending oneself or family is allowed.

3—It is generally agreed that even the "winners" in an all out war nuclear war would lose due to vastly increased radiation, seriously changed global climate ➔ what could be the extinction of the human species.

4—Voting "Yes" here would be a vote to have a say in one's elected government and to exercise one's freedom responsibly by always respecting the rights of others. Voting "No" would be for authoritarianism.

5— Human rights can be defined as basic rights and freedoms to which all humans are entitled. Basically these are held to include the right to life and liberty, freedom of thought and expression, and being treated equally by the law.

6—Voting "Yes" would commit one to an environmental ethic: your impact on the Earth's biosphere should be limited to a fair ecoshare, based on assessment of available resources, environmental impact, computer models, and limits imposed by sustainability criteria. Widespread acceptance of it would not tolerate a human family in which a relatively few rich people have millions of times more wealth than billions of poor!

Comment: this theme may have value as emotional armor. Belief that, regardless of differences, "people are people" can lessen your fear when encountering strangers and in traveling far from home.

Worldview Theme—TFJD CODE: 3331 VI=27 Original Tune Era: 1970s   **RS Top 500 List:** Yes

Worldview Theme #38: Valuing Family

Worldview Theme Summary: for more: www.projectworldview.org/wvtheme38.htm

I believe that love and life are linked in a way most naturally expressed by marriage and family. I know that family is what's most important in life. Not only is it where life's great joys are to be found, it's a big part of the "glue" that holds society together. Accordingly, I feel that government policy should strengthen the family—in particular giving parents more childcare options, and the right to choose the kind of education their children receive. Personally, I value spending time with my family above all else. Of course, family brings obligations. I feel it's the parents' duty to sacrifice and do their best for their children, even at the expense of their own well-being. Another duty: regardless of the qualities/faults of one's parents, I feel one must love and respect them, and, if needed, help care for them as they age.

SONG

"Jean, My Mother in Law" by Stephen P. Cook
to be sung to the tune of "Mother in Law" by Allen Toussaint / Ernie K Doe

The best people I know[1]	She said at age sixty-one
Mother in Law, Mother in Law,	She felt like she was twenty and looking for fun
She's been good to me so	And wat----ch out my Son
Mother in Law, Mother in Law,	Mother in Law, Mother in Law
Many times she'd speak her mind	Mother in Law, Mother in Law
Telling me I'm doing fine	My marriage to Jean's daughter didn't last
I'm gonna miss her so	Mother in Law, Mother in Law,
Mother in Law, Mother in Law	A family life consigned to the past
Mother in Law, Mother in Law	Mother in Law, Mother in Law,
She was married to William Moore	This le----ft me alone
Mother in Law, Mother in Law,	I had to find a new home
Berkeley Law School lawyer galore	No longer was Bonnie Jean my
Mother in Law, Mother in Law,	Mother in Law, Mother in Law
He died with legal shoes to fill	Mother in Law, Mother in Law
She did it with considerable skill	Jean's daughters had kids of their own
For awhile she truly was a	Grandma in Law, Grandma in Law,
Mother in Law, Mother in Law	Their laughter filled her home
Mother in Law, Mother in Law	Grandma in Law, Grandma in Law,
She had old country roots Bonnie Jean	The joys of child---hood loomed large
Mother in Law, Mother in Law,	Her favorite toy parked in the garage
She loved Scotland something mean	Bonnie Jean had it all
Mother in Law, Mother in Law,	Grandma in Law, Grandma in Law,
Robert the Bru----ce was she felt	Grandma in Law, Grandma in Law
Superman dressed in a kilt	Her life ended with a final treat
A Highland Games homecoming queen my	Grandma in Law, Grandma in Law,
Mother in Law, Mother in Law	A new baby she got to meet
Mother in Law, Mother in Law	Grandma in Law, Grandma in Law,
Many nights I watched Bonnie Jean	Grandson Casey and Jen brought Annie
Mother in Law, Mother in Law,	To smi----le for their granny
Sipping scotch, her eyes had a gleam	She was something else
Mother in Law, Mother in Law,	GreatGrandma in Law, GreatGrandma in Law
	GreatGrandma in Law, GreatGrandma in Law

SONG—NOTES / COMMENTS (this song is part of the author's personal story)

1—This autobiographical song was sung by the author at a 2013 memorial wake honoring his long-time mother in law.

Comment: this theme has value as emotional armor: family shelters, gives comfort, lessening fear, suffering.

Worldview Theme—TFJD CODE: 1332 **VI=**486 **Original Tune Era:** 1960s **RS Top 500 List:** No

Worldview Theme #39A: Tough Love

Worldview Theme Summary: **for more:** www.projectworldview.org/wvtheme39.htm

Sometimes kindness does more harm than good. If I care about another's development and learning to accept responsibility then I shouldn't pamper, spoil, mollycoddle, or indulge. Often, helping in a way that does not involve outright giving or meeting all needs is a better approach. Similarly, not explicitly instructing, but rather fostering conditions that allow independent discovery (even if that means learning from mistakes) can provide more meaningful lessons. Rather than accepting excuses or shortcomings, I should confront this person and communicate my expectations as to rectifying behavior.

SONG

"You Can't Always Say What You Want" by Stephen P. Cook

to be sung to the tune of "You Can't Always Get What You Want" by Jagger & Richards/The Rolling Stones

Facing my soon to be ex-wife[1]
I planned some verbal abuse
Saying I carried you for years in our marriage
Now get a job so I can cut you loose
Such mean words I couldn't say to her
Though they were what she needed to hear
Doing a tough love number on my ex-wife
In her eyes looking at me I'd see tears

You can't always say what you want
Nice words can be hollow, thin, and gaunt
Mean ones so aggressive they taunt
But if you speak your mind
You'll do just fine
And say what you need to…All right!

As professor I had student workers
A poor supervisor was I
Some would half ass and cut corners
Which I might ignore, not let words fly
But doing that did them no favor
They needed confronting, looked in the eye
Hey man you're slacker and bad actor
You're half assin' here, tell me why?

You can't always say what you want
Nice words can be hollow, thin, and gaunt
Mean ones so aggressive they taunt
But if you speak your mind
You'll do just fine
And say what you need to… All right!

As for unquestioning obedience[2]
Instilling it can take much work
Parents should be consistent and firm
But not fascist dictator jerks
My daughter only got one spanking
And she's turned out pretty well
But after being caught big time lying
Her three year old ass hurt like hell

You can't always say what you want
Nice words can be hollow, thin, and gaunt
Mean ones so aggressive they taunt
But if you speak your mind
You'll do just fine
And say what you need to…All right!

Learning from mistakes and feedback
Is especially meaningful
Parents can use teachable moments
To help their kids outta some hole
My son I helped escape jealousy
And his life's been a pretty good ride
Threatened by his sister's success
I helped him feel good, take pride

You can't always say what you want
Nice words can be hollow, thin, and gaunt
Mean ones so aggressive they taunt
But if you speak your mind
You'll do just fine
And say what you need to… All right!

SONG—NOTES / COMMENTS   (this song is part of the author's personal story)

1—This is an autobiographical song. For the record, the author has more than one ex-wife!

2—While instilling this could be a valid parenting goal for their very young children, many parents will be more comfortable eventually teaching them (as teenagers) to question authority, and think for themselves when appropriate.

Comment: ill planned tough love approaches can emotionally scar the loved ones they are supposed to help
➔ their suffering ➔ their acquiring emotional baggage. (Also see comment for theme #2B.)

Worldview Theme—TFJD CODE: 2121 **VI=8 Original Tune Era:** 1960s   **RS Top 500 List:** Yes

Worldview Theme #39B: Scapegoating

Worldview Theme Summary: **for more:** www.projectworldview.org/wvtheme39.htm

In my anger over an outrage I've suffered, I will sometimes single out some person or group to blame. (Note: scapegoating often involves discriminating by unfairly blaming others for some (real or imagined) offense. It happens at all levels: from sport fans blaming a particular player for their team's loss, to parents targeting an unwanted child, to prejudiced individuals targeting someone whose looks, race, or sexual orientation they don't like, to organized groups committing hate crimes, to nation states targeting whole populations for genocide.)

SONG

"Dirt's My Name" by Stephen P. Cook
to be sung to the tune of a medley of "Sympathy for the Devil" and (chorus only) "Jumping Jack Flash"
by Mick Jagger and Keith Richards / The Rolling Stones

I grew up with a loving mother
And I learned to value fair play
But they were times she was mean
'Bout Grandpa she'd nothing good to say

We seldom visited this supposed bad man
Years later this became a bummer
When I learned how respected he was
This man the Golden Rule Plumber[1]

This wasn't right pal
Was not a fair game
It wasn't right—
She said dirt's his name
He's to blame, blame, blame

Took a trip many hundreds of miles
By car with my children and wife
She brought the caged up cat along
Guess she needed the creature in her life

I supposedly let him escape
Out motel room door—my wife had a cow
The kids heard her dump on me real bad
'Till from the bed springs there came a meow

This wasn't right pal
Was not a fair game
It wasn't right—
She said dirt's my name
I'm to blame, blame, blame

My mother grew up not liking her nose
"Makes me look Jewish" she once said
Later I found in the family tree
A Jewish name among long ago dead[2]

If my mom had grown up in Germany
Instead of in the USA
Would Hitler[3]'s men have gassed her
In hellholes where he made Jews pay?

This wasn't right pal
Was not a fair game
It wasn't right—
He said dirt's our[4] name
We're to blame, blame, blame

SONG—NOTES / COMMENTS   (this song is part of the author's personal story)

1—This is an autobiographical song. The author only saw his Grandpa a few times—the latter died when the former was ten years old. Many years latter the man's business cards displaying this logo were discovered.

2—The supposed Jewish ancestor died in 19th century Germany. The author has since enjoyed speculating about this being the genetic origin of his talent in math and physics. (While regrettably reinforcing stereotypes about Eastern European Jews, he viewed this supposed ancestry as a sort of status symbol!)

3—Tragically a hateful man whose worldview was built around scapegoating perpetrated horrible genocide.

4—Use of "our" suggests what many feel: in the desire to end genocide, "we are all Jews."

Comment: this theme can promote carrying emotional baggage. For this theme's value as emotional armor see the comment for theme #17A. Avoiding looking for others to blame may signal emotional maturity.

Worldview Theme—TFJD CODE: 1311 **VI=81 Original Tune Era:** 1960s **RS Top 500 List:** Yes/Yes

---

Worldview Theme #40: Environmental Economics

Worldview Theme Summary: **for more:** www.projectworldview.org/wvtheme40.htm

I believe that assessing economic health must necessarily factor in environmental health. Economic analyzes must not 1) ignore loss of natural capital—soil, fish, biodiversity, fossil fuels, etc—or fail to depreciate resources as they're used up or polluted; 2) pretend that waste has no ill effect; 3) put no value on natural beauty. Very efficient industrial activities that resemble natural processes with matter recycling in closed systems should be "winners"; wasteful ones should also be economic "losers". Use of Earth's "commons" — air, water, land, soil, trees, minerals, etc—should be regulated so that the right to use the commons is linked to responsibility to protect it. Markets (some based on "cap & trade") providing incentive for environmental good & investment in restoring/protecting natural capital should be encouraged.

SONG

"The Battle Hymn of New Economics" by Stephen P. Cook
to be sung to the tune of "The Battle Hymn of the Republic" by William Steffe/Julia Ward Howe / traditional

Let us join together
To enact a carbon tax[1]
And to hard working poor people
Rebate this money back
Big greedy corporations
And polluters we'll attack
Fight greenhouse gases[2] now

Sustainability Forever
Earth First Forever
Solidarity Forever[3]
United We are Strong

Energy from renewables
More of that's our goal
Let's stop building power plants
Fired by dirty coal
Stop C O two from rising
That we shall patrol
Value natural capital[4]

Sustainability Forever
Earth First Forever
Solidarity Forever
United We are Strong

Indicators should not rise[5]
As more and more we trash
Keep ignoring hidden costs[6]
And our economy will crash
Winner Take All Society[7]
Hey, that's something rash
Work for social justice now

Sustainability Forever
Earth First Forever
Solidarity Forever
United We are Strong

SONG—NOTES / COMMENTS

1—A carbon tax would be levied on carbon dioxide pollution that fossil fuel dependent activities of people and business put into the atmosphere. Such taxes seek to factor environmental costs into the market system.

2—Most notably carbon dioxide (CO_2), whose rising levels (passing 400 ppm in 2014) gets the attention, but human activity (especially agriculture) releases lots of methane, which is many times as potent as CO_2.

3—This is the title of a 1915 song written for labor unions but often used for other progressive causes.

4— Natural capital includes natural resources (air, water, soil, forests, minerals, fossil fuels, fish, etc) and the biodiversity of natural living ecosystems (grasslands, wetlands, ocean coral reefs, etc).

5— Gross domestic product (GDP) is the annual market value of a country's total domestic economic output, including all end goods and services purchased. It is often used to gauge economic well-being.

6—GDP doesn't measure decreases in natural capital or many other things important to sustainability.

7—Seems capitalism is good at generating wealth but poor at evenly distributing it. The phrase used to characterize the disturbing societal trend toward greater inequality is "Winner Take All Society". In such a society, in the words of Molly Ivins, "A few people get ungodly rich, and the rest of us fall behind!"

Comment: Critics of business as usual / economic growth (theme #22A) who charge that theme represents a societal maladaptive coping strategy (see comment theme #22A) like this theme better. Some would prefer a quality of life index—which includes emotional well being—replacing % GDP growth/yr to gauge progress.

Worldview Theme—TFJD CODE: 3233   **VI=36   Original Tune Era:** 1800s   **RS Top 500 List:** No

Worldview Theme #41: Struggling With a Basic Need: Self Esteem

Worldview Theme Summary: for more: www.projectworldview.org/wvtheme41.htm

I'm struggling to find the road to emotional maturity and make peace with myself. I seek a sense of my own intrinsic value, self-respect, confidence in my ability to handle life and being able to enjoy it in relaxed fashion. I want to leave behind what's inside me too often now: feeling unworthy, that I can't cope, that I'm a failure; being too concerned about what others think of me; anxiety, fear, and self doubt. When I'm really down, on myself and others, it seems like a battle rages inside. (Note: some lose the battle, descending into a hell of bitterness/self hatred. Others compensate for unworthiness by excessively self sacrificing/doing things for others—often full of sorrow for themselves. A few find the strength to change and grow.)

SONG
"Me and Myself" by Stephen P. Cook
to be sung to the tune of "Nights in White Satin" by Justin Hayward / The Moody Blues

I'm hurting and scared—I need a friend
And this war inside me, I know it must end[1]
What do I care, what others may think?
Make peace with myself, without it I'll sink

End the war [echo] the war[2]
Me and myself [echo] myself
End the war [echo] the war

I grew up unwanted—unloved, insecure[3]
Can I transcend this? I'm really not sure
Reasoned belief tells me, a good person I am
Then feelings of worthless hit with a slam

Find self esteem[4] [echo] esteem,
Strength through self esteem [echo] esteem
Find self esteem [echo] esteem

Questioning choices, decisions I've made
Blaming myself, with tears I have paid
When things go wrong, or needs go unmet
Life can be like that—start over, forget

Find self esteem [echo] esteem,
Strength through self esteem [echo] esteem
Find self esteem [echo] esteem

Life's not a crisis, I need to relax[5]
Attend to my real needs, get back on track
I know I can make it, that I can cope
Grow positive, weed negative[6]— this gives me hope

Find self esteem [echo] esteem,
Strength through self esteem [echo] esteem
Find self esteem [echo] esteem

All that I've been through, what I've overcome
I'm older and wiser, not helpless and dumb
We care and we're sensitive, on the same team
Thank you my friend, for helping me believe

In myself [echo] myself
We're on the same team [echo] same team
Strength through self esteem [echo] esteem
On the same team [echo] same team
Me and myself

SONG—NOTES / COMMENTS   (this song is part of the author's personal story)

1— This semi autobiographical song is based on a 1973 poem and on long-time discussion / empathizing with / consoling others.

2—For many, introspection—the process of looking inside one's mind, recalling events, memories, sensory experiences, etc, and reflecting—can be a healthy activity. But for those with harsh critical "inner voices" it can be a debilitating battle, like fighting a war. This song is about ending the war and making peace!

3— Insecurity refers to lacking confidence and assuredness, feeling uncertain and unsure—perhaps even unprotected and unsafe. Feelings of anxiety often accompany feelings of insecurity. (For the record, the author grew up feeling loved!)

4—Self esteem refers to one's self-appraisal. It provides a measure of personal worth or worthiness.

5—Many people with low self esteem and lots of anxiety operate in a self-created state of emergency.

6—Replacing negative messages, often planted in one's brain during a difficult childhood, with positive ones can be a difficult process that, even with determined conscious effort, can take years.

Comment: the struggle for self esteem ➔ acquiring emotional baggage, but winning it provides emotional armor (defense against self and other inflicted painful stabs) as the song suggests. In winning this battle, your emotional intelligence may increase. Basically this is being aware of and in control of your own emotions, being aware of and helping nurture others' emotions, and being able to soothe yourself when distressed.

Worldview Theme—TFJD CODE: 2323 **VI=216** **Original Tune Era:** 1960s   **RS Top 500 List:** No

Worldview Theme #42: Ethical Orientation

Worldview Theme Summary: for more: www.projectworldview.org/wvtheme42.htm

I'd say ethics starts with honesty and respect for laws, extends in earning a living to adhering to professional ethical codes and avoiding conflicts of interest, and can, for those especially concerned with social justice, even come to include applying principles which involve asking questions. I offer three of them: 1) Greatest General Good Principle: "In deciding whether a proposed action is morally right, am I comfortable with its perceived social benefit and the extent to which it produces the greatest good for the greatest number of people?" 2) Principle of Fraternal Charity: "If I were in the shoes of someone affected by this, facing similar circumstances, could I live with the consequences of what this decision involves?" 3) Principle of Universality: "What would be the results if everyone acted in this manner?"

SONG
"Ethical Man" by Stephen P. Cook
sung to the tune of "Piano Man" by Billy Joel

Share your wisdom you're an ethical man[1]
Principles for living today
Help us to ask the right questions
Help us to find our way

Find a home in your head for honesty
Install it there on a throne
Learn to value the truth
Don't be aloof
With good conscience[2] you're never alone

Respect the law or work to change it
Abide by professional code
Give it your best
Avoid conflict of interest
March for justice don't be slowed

Apply the Greatest Good principle[3]
With a question to ask before you act
Perceived social benefits
All those good hits
Will they reach great numbers in fact?

'Bout the Fraternal Charity principle
A question for the affected
If I'm in his shoes[4]
Would this I choose
Given consequences and what's been neglected?

'Bout the Universality Principle[5]
I've this question from the first
What can you say
If all acted this way
Would it be for the best or the worst?

Share your wisdom you're an ethical man
Principles for living today
Help us to ask the right questions
Help us to find our way

SONG—NOTES / COMMENTS

1—Human ethical behavior has evolved. When people were little more than animals their behavior was dictated by self-interest in meeting basic needs to survive. Among pre-civilization it extended to include family and biological relatives. As culture developed and survival pressures eased, ethical behavior was extended to include community, tribe, regional neighbors, ethnic group, and nation. Today a few feel a sense of belongingness to the whole human species and to the planet and behave accordingly. (See theme #37B.)

2—Conscience involves a sense of right and wrong. H.L. Mencken has called it "the inner voice that tells us that somebody might be watching." When behavior falls short of what is idealized as "right," guilt can result.

3—Utilitarians, who judge "rightness" by benefits for the greatest number of people, apply this principle.

4— Those with great empathy can better imagine being someone else and experiencing his or her feelings.

5—A key goal for those working in the field of normative ethics is to identify universal (meaning they apply to everyone) rules (or norms) that should (use of this word implies value judgment!) guide human behavior.

Comment: An honesty / high ethical standards mindset arms you emotionally against guilt producing sleaze. It reduces anxiety: if you never lie, cheat, steal, etc.you don't fear an unethical side of you being exposed — because there is none! And your social justice inspired ethical principles surround you with good karma.

Worldview Theme—TFJD CODE: 3221 VI=8 Original Tune Era: 1970s   RS Top 500 List: Yes

Worldview Theme #43: Seeking Wealth and Power

Worldview Theme Summary: for more: www.projectworldview.org/wvtheme43.htm

Whenever I find myself unabashedly pursuing all the wealth, luxuries, comfort and power, that anyone could ever dream of, if doubts about the "rightness" of this pursuit creep in, I give myself a pep talk. It goes like this: "As a creature in the economic jungle, you must pursue your own gain, otherwise predators will crush you. The strong survive, the weak don't—it's a natural law—just as seeking to maximize your own happiness and pleasure comes naturally—not sacrificing for others. Pursuing your own needs insures you are master—no one is pulling your strings. Rather than saying "I have enough" and retreating from still more wealth and power, living in even more luxury, see your material success as evidence of your superiority. The meek won't inherit the Earth. Those who have the gold make the rules!"

SONG
"Give My Regards to Wall Street" by Stephen P. Cook
to be sung to the tune of "Give My Regards to Broadway" by George M. Cohan / James Cagney

Give my regards to Wall Street
On my way to billionaire
Tell 'em down at Goldman Sachs[1]
That I will soon be there!

Could stock options or junk bonds
Buy our waterfront home?
Or we float an IPO[2]?
Stick with me, don't you roam!

The big one[3] won't get away
We'll laugh all the way to the bank
The bulls are running today
No mercy, don't break rank!

Give my regards to K Street[4]
On my way to power elite[5]
Let 'em know whose in charge
Big money talks, I repeat!

Show 'em what we're made of:
The strength to get what we want
We'll bring down the most upright[6]
Their ideals we will taunt!

Give my regards to Wall Street
On my way to billionaire
Tell 'em down at Goldman Sachs
That I will soon be there!

Give my regards to K Street
On my way to power elite
Let 'em know whose in charge
Big money talks, I repeat!

SONG—NOTES / COMMENTS
1—A multinational investment banking firm. Many of its executives have become extremely wealthy and many of its alumni have moved into key government leadership positions in steering the US economy.
2—An initial public offering is how a privately owned company issues stock and becomes publicly owned.
3—A big pay day—like selling one's idea, an IPO, having one's startup bought by a big name company, etc.
4—If Wall Street is associated with those who run the US economy from its financial center in New York City, K Street is associated with the non-elected lobbyists and influence peddlers who help run the US government from Washington DC by using campaign contributions and the power their money commands.
5— Power elite refers to the class of people in positions of power in the US corporate state. The term was first used in the 1950s as the title of a leftist assessment (a book by C. Wright Mills) of who runs America.
6—This viewpoint supports cynics' contention that "everyone has their price" and that every politician is potentially corruptible: their vote for sale if the amount of money dangled in front of them is big enough.

Comment: this theme has value as emotional armor. Viewing one's success as simply part of the way nature works and beyond one's control, provides a defense against both feelings of guilt and others' charges. Also see comments for themes #19A and #50A.

Worldview Theme—TFJD CODE: 3323 VI=54 Original Tune Era: 1900s   RS Top 500 List: No

Worldview Theme #44A: Sanctity and Dignity of Life

Worldview Theme Summary: **for more:** www.projectworldview.org/wvtheme44.htm

I believe that life is a sacred, mysterious gift. I stand in awe of the conscious, feeling, vibrant expression of life. Accordingly, I will not engage in any behavior, nor sanction any acts that terminate such life, or needlessly inflict pain on such living things. My respect for the sanctity, integrity, and dignity of life is such that I will oppose certain medical, biotechnological, or agribusiness practices that I see as tampering with it or degrading it.

SONG
"Momma, Love Me" by Stephen P. Cook
Sung to the tune of "Landslide" by Stevie Nicks / Fleetwood Mac

To life's creative impulse I let go
What began with love should I let grow?
A man and woman and vital spark
Divine light shining there in the dark[1]
The dark [echo]

This life inside me I can't put down
Not yet a beating heart, not a sound[2]
But I'm hearing a new borne baby cry
Momma, love me, don't ask why[3]
Ask why [echo]

Does the world need this mouth to feed?
Should I honor you or pull this weed?[4]
Should I respect your fledgling human rights?[5]
Or ignore my conscience and end the fight?[6]
The fight [echo]

Reasons to end this life or let it be
Saddled with a child I won't be free
But you down there with no hand to wave[7]
I can't choose for you an early grave[8]
Early grave [echo]

This life inside me I can't put down
Not yet a beating heart, not a sound
But I'm hearing a new borne baby cry
Momma, love me, don't ask why
Ask why [echo]

This life inside me I can't put down

SONG—NOTES / COMMENTS

1—This and the previous line suggest a belief in vitalism (theme #5B) and that new life requires God providing a divine spark or blowing the "breath of life" into inanimate matter. Those holding such beliefs would be less likely to end unwanted pregnancy with abortion in comparison to those valuing scientific materialism (theme #5A) and believing that molecular biologists will soon succeed in creating life in the lab.

2—The heart of a developing human embryo (fetus) typically starts beating around twenty-one days after conception but is not audible to a doctor listening with a stethoscope until week twenty-one or so of pregnancy.

3—The maternal love most mothers feel is unconditional love.

4—A 1980s *Sesame Street* program with a segment about explaining the need to thin cramped marigolds in a garden by noting that they need nutrients, water, light, and space to grow properly—just like children—brought complaints from Pro Lifers. They suggested that the marigolds be transplanted, not killed.

5—Human rights are held to include the right to life and liberty—but a key question relevant to the Pro Life/Pro Choice issue is when do those rights begin? The former argue that life and the rights associated with it begin at the moment of conception.

6—With conscience being a sense of what is morally right or wrong, if conscientious behavior dictates an unwanted fetus be allowed to live but actual behavior results in abortion, the huge gulf between these behaviors not surprisingly can produce lots of guilt and great feelings of remorse.

7—Developing fetuses have tiny hands that can curl fingers to make a fist by sometime around weeks #10 to #12 of pregnancy.

8—She has a choice. If abortion was illegal, she'd also be agonizing over risking jail, bleeding to death after a botched job, etc.

Comment: this theme may have value as emotional armor. As the song suggests with reference to "conscience," it can provide a defense against feelings of guilt. (See also comment for theme #32.) While the strong (generally joyous) emotions that surround the birth of a baby are both expected and often on public display, strong private emotions (sometimes anguished guilt) can surround the intentional death of a fetus. (Also see comment for theme #44B.)

Worldview Theme—TFJD CODE: 2321 **VI=72 Original Tune Era:** 1970s   **RS Top 500 List:** No

Worldview Theme #44B: Animal Rights

Worldview Theme Summary:	for more: www.projectworldview.org/wvtheme44.htm

I too believe life is to be respected. But unlike anti-abortion activists, those battling euthanasia, opponents of capital punishment, etc, my focus is on extending that respect to animals. I believe if we link morally wrong to evil, evil to pain, pain to certain behavioral reactions we see in higher animals, then a desire to do the morally right thing dictates recognizing that animals have rights and extending ethical treatment to them.

SONG
"Expecting to Die" by Stephen P. Cook
Sung to the tune of "Expecting to Fly" by Neil Young / The Buffalo Springfield

Confined you are to gestation crate[1]
Expecting to die[2]
Uncomfortable you can't turn around
You won't even try
Factory farm breeding pig
By the winter you are nursing
Piglets you can't see
Confined to farrowing crate[3]
To spare injury
Babe, piglet you can't see[4]
Babe, piglet you can't see

Your life cycles on and on
Three litters a year and you're spent
To the slaughterhouse you smart animal
To market holiday ham is sent
Pork production farm[5]
Ham and bacon
I'll live without you[6]
For me, pigs won't die
Give animals like Babe respect
Please give it a try
Babe, please give it a try
Babe, please give it a try
Babe

SONG—NOTES / COMMENTS

1—Metal crates measuring 6.6 ft long by 2.0 ft wide used in intensive pork production to house the sow (which may weigh up to 900 lbs) during pregnancy (meaning most of her adult life). Typically lined up row after row in large sheds, to opponents of such factory farming they are unhealthy and inhumane. Given floors made of concrete slats that manure falls through, the animals live directly above their own waste.

2—In the 1983 novel *The Sheep Pig* (which the 1995 movie *Babe* was based on), the border collie Fly, who comes to treat the precocious pig Babe like her son, is glad Babe has no idea of the fate in store for him: his owners initially plan on fattening him up to be a Christmas ham. So despite his intelligence, Babe is thankfully spared from learning this knowledge by the other farm animals and is not "expecting to die." Happily both his intelligence and social nature make him so useful and win him respect that his life is spared. Unlike factory farm pigs, Babe is not confined to a tiny space but mostly runs free. The remarkable intelligence and behavior of feral hogs, whose growing numbers infest places like rural Texas, suggest they know the fate in store for them if caught —explaining the extreme precautions they take to avoid capture. Of course whether pig "intellect" and consciousness is such that they expect to die if caught is debatable!

3— A few days before giving birth, sows are moved to farrowing crates. Here piglets will be nursed. Despite providing room for piglets to play, they are designed to separate piglets from their mothers, whose weight might otherwise crush them. So they restrict the sow—and she can't turn around to see her piglets.

4—This line imagines Babe's life beginning as a piglet on a factory farm with a confined mother who, although able to provide nursing, is unable to see him.

5—Every year around six million breeding sows populate factory farms in the United States.

6—Not surprisingly, many who respect animal rights are vegetarians!

Comment: The behavior associated with this theme provides emotional armor in that it allows those who empathize with and feel compassion for animals (as in the song) to better sleep at night knowing their feelings and actions align. Beyond that, one doesn't have to look far to find the strong emotional driving force behind both anti-abortion and animal rights movements. It could be that among the strongest defenders / advocates for both protecting the unborn (theme #44A) and extending humane treatment to animals are people who have themselves felt unwanted, unloved, weak, powerless, and generally at the mercy of stronger adults. Living for so long with those feelings, they often identify strongly with unwanted fetuses or animals.

Worldview Theme—TFJD CODE: 2233 VI=144 **Original Tune Era:** 1960s | **RS Top 500 List:** No

Worldview Theme #45A: Borrowing Mentality

| **Worldview Theme Summary:** | **for more:** www.projectworldview.org/wvtheme45.htm |

I prefer having or doing something today, and borrowing money (or becoming obligated) to make that possible, rather than waiting until a future time when I've saved enough money to (or can otherwise) have/do it. In general, I have no problem with individuals or governments contracting monetary, personal or ecological debts against tomorrow so that I (or society) can have/do something today.

SONG

"Credit Card" by Stephen P. Cook

to be sung to the tune of "Different Drum" by Michael Nesmith / Linda Ronstadt

You and I argue if I run up credit card debt[1]	You joke I'm banking on The Rapture[3]
How can you be my sweet loving pet	To avoid debtor prison[4] capture
When you so often lecture me?	But with bankruptcy[5]
Who—oa	Couldn't I become debt free?
You laugh and then suggest big debtors	Whoa—No way! That'd be cheating[6]
Once were chronic bed wetters[2]	You say we can do some dealing
And the girl you marry will be debt free	We'll both be happier
	If I avoid bankruptcy
Oh with your good salary	
What's the big deal?	So goodbye my credit cards[7]
And why all of your budgeting zeal?	I'm cutting you up, this isn't hard
Seems you prefer your money to me?	So you'll pay off my debts
	And then marry me[8]

SONG—NOTES / COMMENTS

1—Purchasing using a credit card is an example of unsecured consumer debt. This debt can grow beyond the original cost of the purchases with the addition of interest charges—levied on debt not paid in timely fashion, typically about 16 % / year—and late fees. Overall as 2013 ended, the typical USA household owed $6690 in unpaid credit card charges. Nationally such debt stood at just over $800 billion.

2— Perhaps connecting debt and bed-wetting and is mere silliness, but one can argue otherwise! Bedwetting has been called "the hidden problem of childhood." Certainly high levels of (not immediately visible) debt can cause economic problems. Buying things one can't afford involves instant gratification: the thrill that comes when you immediately get a desired something. Driving this, some would argue, is a childish "I want that now!" force. For some, this force is powerful enough to overcome the opposing force: a rational, restraining adult attitude questioning whether it's really needed / if there's money to pay for it.

3—To many Christians, this is when life as we know it ends with Jesus' return and the final resurrection.

4—Debtor prison was where people unable to pay their debts ended up in England (Charles Dickens wrote about them) and western Europe up until the mid 19th century. Eventually bankruptcy laws helped do away with debtor prisons although they remain in a few places (including the Middle East, Greece, Hong Kong).

5—While bankruptcy courts can rule that people can walk away from some debts, usually this is a last resort for debt strapped consumers. Those declaring bankruptcy will typically be unable to borrow money for years —not surprising given that the card issuers and retailers are often big losers in personal bankruptcy verdicts. In the 2008—2013 time period, USA consumers defaulted on $261 billion in credit card charges.

6—If the intent, when the debt was contracted, was not to repay, then yes, this would be cheating. More typically unforeseen circumstances (like unexpected health emergencies) are behind bankruptcy. But it does represent reneging on a promise!

7—While a typical USA adult has three or four credit cards some people have many more.

8—This song has a cute twist. Whereas going into debt helps untold numbers of people have something they want now without waiting, here what is desired (marriage!) won't occur until the credit card debt is paid!

Comment: Those running up big debts may be financially irresponsible, but are they emotionally immature? The first sentence in this theme's description suggests those who value it may be lacking in the ability to delay gratification (see note 2), which some link with emotional maturity. Indeed, a 1988 research report authored by Mischel, Shoda, and Peake, found that "pre-school participants' ability to delay gratification …was a strong predictor of their coping ability in a ten year followup study."

| **Worldview Theme—TFJD CODE:** 1222 **VI**=144 **Original Tune Era:** 1960s | **RS Top 500 List:** No |

Worldview Theme #45B: Work Hard, Pay As You Go

Worldview Theme Summary: for more: www.projectworldview.org/wvtheme45.htm

I believe that personal debts or obligations, if not honored, can lead to guilt. Ecological debts can produce guilt if one knows that disrupting natural cycles leaves future generations with damage to repair. To avoid feeling guilty or obligated, worries about unpaid bills, or interest charges, to some extent in my life as a whole I adopt a "work hard, pay as you go" approach.

SONG

"Pay As You Go" by Stephen P. Cook
to be sung to the tune of "Stand By Your Man" by Billy Sherrill / Tammy Wynette

Don't give in to borrowing money
Digging a financial hole for yourself
Get with working hard
Make do best you can
Lose obligation
Step up to wealth

Don't give in to wanting it all now[1]
Losing peace of mind with unpaid bills
Instead be patient
Work hard to get ahead
And someday you'll have your thrills

Pay as you go
Test out your constitution
Find creative solution[2]
When times are tough[3]

Pay as you go
Don't discount the future[4]
Don't let guilt[5] lay you low
Pay as you go

Pay as you go
Don't discount the future
Don't let debt lay you low
Pay as you go

SONG—NOTES / COMMENTS

1—Some would argue wanting it all now is an aberrant desire: a combination of greedy acquisitivity and childish instant gratification. Others would say it's just human nature!

2—Many people feel that finding solutions to problems is at the heart of what being human is about!

3—As famed UCLA basketball coach John Wooden liked to say, "When the going gets tough, the tough get going." The getting going here means working to make money that might otherwise be borrowed or using one's own labor in lieu of paying someone else to provide the service that your labor can provide.

4— Discounting the future involves doing or having (consuming) something now, rather than waiting, or rather than investing the money you would have spent and getting a high return on the investment.

5—Guilt and money is a complicated subject! While in affluent countries the rich may feel guilt over their good fortune, that isn't what is alluded to here. Rather, the reference is to agonizing over the inability to pay debts and reneging on the promise originally made to repay. Religious folks interpret biblical verses (like *Romans* 13:3 "Owe no man anything" or *Psalms* 37:21 "The wicked borrow and do not repay") as not connecting borrowing money with sin, but rather linking sin with breaking the promise and failing to repay.

Comment: To the extent that this theme represents self restraint (see theme #29A comment), it may signal some emotional maturity. It has value as emotional armor. As the song suggests, it can provide a defense against feelings of guilt. In this regard, also see note 5 above. Before the "pay as you go" can happen though, you need to "work hard." Losing yourself in hard work is one strategy for escaping other stresses and having to confront unpleasant grim realities about yourself and your situation. If that work hard ➜ money and facilitates pay as you go, it's probably inappropriate to label the hard work as a maladaptive coping strategy!

Worldview Theme—TFJD CODE: 3213 VI=12 Original Tune Era: 1960s   RS Top 500 List: No

Worldview Theme #46A: The Technological Fix Mentality

Worldview Theme Summary: **for more:** www.projectworldview.org/wvtheme46.htm

In looking for solutions to problems, whether they be pressing societal problems or those causing minor human inconvenience, I look first to human technological ingenuity, and engineering design/problem solving skills. It is in the demonstrated ability of engineers and planners using technology assessment to find technology-based solutions to such problems that I put my faith and trust. Their efforts have steadily brought nature under human control and increased human comfort.

SONG
"Technology Runaway" by Stephen P. Cook
sung to the tune of a medley of (first nine verses) "Runaround Sue" by Ernie Maresca and Dion DiMucci
and (last three verses) "Runaway" by Del Shannon

What I value, the way it oughta be
Solving problems with technology
Bringing nature under our control
More human comfort, that's our goal

We started making tools long ago
Then tamed fire, made it friend not foe
Lives made better harnessing energy
The story of our technology

With technology
We break new ground
If it doesn't work we put it down[1]
Learning from mistakes we get wise
That's why our species
Our species it flies

Industrial revolution made with steam
Then computer age, living our dream
Smart technology using our brain
Easier lives, living with less pain

Third world poor
May be digging a ditch
But Wall Street folks
They're getting rich
Running it all
With cheap fossil fuel
They see the profits, not the C O two

With technology
We break new ground
If it doesn't work we put it down
Learning from mistakes we get wise
That's why our species
Our species it flies

I know you worry
'bout climate change
We'll set our sights on it, get it in range
We'll put giant mirrors up in space[2]
Hey, don't doubt the human race

I know you worry 'bout inequality
And injustice causing instability
We can reprogram human DNA[3]
Make us kinder, make greed go away

With technology
We break new ground
If it doesn't work we put it down
Learning from mistakes we get wise
That's why our species
Our species it flies

I imagine looking back
Seeing we got off track
Our technology, what did it lack?
This world's getting too hot
A few rich, many have not
I don't like
What our money's bought

I see it going down the drain
More people feeling real pain
I'm asking you to think with me
About remaking technology
As I ponder
I pah-pah-pah-pah ponder
A way
A wah-wah-wah-wah way
Us finding a way
To stop this runaway
Technology runaway
I hope we can find a way

I'm asking you to think with me
About remaking technology
Giving it a more human face
Us living with dignity and grace
As I ponder
I pah-pah-pah-pah ponder
A way
A wah-wah-wah-wah way
Us finding a way
To stop this runaway
Technology runaway
I hope we can find a way
I hope we can find a way

SONG—NOTES / COMMENTS

1—This line and the next one provide the rough idea behind feedback, the heart of the scientific method.

2—A geoengineering proposal to combat Earth's manmade enhanced greenhouse effect induced global warming using space-based mirrors to reflect unwanted solar radiation back into space and cool the planet.

3—Scientists have begun modifying genes—a technology with great potential benefits and risks. Given bioethical concerns, society may outlaw certain human genetic engineering procedures such as cloning but permit some tweaking of human DNA.

Comment: Personalities built around "can do" optimistic confidence—those that tend to respond to certain stresses as challenges to overcome, rather than as insurmountable obstacles—might value this theme.

Worldview Theme—TFJD CODE: 3113 **VI=3** **Original Tune Era:** 1960s   **RS Top 500 List:** Yes / Yes

Worldview Theme #46B: Militarism

Worldview Theme Summary: for more: www.projectworldview.org/wvtheme46.htm

I think of militarists as exalting military virtues/symbols, being comfortable following orders and the military chain of command, advocating military preparedness, being the first to call for war, etc. —and I think of myself as one with some hesitancy! While I don't doubt that waging modern war is the ultimate technological solution to problems essentially based on disputes between people, I know that great military leaders can nonetheless prefer diplomacy and see war as something to be avoided.

SONG

"Tough and Strong" by Stephen P. Cook
sung to the tune of "Caissons Go Rolling Along" by Edmund L. Gruber / John Philip Sousa

On the land, on the sea,
In the air, let it be
Our military must be kept strong
On the earth, out in space[1]
We'll command any place
Our military must be kept strong

So its hi dee hi dee ho
Hey army say "Bravo!"[2]
Be proud that you belong
For where ever you go
You will always know
Our forces are tough and they're strong

With marines, with Seals[3]
Special ops, made of steel
Our military must be kept strong
Stealth fighter[4], all nighter
Moving fast, much lighter[5]
Our military must be kept strong

So anchors aweigh[6]
Our navy saves the day
Be proud that you belong
For where ever you go
You will always know
Our forces are tough and they're strong

Bring 'em shame, those to blame
Fight with flame, live in fame
Our military must be kept strong
Honor code, proud and bold
Tradition rich and old[7]
Our military must be kept strong

So heading for blue sky[8]
Our air force flying high
Be proud that you belong
For where ever you go
You will always know
Our forces are tough and they're strong

SONG—NOTES / COMMENTS

1—Since the late 1950s launch of the first earth-orbiting satellites, a high % of them have had military uses: for intelligence, navigation, and communication. A 1967 treaty outlawed space-based weapons systems.

2—A term with various connotations: bravery, celebratory gusto, machismo, unambiguous code for letter B, etc. The author connects it with Fort Bliss, a US army base near the Rio Grande—the Rio Bravo in Mexico.

3—The USA Navy's Sea Air Land teams are typically employed in covert special warfare operations.

4—This refers to both the aircraft technology that allows planes to escape radar detection and to the individual combatants equipped for seeing in the dark, avoiding detection, etc. in special covert combat operations.

5—A recent USA military trend favors increasingly mobile forces using precision smart technology.

6—"Anchors Aweigh," written in 1906, is the fight song of the USA Naval Academy.

7—Military tradition in general refers to long-time practices of family service, procedures/protocols including drills, dress, military courtesy, etc., and military lore including battle tales, songs, etc. In the USA the tradition dates from the Revolutionary War (1775-1781) era, elsewhere it can be much longer.

8—Refers to the first line of the USA Air Force Song, written in 1938, "Off we go into the wild blue yonder!"

Comment: While those seeking camaraderie may be drawn to military service, the need to rein in impulses and follow orders can present some with difficulties. This theme can have value as emotional armor. Military service can be linked to the strength that weapons and working as part of a team brings. And to providing leadership skills. Both can aid those who served later in life as civilians facing stressful situations. Facing the emotional challenges combat presents—beginning with overcoming fear—is a theme behind great literature. Sadly some veterans (with PTSD) never mentally recover from their traumatic combat / war experiences.

Worldview Theme—TFJD CODE: 3313   **VI=27**   **Original Tune Era:** 1910s   **RS Top 500 List:** No

Worldview Theme #47A: Attitudinal Fix

Worldview Theme Summary: for more: www.projectworldview.org/wvtheme47.htm

In looking for solutions to problems, whether they be pressing societal problems or those causing minor human inconvenience, I look first to changing human attitudes and associated behaviors. This is done through education, drawing heavily on existing social infrastructure and institutions. It is in the ability of people to come together in a spirit of co-operation in an atmosphere of learning constructively from each other, sharing worldviews, articulating values and goals, and finding mutually acceptable non-technology (or soft technology) based solutions, that I put my faith and trust.

SONG
"Stingy" by Stephen P. Cook
sung to the tune of "Cloudy" by Paul Simon and Art Garfunkel

Stingy[1]
More hoarding, less giving I call it stingy
It's not the way I want the world to be
Greed and giving just don't mix
We need an attitudinal fix
Not money gaming tricks
Those with gold rule or Golden Rule take your pick

Hello what's right
I haven't seen you through the dark night
Won't you come out into the light?

Stealing
Taking what you've no right to that's stealing
It's not the way I want the world to be
Rip-off and right-on just don't mix
We need an attitudinal fix
Not pirate plundering tricks
Me first, our children's future take your pick

Hello what's right
I haven't seen you through the dark night
Won't you come out into the light?

Lying
Saying what you know is false that's lying
It's not the way I want the world to be
Uncouth and truth just don't mix
We need an attitudinal fix
Not muddying the waters tricks
Bullshitting or enlightening take your pick

Hello what's right
I haven't seen you through the dark night

Won't you come out into the light?

Prejudice
Not giving someone a chance that's prejudice
It's not the way I want the world to be
Not my kind and kindness just don't mix
We need an attitudinal fix
Not ethnocentric tricks
Racist or color blind justice take your pick

Hello what's right
I haven't seen you through the dark night
Won't you come out into the light?

Bad Karma
Bad comes back to bite that's bad karma
It's not the way I want the world to be
Hard knocks, soft kisses just don't mix
We need an attitudinal fix
Not hard sell huckster tricks
Wham bam or thank you, ma'am take your pick

Hello what's right
I haven't seen you through the dark night
Won't you come out into the light?

So my friend please don't lie
And let's divide that pie
Give the ol' Golden Rule a try
Lets remake the world, not let our dreams die

Hello what's right
I haven't seen you through the dark night
Won't you come out into the light?

SONG—NOTES / COMMENTS
1—This song is about promoting behavior changes: like from being unwilling to give, to being generous.
Comment: Those with both "can do" personality and brighter view of human nature might value this theme.

Worldview Theme—TFJD CODE: 2132 **VI=24 Original Tune Era:** 1960s   **RS Top 500 List:** No

Worldview Theme #47B: Pacifism

Worldview Theme Summary: for more: www.projectworldview.org/wvtheme47.htm

I think of pacifists as 1) opposed to using guns, war, and violence to settle disputes and 2) preferring use of non-violent means to combat wicked and evil acts rather than violence, vengeance, capital punishment, etc—and I call myself one with some hesitancy! While I see fighting violence with more violence as both morally wrong and contradictory, and don't believe good can come out of evil, I nonetheless see merit in arguments that if evil is left unchecked, unpunished, and not countered with strong action, then more evil will result. Note: avoiding war through diplomatic efforts—something pacifists applaud—is the ultimate attitudinal fix.

SONG

"We Gotta Bring An End to War" by Stephen P. Cook

Sung to the tune of "We Gotta Get Out of This Place" by Cooper, Ezrin, Hood / The Animals

In this sorry sad part of the world
Where people can't reconcile[1]
How 'bout you stop killing for awhile?
Hey my son you're so strong and gritty
So why not to peace be true?
With lasting peace life can start anew
Could be

Old man that's easier to say than do
We can't sit down with those we hate
We're planning vengeance, talking peace can wait
Revenge, we want it[2]
We've been fighting so long
There's one thing on our mind
There all the time:
War War War War

We gotta secure lasting peace
With the best effort we can mount
We gotta secure lasting peace
Let's not waste lives but make them count

Hey my son you're so smart and caring
Don't you feel deep in your heart
Choosing love not hate is where to start?
Think now

Old man I know what you say is true
I've read it in the good book[3]
Searching our hearts, opening to look
For peace, we want it
We've been fighting so long
There's one thing on our mind
There all the time:
Peace Peace Peace Peace

We gotta secure lasting peace
With the best effort we can mount
We gotta secure lasting peace
Let's not waste lives but make them count

Somehow old fella
Like Gandhi, King, Mandela[4]
We gotta bring an end to war
Hey there UN—that's what you're for!
No more games: bring an end to war
War: We all lose! Know the score!

SONG—NOTES / COMMENTS

1—Reconciliation often requires conflict resolution: settling a conflict characterized by tension/antagonism and sides whose motives, purposes, and intentions seem totally at odds and perhaps irreconcilable. The process can involve informal discussion or a formal procedure with rules and mediator(s).

2—As this song was being finalized in February 2014, a Pakistani Taliban spokesmen, after taking credit for killing twenty three government soldiers, said, "We want to make it clear…that we know how to take revenge."

3—Refers to the Christian *Bible*, not the 2011 humanist book with this title. Most religious texts preach peace and condemn violence: the *Bible's Old Testament* and the *Qu'ran* are possible exceptions.

4—Great 20th century men of peace, reconciliation and non-violence: Mahatma Gandhi (1869-1948) of India, Martin Luther King, Jr. (1929-1968) of the USA, and Nelson Mandela (1918-2013) of South Africa.

Comment: Nonviolent resistance is a strategy for coping with stresses continually inflicted on subject people by a stronger, more powerful authority who dominates them. It may be the only option if armed resistance would simply lead to futile slaughter. True pacifists also adopt it when that other option is viable.

Worldview Theme—TFJD CODE: 1122 **VI=36 Original Tune Era:** 1960s **RS Top 500 List:** Yes

---

Worldview Theme #48: The Co-operative, Decentralized Society Advocate

Worldview Theme Summary: **for more:** www.projectworldview.org/wvtheme48.htm

I prefer cooperation to competition, since the latter can bring out the worst in people. I prefer locally controlled economic arrangements involving a mixture of cooperative, employee-owned, and private businesses. I like voluntary, democratic organizations in which people join hands in promoting community, common good, and self reliance. I prefer decentralized economic or government structures, since they can better respond to local needs. I dislike big, authoritarian, centralized corporate or government structures. Instead, I think that, while planning can involve a whole bioregion, power and decision making should diffuse down to the lowest level possible, ideally to community, neighborhood, individual—and all would participate.

SONG

"Take Me to the Food Co-op" by Stephen P. Cook

to be sung to the tune of "Take Me Out to the Ball Game" by Jack Norworth, Albert Von Tilzer

---

At Big Business Miss Liz was mad:
"Greedy absent owners—too bad!"
Big on community[1], Liz spent
Every cent
She would vent.
To local owners she gravitated
With corporate chains got frustrated
"I'm telling you I want to see
Social responsibility[2]!"
So…
"Take me to the food co-op[3]
Down to the credit union[4]
Owned by good folks like you and me
Go economic democracy[5]!

Let us root root root for the home team
When profits depart it's a shame
Let workers keep more more more moola[6]
In a brand new game

Sign me up with the farm team
Give me my share of the crop
Small farmers are good guys, that's for sure
Go community agriculture[7]

Let us root root root for the home team
When profits depart it's a shame
Let farmers keep more more more moola
In a brand new game"

SONG—NOTES / COMMENTS

1—Community, according to Ferdinand Tönnies in his 1887 book *Gemeinschaft und* Gesellschaft, is built around the personal, family, and neighborhood relationships and feelings of togetherness that one expects in a place where people have direct, face to face contact. It is to be distinguished from "society" — where self interest motivated individuals are held together by formal regulation and legal framework, relationships between people are more impersonal, and there is less cohesion and less dependence on each other.

2—Social responsibility is an ethical theory according to which organizations, businesses, and individuals are obligated to act in a way that benefits society at large. According to Lord Holme and Richard Watts, in their article "Making Good Business Sense," businesses should "behave ethically and contribute to economic development while improving the quality of life of the workforce and their families as well as the local community and society at large."

3—A food distribution consumer co-operative outlet typically offering natural foods to its members

4— A member-owned co-operative association that accepts deposits from and loans money to its members

5—Economic democracy generally refers to a socioeconomic system doing some or all of the following: 1) transferring economic decision-making from the few to the many through worker management/ownership of productive enterprises, 2) promoting democratic local/regional control over corporate state central planning, 3) entrusting the central government with levying taxes that allow social control of investment carried out locally/regionally, and 4) retaining the market system but abolishing private or absentee ownership of productive resources, and wage labor. In worker run enterprises workers are paid by sharing in profits.

6—A slang term for money

7—Community supported agriculture provides an alternative model for growing and distributing food.

Comment: This theme, taken together with Left Anarchism (theme #50B), represents a much different way of organizing society/economic activity—an alternative to themes #19A/ #19B. Some argue it would give "little guys" a greater sense of empowerment than beings cogs in the corporate state machine does.

Worldview Theme—TFJD CODE: 2133 **VI=36 Original Tune Era:** 1900s   **RS Top 500 List:** No

Worldview Theme #49A: Social Welfare Statism

Worldview Theme Summary:	**for more:** www.projectworldview.org/wvtheme49.htm

I am a believer in the concentration of economic controls and planning in the hands of a highly centralized government (statism). I prefer a strong national government that: 1) takes responsibility to ensure that everyone is looked out for by providing extensive social services, and 2) assures environmental quality, workplace safety and societal stability through appropriate regulations. (Note: While social welfare states heavily tax private property, they don't challenge its sanctity as socialism does.)

SONG

"Building The Common Welfare" by Stephen P. Cook
to be sung to the tune of "I Heard It Through the Grapevine" by N. Whitfield and B. Strong / Marvin Gaye

I'm tired of hearing you
Talking 'bout the free lunch crew[1]
Putting down the welfare state[2]
Jesus preached love, not hate
If your son was hungry poor,
Would you slam the kitchen door?

Building the common welfare
To lift up some, we must share
Building the common welfare
Someday you may need our care

Please don't you bitch to me
'Bout that housing subsidy[3]
Valuing your tax dollar
Putting down those in squalor
If your daughter was homeless,
Would you ignore her duress?

Building the common welfare
To lift up some, we must share
Building the common welfare
Someday you may need our care

You put down markets not free
And social security[4]
You'd shred the safety net
On big business stake your bet
Damn your socialism scare!
We need national health care![5]

Building the common welfare
To lift up some, we must share
Building the common welfare
Someday you may need our care

SONG—NOTES / COMMENTS

1—Free lunch is often applied to poor people using state provided welfare program services. The more general economics term is free rider, where people benefit from resources and services they don't pay for.

2—At the heart of such governments is a commitment to welfare assistance in the form of monetary or other help with services designed to provide an economic or social safety net for those disadvantaged members of society who are unable to support themselves. Eligibility is determined by income below the poverty level and other "means tests." Recipients may be required to demonstrate that they are seeking employment or have enrolled in job training.

3—This refers to tax dollars going to provide affordable housing to the poor in government owned structures

4—The USA social insurance program for the elderly and disabled established during the New Deal era.

5—The last two lines refer to the debate over the USA health care insurance compromise known as "The Affordable Care Act" passed in 2010. Opponents fought against this legislation, which builds on the existing private insurance/health care provider system, by charging that the new scheme, in which all people would eventually be required to have health care insurance, amounted to "socialism." At the other extreme were those who unsuccessfully sought to expand the widely popular government administered Medicare program so that everyone would be eligible—not just those of age 65 and over!

Comment: Being poor, a recipient of government welfare aid, and a believer in this theme leaves one open to attacks questioning one's character, work ethic, etc. This song provides emotional armor against that. The government "safety net" that supposedly social welfare states have in place to catch those in need (who might otherwise fall into some oblivion of suffering), employs what many see as a psychologically comforting metaphor for those struggling to cope. Critics charge that the safety net is full of holes punched by those who wish to gut the welfare system.

Worldview Theme—TFJD CODE: 3232 **VI=24 Original Tune Era:** 1960s **RS Top 500 List:** Yes

Worldview Theme #49B: Socialism

Worldview Theme Summary: **for more:** www.projectworldview.org/wvtheme49.htm

I believe in a centrally planned socialist economic system in which, not only does the state control all means of production but, production and distribution are designed to directly satisfy economic demands and human needs with the common good, rather than private profit and accumulation of wealth, in mind. (Note: socialist economies can take different forms: some retain aspects of capitalism, some reject central planning, some embrace democracy, etc. Communist states have all property held in common for the public welfare.)

SONG

"A Socialist Economy (The Fight Continues)" by Stephen P. Cook
to be sung to the tune of "Happy Christmas (The War is Over)" by John Lennon / John Lennon & Yoko Ono

What is socialism?
Jack London did ask[1]
A brotherhood of man
Getting there's our task
Capitalist engines
We'll take over and run
For people not profits
With our votes not guns

A socialist economy
Toward this let's steer
With full employment
Not losing job fear

I'm a socialist
Albert Einstein said[2]
People not predators
Keep that in your head
Do away with profits
Limit competition
We need stability
Not depression

A socialist economy
Toward this let's steer
With full employment
Not losing job fear

What is socialism?
Asked our comrade Che[3]
Ending exploitation
Making oppressors pay
We fight to end misery
And alienation
To help people achieve
Their liberation

A socialist economy
Toward this let's steer
With full employment
Not losing job fear

The fight continues
Won't you join us?
The fight continues…Yeah!

SONG—NOTES / COMMENTS

1—American writer Jack London (1876-1916) provided a book length answer to this question with his 1908 novel *The Iron Heel*. Its plot involves centuries of domination of monopoly capitalists/robber barons eventually overthrown in a socialist revolution. Many who read London's *Call of the Wild* and *White Fang*—which seemingly celebrate survival of the fittest and rugged individualism—are surprised to learn of his abandoning individualism and embracing socialism. Through life experience he came to strongly identify with poor people and their struggles to make a decent living.

2—Albert Einstein (1879-1955), the great physicist and *Time* magazine's "Man of the Century," embraced socialism. His views are summarized in his 1949 essay "Why Socialism?"

3—Che Guevara (1928-1967) was an Argentina born revolutionary who became a leader of the Cuban communist revolution and sought to export it elsewhere. His conversion to believing the status quo was rotten and revolutionary change was needed can be traced to his travels as a medical student, through South America and seeing widespread poverty, misery and disease.

Comment: This theme represents a much different way of organizing society / economic activity—an alternative to themes #19A/ #19B. Based on grim realities of how the Soviet Union operated, many argue that, besides making everyone poor, such a system would put those (like libertarians, theme #50A) who value individual freedom, liberty, private property, etc. in a psychological hell. Others, with a brighter view of human nature, argue the Soviet system was an aberration and socialism is a viable alternative to capitalism.

Worldview Theme—TFJD CODE: 3231 **VI=12** **Original Tune Era:** 1970s   **RS Top 500 List:** No

Worldview Theme #50A: Libertarian

Worldview Theme Summary: **for more:** www.projectworldview.org/wvtheme50.htm

I oppose 1) taxes beyond those needed to provide law enforcement / national defense, 2) government interference with free market forces, and 3) laws limiting individual freedom—restricting speech/public expression, limiting firearms, requiring military service, making certain acts crimes where there's no victim, restrictions on private property use, etc. Freedom is protected by such property, so governments should not appropriate it for public welfare. (Note: Libertarians preaching abolition of government are often called anarcho-capitalists.)

SONG
"Live and Let Live" by Stephen P. Cook
to be sung to the tune of "Peaceful, Easy Feeling" by Jack Tempchin / The Eagles

I like the non-aggression principle[1]
And don't like coercion
Respect my rights, my property, leave me alone
Unless I want interaction

I just wanna live and let live[2]
Please don't come looking for me
Enjoying my freedom and liberty

Don't threaten or assault my property[3]
My family or my person
If you do you're liable to meet
My good friends Smith and Wesson[4]

I just wanna live and let live
Please don't come looking for me
Enjoying my freedom and liberty

If you've come to tax or restrict
Or search for victimless crime[5]
We're all consenting adults "free to choose"[6]
So you'll just be wasting your time

I just wanna live and let live
Please don't come looking for me
Enjoying my freedom and liberty

Yeah—ah

SONG—NOTES / COMMENTS

1—The non-aggression principle, as expressed by libertarian philosopher and writer Ayn Rand (1905-1982), says coercive physical force or the threat of such force against person or property should never be used first, and only has legitimate use for defensive purposes by individuals or by governments to punish law-breakers.

2—"Live and let live" is an expression based on the idea that people should be able to live their lives in any way they see fit as long as they aren't bothering other people. How one interprets the "bothering other people" qualifier can determine the extent to which one accepts government regulation of certain activities.

3—Many libertarians believe that individual possession of private property gives people rights that help guarantee their freedom, and that government challenging those private property rights is tantamount to government trampling on their freedom. Americans who put private property on such a pedestal typically oppose government restrictions on how they use their land, and government employees trespassing on their property—perhaps citing the fourth Amendment to the USA Constitution to bolster their legal standing.

4—A USA gun manufacturer. Many libertarians value and exercise their right to keep and bear firearms.

5—Victimless crimes are certain behaviors that most societies frown on, and many have restricted or made illegal, but nonetheless seemingly involve only consenting adults and have no immediately obvious victims. Examples include gambling, marijuana use and prostitution.

6—*Free to Choose* is the title of the 1980 book by economists Rose and Milton Friedman and ten-part television program. The philosophy it is based on promotes free market capitalism and excoriates government intervention and regulation in matters that could be left to market forces alone—arguing that the meddling contributes to economic inefficiency and brings with it a great cost in loss of personal freedom.

Comment: freedom loving, pro "virtue of selfishness" believers in this theme are open to attacks questioning their unwillingness to share, support common good, etc. This song provides emotional armor against that. The dialogue between libertarians and social welfare state advocates is typically emotionally charged.

Worldview Theme—TFJD CODE: 3222   VI=16   Original Tune Era: 1970s   RS Top 500 List: No

Worldview Theme #50B: Left Anarchist

Worldview Theme Summary: **for more:** www.projectworldview.org/wvtheme50.htm

While my brand of libertarianism would abolish the state altogether and abandon or vastly reduce private property rights, it values egalitarianism and order. It would replace government with free associations. Co-ops and communes would be key units in the ideal way to organize society I imagine. (Note: Left anarchism comes in different forms. One is collectivist anarchism where means of production are collectively owned and managed by the producers themselves with labor-based compensation; another might emphasize need-based distribution.)

SONG

"To Get Justice" by Stephen P. Cook

to be sung to the tune of "Rough Justice" by Mick Jagger and Keith Richards / The Rolling Stones

In my hippie days I was a dove
Now I've turned into a hawk
I still don't much like violence
But if we need it I'll raise no squawk

There's no justice[1] today
Governments you're in the way
There's no justice
When the power elite[2] run the show

I like order, I like fair play
We can have them without the state
Time was I thought we could ignore it
But now I think it's just too late

There's no justice today
Governments you're in the way
There's no justice
When the power elite run the show

Urban co-ops, rural communes
I thought they'd leave us alone
From their red tape[3] we can perhaps escape
But inequality[4] we can't condone

There's no justice today
Big money gives us no say[5]
To get justice
Lets clean the slate and smash the state

Organic farms they're taking up arms
Legalized pollution trepasses[6]
Global climate change: their end game
Lawsuits? We've run out of redresses

There's no justice today
Big money gives us no say
To get justice
Lets clean the slate and smash the state

To the corruption and pollution
There's only one solution
To get justice
Lets clean the slate and smash the state[7]

SONG—NOTES / COMMENTS

1— Justice is about implementing what is reasonable, proper, lawful, right, fair, deserved, merited, etc. For left anarchists justice is often connected with fairness, a connection with three dimensions: equal treatment, the degree to which exercising freedom is to be allowed, and reward for contributing to the common good.

2— The power elite refers to the class of people in positions of power in the corporate state. This latter term is used by leftists, who believe that government and large corporations are run by the same people and, being so thoroughly intermeshed, have the same ultimate goals.

3—Government regulation

4—This refers to the huge gap in income and wealth between society's "haves" and "have nots."

5—Those with money pay to have their opinion broadcast, greatly magnifying their influence in elections.

6—Pesticide spray drifts across property boundaries; power plant pollutants cross international boundaries.

7—End the status quo with a revolution that topples the corporate state (see note 2 above, and note 3 theme #19B)

Comment: The terms anarchist and anarchy are so loaded with emotionally charged negative connotations (serious baggage!) they inspire fear in many people. Those working for change who value this theme might consider latching onto more emotionally positive words—like cooperation. (See comment theme #48.)

Worldview Theme—TFJD CODE: 2322 VI=144 Original Tune Era: 2000s   **RS Top 500 List:** No

Worldview Theme #51: Ethical Globalization

Worldview Theme Summary: for more: www.projectworldview.org/wvtheme51.htm

As interaction and integration among the people, businesses and governments of nations accelerates, I think we need authority that transcends nations. This authority could be provided by strengthening/democratizing existing institutions (UN, WTO, etc) and creating new ones. It would mediate disputes, do peacekeeping, and regulate international trade—intervening when worker exploitation, environmental degradation or economic upheaval warranted. It would regulate capital flow, bust monopolies, and promote wealth/technology transfer aiding the poor—giving all at least a minimum living standard and a voice in the decision-making affecting them. (Note: Many don't like the 'ethical' qualifier. They see 'globalization' as extending 'benefits' of free market capitalism to the whole world.)

SONG

"Patience At Its Limit" by Stephen P. Cook
to be sung to the tune of "Take It To The Limit" by Henley, Meisner, and Frey / The Eagles

Protesting at the World Economic Forum	
Where the fat cats meet in the snow[1]	Patience at its limit
I was reading 'bout inequality—that new report	Patience at its limit
It got me feelin' loooooooooooooooow	Patience at its limit: the last stray
The world's richest eighty-five people	Patience at its limit [Please!]
Holding outrageous wealth	Patience at its limit [Come on!]
While billions of poor arrange	Patience at its limit: the last straw
Lives in squalor and filth	
Hey this troubles me greatly:	Patience at its limit [Please!]
Unfair, don't stare, please care, gotta share	Patience at its limit [Come on!]
Something's gotta change	Patience at its limit: the last straw
So we fight for what's right	[starts to fade out]
Our emotions are raw	Patience at its limit
Our patience at its limit: the last straw	Patience at its limit
	Patience at its limit: the last straw
We got capitalists making big money	
We got failure to spread it around	[fades out more]
If the have-nots revolt tomorrow	Patience at its limit [Please!]
They'll have the high ground[2]	Patience at its limit [Come on!]
	Patience at its limit: the last straw
And when you're trying to stay alive	
Somebody needs to care	[fades out still more]
You can't find enough food	Patience at its limit [Please!]
But there's plenty elsewhere	Patience at its limit [Come on!]
With some help you could break in	Patience at its limit: the last straw
So you're looking round for higher ground	
And planning to intruuuuuuuuuuuuuuuuude	[fades out to barely audible]
So we fight for what's right	Patience at its limit [Please!]
Our emotions are raw	Patience at its limit [Come on!]
Our patience at its limit: the last straw	Patience at its limit: the last straw

SONG—NOTES / COMMENTS

1—A phrase used by rock star and humanitarian Bono in describing the WEF meeting in Davos, Switzerland
2—The moral high ground or ethically superior position
Comment: The left has tarred "globalization," the right "socialism," with emotionally negative connotations.

Worldview Theme—TFJD CODE: 3332 **VI=54** **Original Tune Era:** 1970s   **RS Top 500 List:** No

Worldview Theme #52: Independent Living for the Sick or Disabled

Worldview Theme Summary: **for more:** www.projectworldview.org/wvtheme52.htm

Perhaps unlike you, I have a handicap. A physical or mental impairment, chronic illness or pain compromises operation of an integral part of me: my senses, my body, or my mind. This makes my fully functioning and achieving unusually difficult, if not totally impossible. Even at those times when I seemingly overcome this condition, I am still conscious that it exists. I'm aware that people and/or technological "crutches" often help me. I'd like to depend on these less, and more often function independently of them. I have learned lots about my special needs and overcome obstacles once thought insurmountable. Perhaps like you, I value self determination, self respect and equal opportunity.

SONG
"Caring Respect" by Stephen P. Cook
to be sung to the tune of "Seventy Six Trombones" by Meredith Wilson (from *The Music Man*)

[with upbeat loud enthusiastic tempo]

At seventy-six my old bones hope to be keeping up
And at one hundred and ten finally left behind[1,2]
I plan to give it all I've got to call my own shot
Independent Living[3] is what I have in mind

At seventy-six I hope to still be giving back[4]
So they think of me at birthday hundred and ten
Inability to meet my needs will bring me to my knees
It's not a matter of if, but when

[transition to quieter but still enthusiastic tone]

I know this old body will soon break down
Old and sick, old and sick, pain gets in the way
A double wheeled chair for me and stay indoors
My goal, is to delay that day

All of us young and old have special needs
Take care of me, take care of me
Please be extra kind
Help out where I can
Empathize[5] that's been my plan
With caring respect to both give and find

[transition to softer, slower, subdued, quiet]

Helpless when we enter this world
That's how we leave[6]
Humbly, humbly we end up where we start
If I'm helpful to others along way
With caring respect
I'll die having done my part

SONG—NOTES / COMMENTS   (this song is part of the author's personal story)

1— Perhaps this song should be classed as semi-autobiographical? It honors the author's father—who, when his young children told him he was really old, told them he felt like he was one hundred and ten. In latter years the joke was he would live to that age (he died just short of ninety-two). Just a couple of years before his death, he announced he really loved musicals. Perhaps *The Music Man* was especially a favorite!

2— According to a Vanguard Group retirement planning calculator, the chance that a married couple—each 76 years old, call them John and Mary—will live to be 110 years old are: 0.01% for John, 0.16% for Mary.
Other research suggests that today's British sixteen year olds have a 25% chance of living to at least age 100.

3—Independent Living typically refers to the expressed desires of elderly people and people with disabilities to 1) have the opportunity and responsibility to make their own decisions and 2) exercise their right to control their own lives.

4—Being socially responsible—meaning acting in a way that benefits society.

5—Empathy refers to "fellow feeling", that is imagining that you are in the other person's shoes and experiencing his or her feelings, struggles, fears, pain, etc. Often empathy ➔ compassion. Using a phrase from a yoga sutra, cultivating an attitude of "compassion for the unhappy" is a plan that for many is worthy of consideration.

6—Human beings just after birth or just before death are typically helpless.

Comment: this theme may have value as emotional armor in that feeling independent and self reliant can help overcome fears of an unknown (perhaps totally dependent) future. Watching elderly people deal with stress spawned a new term among social science researchers. As Carver and Connor-Smith describe it, "The notion of accommodative coping derives from the process of successful aging…It refers to adjustments within the self that are made in response to constraints. [Adjustments include] acceptance, cognitive restructuring, and scaling back one's goals." The disabled can also benefit from aspects of this coping style.

Worldview Theme—TFJD CODE: 2212 **VI**=32 **Original Tune Era:** 1950s   **RS Top 500 List:** No

A. More on Worldviews, Emotions, Music
Emotional Armor & Adopting Healthy Beliefs

In Part IIIb we'll metaphorically liken someone choosing what to believe in to "Shopping in the Reality Marketplace." But first consider another economics metaphor: depicting stress as what threatens what we value: money, material possessions, our jobs, loved ones, peace of mind, worldview, etc. Coping mechanisms help us deal with stress. Another metaphor, that has a person carrying something, can represent the effects of past encounters with stress or preparing for future ones. Thus we carry emotional baggage and are equipped with emotional armor protecting our feelings.

That emotional armor falls into two categories. 1) Brain function that protects us at times of stress / danger (and can also reward us with "feel good" moments). As discussed in Part I, it has its origin in our genes; 2) key parts of our worldviews, specifically the beliefs / values dear to us, those we turn to for comfort, courage, and inspiration when we are threatened, afraid, hurt, and facing more of the same. This has its origin in our memes (introduced in Part Ic, we turn to them in Part IIIc.)

This armor is hardly perfect! Thus we carry the scars of past disappointments, wrongs, and trauma around with us as emotional baggage. Some of us are weighted down more the others, just as some people are armed with thicker walled defenses. When our emotional armor becomes excessive, and begins to obstruct our personal growth efforts, in a sense it becomes like emotional baggage: something we'd like to get rid of!

There's another reason why we might want to get rid of some emotional armor: it distorts our view of reality, even—in the most serious cases—interfering with the accuracy of predictions we make based on our worldviews. I'm thinking specifically of certain beliefs that people latch onto for emotional reasons, those difficult to logically / rationally justify. Some people know such beliefs are false, but continue to hold them anyway—leaving others puzzled. Thus, in *How the Mind Works,* Steven Pinker writes, "It only raises the question of why a mind would evolve to find comfort in beliefs it can plainly see are false." The reference is to Belief in a Personal God (theme #8B) and other consoling religious beliefs.

I'd answer Pinker's question by noting such beliefs are a key part of our emotional armor. And,

while some will argue that they distort our view of reality, clearly they work more than they hurt— otherwise evolution would weed them out! Good advice to those conflicted about what to believe might be: "Even if you mostly don't believe in something, if believing has psychological advantages, then for you this belief can be a useful fiction. It's related to the practice of adopting healthy beliefs." The latter more generally involves deciding whether to adopt the belief based on the extent to which it will promote your health and the health of the society you live in.

For example, consider belief that all humans are connected via an unseen transcendent dimension. While in the 3D world perceived by our senses humans are separate, unconnected entities, conceivably they could be linked in other ways: in higher spatial dimensions[1], in a spiritual realm, through God, etc.   Suppose, after preliminary investigation, you are still undecided as to its ultimate truth, but do become convinced that if everyone believed it, the world would be a better place. Or at least, if you believe it, your psychological health will be enhanced (you won't feel so alone, alienated, etc.) So this belief becomes part of your worldview because it has psychological advantages, and, if others believed it, could make the world a better place. You don't know if it's part of the ultimate, true description of reality. (We'll return to this heavy topic in Part IIIe.)

Similarly you don't hold some beliefs, not because you're sure they're untrue, but because they potentially are unhealthy to you or society. Example: a young boy decides not to believe that if he behaves badly he will burn in hell, because burning in hell scares him and gives him nightmares. He decides to behave (for other reasons) but not believe in hell and feels better.

It's one thing for you to decide to cast off some emotional armor, and an entirely different matter for someone else to try to emotionally disarm you. "Tread softly. Because you tread on my memes," Richard Dawkins writes (in *The God Delusion*). I can imagine a generally happy but psychologically fragile person saying that to a threatening person.

Importance of Music in Shaping Worldviews

This is similar to the title of a talk[2] I gave in Budapest with one difference. There astronomy was my focus, here it's music. The two come together in the "music of the spheres"—an idea of Pythagoras, who is often credited with discovering the relationship between the length of a plucked string and the pitch of the musical note produced. And in Plato proclaiming astronomy and music were "twinned": one for eyes, the other for ears.

Through our eyes, ears and senses we perceive the world. But perception, as Edmund Husserl put it[3], is "the phase of consciousness that constitutes the pure now, and memory would be every other phase…" Fully realized human consciousness is "constantly fitting things into a story" as Jaynes says. Before this can happen, humans needed to order events in time and gauge time intervals. A concept of time can build on biology (growth, heart beats, etc.) and astronomical observation (interval between sunrises, lunar phases, etc.).

More narrowly one can focus on "our capacity to synchronize to a beat i.e. to move in time with a perceived pulse in a manner that is predictive and flexible across a broad range of tempi"—as Tufts psychology professor Anniruddh Patel puts it in a March 2014 *PLOS Biology* paper "The Evolutionary Biology of Music Rhythm". He suggests that we innately (and perhaps uniquely?) possess a sense of basic time interval. But this doesn't give us the sense of past/now/future that I argue consciousness needs. Thus I don't equate a musical consciousness state with one embodying concepts of justice or morality.

The "music and consciousness" relationship is a complex one. In a similarly titled volume, David and Eric Clarke note[4] how music "combines social, conceptual, technical, perceptual and motor attributes; the way it is distributed in /around societies; the high value that is placed upon it…that it seems not to be the official medium of communication in any culture" as all bolstering the claim for music having "a strong relationship to consciousness." Rather than pursue this, let's focus on how music connects with thinking, feeling, joining, and doing.

The 2009 talk I mentioned in beginning this section was at a scientific conference honoring the 400th anniversary of events that eventually ushered in the triumph of the thinking approach to making sense out of reality. In contrast to doing science, pure music without lyrics does fine without thinking. Words and concepts don't find application in

this pure music realm. On the contrary, in trying to describe "feelings," often language alone is not enough. As Laird Addis put it in his 2004 *Of Mind and Music* book[5], "Certain subtle differences in both the intentions and especially the modes of states of consciousness that are ineffable, that is cannot be captured in language, can be represented to us by music …nuances of mood and other aspects." He notes "a unique isomorphism" between music and emotions.

Society benefits when that relationship involves using music's emotive power to inspire needed social change. But even the simplest music rhythm is capable of leading people to abandon thinking and be swept away by feeling. This can be dangerous! Anthropologist Oliver Sacks[6] notes trance states have been described by ethnomusicologists in nearly every culture. Jaynes, with his Collective Cognitive Imperative—the basis of worldview theme #15 and the anti-thesis of analytical thinking—has detailed how this and similar states (where control of one's actions is ceded to some authority) can arise.

Where this can go is described by John Pfeiffer in his book *The Emergence of Society: A Prehistory of the Establishment*. "What began with a shaman performing in a trance among people around camp fires culminated in spectacles conducted by high priests and their cohorts from platforms elevated above the multitude. There was singing and chanting, words said over and over again, recited in singsong metrical patterns with punctuating rhymes at the ends of lines. Music, setting the pace in the background and echoing and rising to crescendos and climaxes, reinforced the beat. Dancers with masks kept time to the words and the music as they acted out the roles of gods and heroes. Spectators moved with the rhythms and chanted ritual responses."[7]

The joining and doing aspects of music are obvious in the above. Anthony Storr concurs, noting[8] "for most of its history, music has been predominantly a group activity." It began, he writes, "serving communal purposes, of which religious ritual and warfare are two examples." Dancing, the ultimate music—doing connection, provides another. Finally, we mustn't forget the mechanical/ procedural side in moving fingers, hands, vocal cords, etc. in the doing of producing music. Nor all those memes with a musical origin!

Music and the Brain

A new model of the brain has emerged in the last three decades: as an organ that receives information from multiple sensory inputs and synthesizes it to provide us with meaning. This is not bin processing according to whether it comes from eyes, ears, touch, smell, etc. For example, in making sense of the world the brain treats information the ears receive and that derived from reading lips the same in that both activate the auditory cortex. This model recognizes the brain's remarkable plasticity. For example, blind fold a person for as little as ninety minutes and already it seems the visual cortex is activating in a way that heightens our sensitivity to touch!

This model has been informed by studying the role of music in children's brain development. That soothing lullabies can comfort distraught infants and help them fall back to sleep has long been appreciated. And that a majority of young children have imaginary companions. Julian Jaynes regards the latter as "another vestige of the bicameral mind" and says it typically occurs between ages three and seven just before consciousness has fully developed.

What has only recently been appreciated is the large amount of plasticity that young brains possess. Consider blind children. German neuroscientist Hermann Ackermann says children born blind have a visual cortex that is largely unresponsive to stimuli—visual or auditory. His work[9] shows if a young child suffers an accident that results in blindness, the brain is able to make new neural connections and rewire so that otherwise unused portions of the visual cortex get connected to auditory regions. This explains why some blind musicians (such as Ray Charles) can have an almost superhuman sense of hearing.

Consider what musical practice can do. In a November 2010 *Scientific American* article "Hearing the Music, Honing the Mind," the magazine urges schools to add music classes, not cut them. It cites studies showing "assiduous instrument training from an early age can help the brain process sounds better…" and that "discerning subtleties in pitch and timing can help… in learning a new language." And notes increased ability to stay focused in distracting environments is another benefit of practicing music.

Consider an extreme case of such practice.

Before a child turns six he practices music for an estimated 3500 hours as directed by his father, a skilled music teacher. The child grows up able to maintain entire music scores in working memory so he can "survey it, like a fine picture or beautiful statue, at a glance" (in his own words). It seems he has something analogous to photographic memory: one based on storing auditory (not visual) information in a wholistic fashion. His name was Wolfgang Amadeus Mozart.

From a modern neuroscience viewpoint, such extreme practice reconfigures and reinforces neural connections to the point where they matter as much or more than genetic whiteprints. In his 2010 book *Bounce*[10], author Matthew Syed recounts stories ranging from Mozart's to the Williams' sisters—who began practicing tennis at ages three and four and a half. He similarly concludes that much practice (> ten thousand hours), hard work, and fierce determination often trump innate genetic ability.

One might think that the new way to model the brain would doom Jaynes' bicameral mind hypothesis? On the contrary, recognition that neural plasticity can change brain function quickly answers Jaynes' critics who charge needed changes underlying genetic makeup would happen too slowly. Similarly in the last decade, we've learned epigenetic forces produce inheritable changes in gene activity and rapidly drive evolution without changing the gene part of DNA sequences. Epigenetic changes affecting when genes are switched on can occur in response to environmental factors. Perhaps such changes resulted from the traumas of 3000-4000 yrs ago and ancient minds became more flexible, creative and conscious!

Finally, what else can we say about dancing? Besides music and movement, it involves emotional expression and social interaction. In this regard, we contrast similarly titled works: Annis Pratt's *Dancing With Goddesses* and Donella Meadows' "Dancing With Systems" paper (see theme #13.) Both recognize dancing is a dynamic activity. Pratt's work (with mythology / Jungian archetype overtones) is right brain focused; Meadows is more left brained. Whatever the focus, few would disagree that dancing—like all emotional aspects of life itself—has its share of changes. That is, it contains some degree of emotional volatility, our next topic.

B. Emotional Volatility, Creativity and the Reality Marketplace

Emotional Volatility and Worldview Themes

Something that's volatile is likely to change in a sudden and extreme way. Many have applied the term to financial investments. Thus those investing in the stock market need to be prepared for much greater changes (both up and down) in their account's value on a much shorter time scale—that is, much greater volatility—when compared to fixed income investments—say composed of USA government issued treasury bond holdings which typically behave much less erratically.

With respect to "investing" in various worldview themes, we can provide a similar volatility based contrast. Those investing in Passionately Impulsive (theme #18A with TFJD code 1323) and The Artistic Orientation (theme #12 with TFJD code 1333) need to be prepared for much greater changes (both up and down) in their feelings / emotional state on a much shorter time scale —that is, much greater volatility—when compared to less emotionally volatile themes such as Dispassionate (theme #18B with TFJD code 3111) and Scientific Materialism (theme #5A with 3121).

Worldview theme volatility increases dramatically with absence of thinking (T in the code) and increase of feeling (F in the code). Numerically, one gauges worldview theme volatility by using the theme's TFJD code. The 1, 2, or 3 scores for each of the T, F, J, and D components have partly been assigned with the following equation in mind:

$$\text{volatility index} = VI = (4-T)^2 F^2 J D$$

Volatility indices for each worldview theme are shown at the bottom of the theme's Part II page.

Figure #7: Computing the Volatility Index VI

Plugging into volatility index = $VI = (4-T)^2 F^2 J D$ for theme #18A with TFJD code 1323:
$$VI = (4-1)^2 \times 3^2 \times 2 \times 3 = [3 \times 3] \times [3 \times 3] \times 2 \times 3 = 486$$

for theme #12 with TFJD code 1333:
$$VI = (4-1)^2 \times 3^2 \times 3 \times 3 = [3 \times 3] \times [3 \times 3] \times 3 \times 3 = 729$$

for theme #18B with TFJD code 3111:
$$VI = (4-3)^2 \times 1^2 \times 1 \times 1 = [1 \times 1] \times [1 \times 1] \times 1 \times 1 = 1$$

for theme #5A with TFJD code 3121:
$$VI = (4-3)^2 \times 1^2 \times 2 \times 1 = [1 \times 1] \times [1 \times 1] \times 2 \times 1 = 2$$

Just as financial advisors might urge their risk adverse clients to avoid investing in highly volatile offerings, one can imagine parents or counselors urging young people to avoid buying into worldview themes with a high volatility index. While such advice might be well meaning—certainly it would be an attempt to steer one to a smoother ride path with fewer bumps in the road —following it could also have unfortunate life outcomes. Those might take the form of deciding not to have kids / start a family. Or result in a lot less passion, creativity and spontaneity in one's life, a life summed up by "nothing ventured, nothing gained," missing out on some of the greatest rewards, beauty, highest highs life has to offer!

Figure #8: High Volatility Themes

#12   The Artistic Worldview   729
#18A   Passionately Impulsive   486
#38   Valuing Family   486
#17A   Bitterness & Vengeance   324
#7B   Magic   324
#27   Belonging To Nature   324
#28A   Hedonistic Orientation   243
#2A   The True Believer   243
#41   Struggling With Self Esteem   216
#24   Struggling With Sustenance   216
#21B   Service To Others   216
#8B   Belief In A Personal God   216
#33B   Addiction   162
#9A   Religious Fundamentalism   162
#45A Borrowing Mentality   144
#50B Left Anarchist   144

Consider the worldview themes with the highest volatility index (see Figure #8). At the top of the list is The Artistic Orientation (theme #12), followed by Passionately Impulsive (theme #18A) and Valuing Family (theme #38). While there is no doubt that a genetic component predisposes certain individuals to these particular worldview themes more than others, each of them involves significant learned (or learning to avoid!) behavior. Consider impulsive behavior or its self restraint (theme #29A) opposite. In his 2014 book *The Marshmallow Test: Mastering Self Control*, psychologist and experimentor Walter Mischel describes the once thought to be innate lack of self control as "a skill open to modification …[that] can be enhanced through specific cognitive strategies that have now been identified."

Artistic Creativity—Risks and Rewards

Of course worldviews are typically not dominated by a single theme but rather several themes are commonly expressed together in many individuals. Consider artistic creativity. One (stereotyped?) conception of the worldview of an artist might be heavily based on high volatility themes from Figure #8: #12, #18A, #28A, #41, and #33B. The last of these is Addiction. With respect to addiction and creativity, Linda Leonard in her 1990 book *Witness to the Fire–Creativity and the Veil of Addiction*, argues that some parallel process (not a cause and effect relationship) occurs in the heads of both addicts and creative people like writers, artists, etc. Of them she writes, "Both descend into chaos, into the unknown world of the unconscious. Both are fascinated by what they find there. Both encounter pain, death, and suffering. But the addict is pulled down, often without choice...the creative person chooses to go down into the unknown realm... Some creative artists descend with the help of drugs or alcohol and continue to create. Some find they must give up their addictions in order to create."

She speaks from personal experience. In describing her volatile creative relationship with alcohol, Leonard writes, "Like Icarus I soared toward the sun with my wings of wine, not realizing that by flying so high I would fall deeply into the sea as had Icarus and my alcoholic father before me." Even after five years of such behavior and an increasing sense of falling, she nonetheless felt that "the euphoric moments were so powerful that the guilt and humiliation through which I paid for them seemed minimal." And, in likening her and other addiction based creative relationships to a bad bargain made with a "Moneylender" archetypal figure, she connects such experience with another of our high volatility themes: #45A Borrowing Mentality.

Even without addiction, pursuit of artistic creativity—whether in art (as painter, sculptor, etc.) in music (as performer, composer, songwriter, dancer, etc), writer, poet, filmmaker, playwright, etc. —carries great risks and demands great commitment. Beyond having raw talent, on the front end one must invest years in training and

practice—developing skills, honing one's craft. At least here, with hard work and determination, your progress is in your own hands: you steer your own destiny. However, as one's pursuit continues, you soon cede that control.

Successful creative endeavors are not isolated efforts—your success depends on other people: your audience and those who promote your work to that audience. And those other people can let you down. Failure to reach and please your audience ends many aspiring artists' careers. Many of those end even before they start with failure to stand out and get noticed. Even those who initially establish themselves by pleasing an audience typically have bills to pay.

Christopher Moore, in his 2012 both hilarious and cynical book *Sacre Bleu: A Comedy d'Art*, describes what is termed "the artist's dilemma" as follows: "...to paint for filthy lucre was a compromise of principles, but to be an artist who didn't sell was to be anonymous as an artist." The mother of the main character in Moore's book—which seems to irreverently trash all of the high-mindedness expressed in the (part II) prose description of worldview theme #12 The Artistic Orientation and the talk often heard in leading art museums—urges him to abandon being "a useless painter" and concentrate on making bread in the family bakery business.

Even more central to risks associated with pursuing artistic creativity is the emotional commitment required. Undoubtedly for every celebrated creative (or we can broaden this to include intellectual) success, thousands of the dreams / flying machines of dedicated intrepid explorers of new cultural terrain crash and burn. This often occurs after lengthy, single-minded, all consuming passionate pursuit of a creation that seems within reach if just a bit more energy is expended or with ratcheting up the intensity of the chase just a bit more. Casualties are often not limited to just artistic individuals, but their family members also suffer.

There is no doubt that seeking the creative "highest highs" threatens one with "the lowest lows"—crashes marked for many by suicide. Clearly the worldview terrain mapped by high volatility worldview themes is dangerous territory. Is it best left unexplored? Recognizing the tremendous gifts the creative individuals who have dwelt there have given humanity, I would argue no. But in counseling those contemplating a life journey largely set in this realm I would 1) stress that one needs a plan B if things don't work out, 2) prescribe much work in developing and cultivating their own emotional intelligence and 3) urge that where appropriate, in fully expressing their feelings, creative explorers nonetheless make good use of thinking tools.

As we've noted in Part I, often it's difficult to separate human behavior into thinking, feeling, joining, and doing components because they occur together. In addition, it could be that careful examination of many creative leaps will reveal unexpected TFJD contributions. Surprisingly, Robert and Michele Root-Bernstein in their 1999 book *Sparks of Genius*, assert that—even in many scientific advances—"to think creatively is first to feel." Their book, subtitled "The 13 thinking tools of the world's most creative people" names those tools as follows: 1) observing, 2) imaging, 3) abstracting, 4) recognizing patterns, 5) forming patterns, 6) analogizing, 7) body thinking, 8) empathizing, 9) dimensional thinking, 10) modeling, 11) playing, 12) transforming, and 13) synthesizing. Besides spurring creativity, they argue that use of these tools can also help overcome "the problem of living in illusion rather than in reality."

Shopping in the Reality Marketplace

Metaphorically speaking, examining various worldview themes can be thought of as shopping in "The Reality Marketplace." Introduced in my book *Coming of Age in the Global Village*, and given something of an internet presence on the **Project Worldview** website, this is an imaginary place where important ideas, beliefs, values, and worldview themes are bought / sold, and where someone might go to find answers to life's important questions, like: "Why am I here?" "How does nature work?" "How can I find God?" "How should I live?" etc."

Ideally the best answers to be found there—the ones most heavily promoted and thus receiving most attention from shoppers—would be based on the consensus view of what works. In contrast to the random nature of answers (to typically more focused questions) an oracle provides, ideally the best selling goods in The Reality Marketplace—

the most popular worldview themes or whatever—are those that have met the test of feedback and received countless good consumer reviews. Investing in those goods should ideally allow the possessor to most comfortably fit into the reality of the situation he or she faces and best confront the issues for which he or she has been metaphorically shopping for solutions.

Given what happens in actuality it is tempting to say that many shopper purchases suggest they continue to live in a world of illusion rather than reality. Nonetheless I believe concluding that is premature for five reasons. 1) For emotional reasons, many settle for (something valuable to them) useful fiction. 2) The complexity of the human predicament, where so many tradeoffs need to be weighed, is almost overwhelming. 3) In the biggest picture sense, we have incomplete information as to the nature of reality. 4) Even in highly focused views, much of the information we do have is feelings based and can't be easily quantified and analyzed. (In this latter regard it should be obvious that the volatility indices presented here for each of the worldview themes are little better than rough estimates that admittedly involve lots of uncertainty!) 5) Despite its less than ideal operation, perhaps one should accord this metaphorical marketplace we have with some respect and concede it possesses some wisdom?

Having said that, I have no doubt that our metaphorical individual investor—ideally a thoughtful, sensitive, caring, active human being who eagerly seeks and is open to making the best choices—can become better adapted to his or her uniquely complex environment and do better than what the "one size fits all" market consensus of most popular worldview theme buys suggests.

To begin with, each of us uniquely enters the world. For each of us the sum total of our genetic heritage and both the surrounding physical and cultural environment is different. As we grow and begin to accept or question what our parents and teachers give us, we each do so from a slightly different TFJD code 2222 Valuing Traditions and Status Quo starting point. From there, both our formal education and experiences in "The School of Hard Knocks" shape us differently. That is, the memes and memeplexes (including worldview themes) we latch onto—our culturally derived individual memetic heritage—often varies widely.

C. Toward a Memetic Code or Something More Immediately Useful

Genes, Memes, Neuroscience / Search for Rules

The search for the genetic code began very slowly with Gregor Mendel's classic 1865 paper. There, from observed characteristics (phenotypes) of the pea plants he studied in breeding experiments, he concluded that hereditary instructions (genotypes) are carried and passed on in discrete units. The whole number ratios he found when comparing numbers of plants with different phenotypes led him to this finding. His paper basically went unnoticed for thirty-five years. It took another fifty years before biologists shifted their focus from human chromosomes to the DNA molecules those chromosomes housed. Once this molecule's structure was worked out, it was soon identified as the genetic information repository.

By the 1960s it was appreciated that the genetic information that propagates from organism to organism, and guides everything from protein synthesis to cell metabolism to reproduction to biological evolution, consists of a long code written with four letters: T, C, A, G. The letters come from the names of four nucleotides—large molecules composed of phosphate group(s), five carbon sugar, and ring of nitrogen, carbon and oxygen atoms—named thymine, cytosine, adenine, and guanine. Thus a tiny segment of genetic code physically realized in DNA's structure might be written something like AAAAGAGGT. In actuality a single long, double helix twisted DNA molecule would more typically encode genetic instructions consisting of anywhere from hundreds to billions of letters. Every string of three letters —called a triplet— codes for an amino acid, which proteins are built from. The "AAA" triplet or tri-nucleotide sequence is the codon that specifies the amino acid Lysine. "AGA" and "GGT" code for amino acids Arginine and Glycine.

Just as life propagates based on a code carried in genes, it's asserted that human culture propagates via memes. A meme is a theoretical unit of cultural information such as a word, an idea, gesture, story, particular behavior, etc. that propagates from mind to mind guiding human cultural evolution. Biologist Richard Dawkins first described them and their supposed functioning in his 1976 book *The Selfish Gene*.

Examples he's cited include a particular melody in a song, the know-how needed to build an arch, and the notion that "You will survive your own death." Note, for something to qualify as a meme it has to be capable of being passed on by people and replicated again inside human minds.

The religious meme cited above builds on an appreciation of the concept of death. Likewise this concept depends on other concepts, most notably the concept of something being alive. Describing memes often requires lower level components and processes—notably language, other concepts, and linking concepts internally to make conceptual maps. Concepts replace sensory experiences and memories. Language facilitates describing them and conceptual map making. Certainly the meme "You will survive your own death" and variations of it like "If you behave a certain way while you're alive, you will survive your own death" (a key part of worldview theme #14A Moralistic God) have successfully replicated and propagated from human mind to mind over the last two thousand years.

Memes have been both widely embraced and severely criticized in the four decades since their introduction. We mentioned one criticism in Part Ic: "meme" is an unnecessary synonym for the term "concept". Others have inappropriately linked memes to "stimuli" and "learnt associations." A second criticism is that unlike genes, which have a real embodiment in matter, memes are something abstract. A third criticism of memes: there isn't a code script for them analogous to the DNA genetic code.

In defending memes, it seems that accepting the charge in the first criticism makes rebutting the second and third ones easier. Recall discussion in Part Ib of how links between neurons in mice brains are associated with specific concepts. It seems that efforts to find a memetic code script could begin with investigating such real neural network connections associated with concept mapping inside brains. While many connectionists and constructionists among neuroscientists might half-heartedly agree that the search for something like a memetic code should head in this direction, symbolists and locationists would not.

In general, it seems that neuroscientists have been rather standoffish about memes, and haven't fully embraced investigating them. Before considering what direction the quest for a memetic code should take, let's consider neuroscientists' search for rules as to how the brain works in processing information and learning.

Many symbolists and locationists are excited about cognitive architecture efforts to build working models that represent brain organization and basic, irreducible cognitive and perceptual operations. One such effort had its beginnings in the early 1970s at Carnegie Mellon University and is known as ACT-R (adaptive control of thought). The latest[1] (December, 2013) version of the code (written in Lisp) provides a modeling framework based on cognitive psychology experiments and brain imaging results that can be used to simulate human behavior.

Representing declarative knowledge in chunks (using vectors), ACT-R employs modules (for such things as declarative memory, procedural memory, and various perceptual motor functions) to represent brain structures. Its modeling breaks down various human cognition and mental processing tasks into a series of discrete operations based on assumptions of how the involved brain areas work. Models can be created to provide step-by-step simulation of specific tasks to test understanding.

Steadily refined over the last four decades, the methodology has advanced to where model predictions of the blood oxygen level dependent responses of fMRI brain scans can be compared to actual data in brain areas such as the prefrontal cortex, hand and mouth areas in the motor cortex, anterior cingulate cortex, and the basal ganglia. Despite its cognitive architecture classification, ACT-R is one of several modeling efforts recently expanded to encompass the affective neuroscience territory of processes and states involving attitudes, motivation, and emotions.

Both connectionalists and constructionists among neuroscientists have long been interested in using computational neuroscience tools to model higher order cognitive functions and better understand consciousness. They have used both artificial neural networks (ANN) and biological neuron models. The former typically consist of layers of processing elements or units termed "neurons." These send data to succeeding layers through "synapse" connections. They employ a

pattern for interconnecting them, a learning routine for updating the strength of the connections, and an activation ("firing") function that converts weighted input to output. Like the human brain, neural networks are designed to learn from experience. Just as the brain can compare data stored in working memory to that in long-term memory, neural networks use pattern recognition routines. They accomplish machine-learning tasks using algorithms (recipes for procedures) to optimize something of interest, given constraints provided.

In contrast to ANNs, which are designed with computational effectiveness in mind, mathematically realized neurons of biological neuron models are constructed to be more like real nerve cells. Whereas ANNs have been widely applied to solve problems like image acquisition and processing, handwriting and speech recognition, biological neuron based models of an entire human brain are in their infancy. Right now the understanding needed to successfully model neural network connections and functions behind encoding and retrieving even the simplest concepts in our brains is beyond our capabilities.

One Neuroscientist's Work on Memes

One of the few neuroscientists enthusiastic about memes is University of Surrey psychology professor Adam McNamara. His 2011 paper[2] begins with recalling the excitement generated by the 1996 discovery of mirror neurons "located in regions highly involved in imitation." Following the suggestion that these "were the neural substrates upon which language could have evolved," he notes the growth of the field of memetics over the next dozen years —spurred by the work of S. Blackmore, F. Heylighten, K. Chielens, etc.

He singles out the "non-measurable, indefinable" nature of memes as presenting challenges, and laments current efforts to meet those challenges. "Mendel did not discover the fundamentals of genetics," he writes, "by throwing his hands in the air and exclaiming that it was all too complex and immeasurable. It appears this is the current scientific stance on memes." Could it be that unraveling something like a memetic code similarly needs another century?

I don't doubt the complexity of the task of figuring out how the brain works in processing information and learning. But I am skeptical that future developments will bring us any closer to a simple, elegant memetic code analogous to genetic code that specifies something fundamental like protein-making instructions.

I don't doubt that, like genes, memes are involved in a fierce competition to survive and replicate, or that similar Darwinian type principles apply. And it seems reasonable, as McNamara describes, that there are four stages in meme replication: 1) perception and assimilation by an individual, 2) retention in the individual's memory, 3) expression by an action involving the individual's motor system producing communicable output, and 4) transmission to another individual who responds to the output.

And I think specific memes are often both found and passed on grouped together with other specific memes in what are called memeplexes. (Worldview themes are an example). And I've already mentioned (in Part Ic) that I like the thought of competing worldviews. Nonetheless I'm skeptical given the nature of memes and the complexity and vastness of the knowledge—both explicit, procedural, tacit, etc.—they can pass on.

Consider the challenge of using memetic code to represent physical world concepts that go far beyond the simplest ones in complexity. For example, what is needed to get from concepts of "Earth," "rotates," "day," and "night," to the meaning of "The Earth rotates and causes day and night" (memeplex)?

Following McNamara, we consider this with use of production rules having form "if condition, then action" in describing the memetic units involved. He uses the concept of "God" as an example and cites rules such as "if God, then omnipotent," "if God, then good," and "if God, punish bad" as rules behind such a concept. Note these rules themselves contain concepts ("omnipotent," "good," "punish," "bad") that need coding and connecting to. Our memeplex example above would similarly need rules for the four concepts cited and for more coding/connections for concepts those rules invoked.

In thinking about writing memetic code for these examples, we need to consider other connections between constituent concepts and more emotionally laden ones important to replication. This may not amount to much for a concept like "rotates," but for "God" (as "punish

bad" suggests!) it is enormous! Even for our memeplex example seemingly squarely set in the physical world, one can argue that emotional factors (including fear of falling off a spinning Earth!) partly explain the lengthy period (over two thousand years) between its initial conception by the ancient Greeks and its widespread replication in human heads. Certainly coding memes and memeplexes built on social science, psychological or other concepts based on a diverse history of human experience, is much tougher than ones confined solely to the physical world!

McNamara takes defining memes beyond production rules and helps us better approach some of the concerns raised by the above examples. He distinguishes between two types of memes: i-memes, whose transmission and storage occurs internally in our central nervous system, and e-memes, whose transmission and storage occurs externally in the world. He is not concerned with challenges posed by e-memes (which he notes with terms like "fidelity of media reproduction," "copyright law," "marketing," "technological," and "public relations.")

In moving toward a neural connectivity profile based description of memes, he stresses "all i-memes will include (direct and/or indirect) connectivity between perceptual related brain regions and motor related brain regions." After writing, "An i-meme cannot be solely an emotional experience, yet …may contain an emotional component," he envisions their primary connections as "cortical and limbic." Saying "an i-meme comprises the neural network which encodes it" currently doesn't help in deciding what is or isn't an i-meme. McNamara argues this isn't important. What's important, he says, is "whether changes to an i-meme can be measured directly by measuring changes in the connectivity profiles of brain regions as a result of changes to e-memes."

He claims neuroimaging fMRI technology is good enough to make such measurements as part of controlled experiments. "Producing such profiles and observing changes in these profiles may be used to describe memetic processing at each stage of meme replication," he writes, before referring to using statistical procedures to assess connectivity strength. He sees data from similar experiments being used to gauge changes to i-memes over time as they evolve.

McNamara provides several examples of crude neural connectivity profiles for various memes. The one for the meme "Error tone on PC" serves as the basis for Figure #9. These are drawn with the width of the straight lines proportional to the strength of the neural connection, with "internal states" representing emotional states.

Figure #9

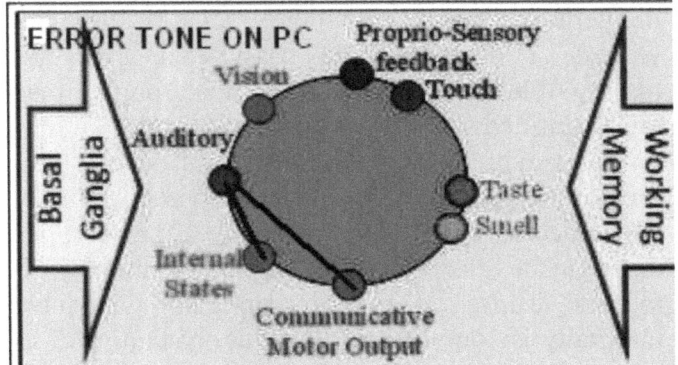

McNamara tries to put a positive spin on his approach by writing, "Viewing cognitive skills as part of a whole evolving 'memetic system'" provides a framework offering important advantages in studying "how these processes interact...to allow humans to function as single and social cognitive units." But to me this look at how connectionalists might proceed in searching for a memetic code underscores the primitive current state of affairs and hardly inspires confidence. Perhaps the symbolists refining the ACT-R model have the better approach, but I doubt it!

Not a Memetic Code, But Immediately Useful!

It may be that modern neuroscience will fail to find a shorthand, useful memetic code that concisely gets at something universally important and fundamentally behind replicating memes /transmitting human culture because none exists. Perhaps the best we can do in concisely summarizing a vast, steadily evolving conceptual framework is simply to continue external conceptual mapping and otherwise describing regions of interest using symbols, words, syntax rules, equations, images, etc. These maps can be a great help in understanding relationships, spurring brainstorming, communicating ideas, and fostering creative innovation. From what I've seen, they often are a "small picture, high resolution" tool. Certainly many "big picture, low resolution" efforts at summarizing human nature and pointing

the way toward future developments have been made. Some, like the "Myers—Briggs Personality Types" classification scheme, are based on the work of Carl Jung (1875-1961). Others have been inspired by Abraham Maslow (1908-1970), with his pyramid-shaped "Hierarchy of Needs" diagram, etc. More recently the work of psychology professor Clare Graves (1914-1986) spawned the spiral dynamics approach of Don Beck and Chris Cowan. It focuses on v-memes, which provide core value system for building the conceptual models that people use to understand the world.

Project Worldview offers another "big picture, low resolution" approach. Initially the idea was limited to quantitatively assessing a worldview by turning it into a series of eighty (later eighty one) scores (on a 1 to 10 scale). To accomplish this, questions (many from opinion surveys) were assembled for each of the worldview themes, and software written to score the related quizzes. By 2012, with versions of The Quick Worldview Analysis Program, this evolved to comparing two worldviews using a mathematically more sophisticated correlation coefficient calculation to provide a single % correlation between them. The TFJD codes and associated Emotional Volatility indices will eventually be used as weighting factors in this program to improve it.

Even without this update, TFJD codes, Figure #2, this book, and concept mapping tools can map a path to change. I see such TFJD code based maps as potentially facilitating what Gaia University's Andrew Langford has described well. "By understanding the processes by which worldviews come about and develop over time we may well be able to map out routes and strategies (unlearning?) for conscious future developments ...As the world we live in is very much shaped by the relative dominance /subordination of various worldviews we might be able to work out how to turn the volume down on some and turn it up on others ..."

Worldviews, mental maps, or internal conceptual frameworks typically result from a lifetime of information gathering in which we constantly "query" the environment. Much of this is done without conscious awareness. In contrast, in recent years the external aid to brainstorming /visualizing relationships known as concept mapping has become increasingly popular. Like using an oracle, our next topic, this can begin with a question.

D. The TFJD Oracle: An Oracle for the 21st Century

Oracles, the Temple at Delphi, the *I Ching*

An oracle is a person or procedure thought to provide wise counsel or good symbolic guidance with respect to questions as to how to proceed at life's important crossroads. It is a form of divination: the art or practice of revealing hidden knowledge, especially the foretelling / predicting future events. The temple at Delphi and the *I Ching* sacred book are two famous and quite different ancient oracles. At Delphi (a site chosen by Zeus who thought it was the center of his "Grandmother Earth" or Gaia), Greeks supposedly received wisdom directly from the gods. This came in the form of verse (dactylic hexameter) from the mouth of an intoxicated young female intermediary. The *I Ching*, initially created as the court oracle of an ancient Chinese dynasty, contains a procedure for using sticks or tossing coins. The results direct one to hexagrams and beautifully written rhyming text.

Typically one gave a carefully conceived question to each of these oracles. Both are truly ancient with roots extending back some three thousand years. While differences in their function are obvious, the oracles also differ in that while the oracle at Delphi is long since defunct, versions of the *I Ching* are still in use. I'd say the oracle based on the worldview themes and associated TFJD codes of this book—with procedure for using it detailed in Figure #10—can be seen as a modern, westernized implementing of the basic *I Ching* procedure. Rather than using stalks of yarrow or coins, it requires one roll of four colored dice.

Oracles, Physicists, Jungian Synchroncity

"God doesn't play dice with the world!" Einstein said in expressing dislike for the role that unpredictable, random events play in quantum mechanics. Yet quantum mechanics' predictions have been extraordinarily well verified and several technologies based on the understanding it provides are widely used. And it seems randomness is not confined to physics. In the last decade molecular biologists have gained new understanding of how chemical alterations to DNA can produce lasting change. "Epigenetics may…amplify individuality by interjecting an element of randomness into how genes are expressed that ultimately affects behavior" reports

Greg Miller in an article in *Science* 5 October 2012. He notes "another potential source of random variation in gene expression in developing brain cells: so-called jumping genes…" It appears in a way God does play dice with the world!

MIT physics emeritus professor Kerson Huang, like most modern physicists, appreciates the world is complex and "there will always be random elements we cannot pin down, even if the underlying laws are known."[1] In 1987 Huang and wife Rosemary finished a new English translation of the *I Ching*, one said to restore "the authentic spirit of the ancient text." Their book includes commentary to help readers appreciate historical, philosophical, and physics connections between the *I Ching* and the modern world.

Careful to not be embracing the predictions made by oracles and fortune-tellers, like he would those made by correct application of physical law, Huang separates the domain in which those laws apply from that in which the *I Ching* and other "nonscientific endeavors" operate. This latter domain is "vast" he writes, "including such diverse phenomena as the stock market, classical music, and love. In fact, it covers all phenomena in which the 'measuring device' is a person."

Wolfgang Pauli (1900-1958) is another famous physicist who has written about understanding random events in people's lives. Not only does quantum mechanics cast off certainty in the realm it governs, the cause and effect relationships that apply in the classical realm also break down. In this regard, Pauli collaborated with Carl Jung in a 1952 paper about synchronicity and "temporally coincident occurrences of acausal events."

Synchronicity refers to events that occur either simultaneously or nearly so in meaningful fashion, but yet they have no evident cause and effect connection. A famous example cited by Jung involved his patient recounting a dream she had involving a golden scarab. Just at that moment an insect very similar to what she was describing appeared outside the window glass next to her! Other examples: clocks spontaneously stopping or pictures falling at the time of someone's death.

Jung and followers believed such events occur much more often than would be expected if they were due to mere random chance coincidence. Many of them might claim that synchronicities provide evidence of a collective unconscious, the existence of connectedness at a higher (normally unperceived) level, and that consciousness contains a "reality structurer" which psychically affects reality. In the last three decades both New Age enthusiasts and a few physicists (including Roger Penrose[2] and refuting him, Max Tegmark[3]) have explored the possibility "that the brain acts as a quantum computer, and that quantum coherence is related to consciousness in a fundamental way."

In a 2003 paper about quantum random walks Julia Kempe[4] explicitly connects oracles—which she thinks of as "a black box that we cannot open" that "we query with some input to get a specific answer"—with quantum computers. With respect to questioning a database oracle in search of an answer (termed "the marked item") and efficient computer design, she writes, "It has been shown that a quantum computer ...can find the marked item with only $\sqrt{N}$ queries, where N is the number of items, whereas a classical algorithm will require of order N queries." Example: suppose we must direct 100 questions to a classical computer based database oracle to retrieve information we desire. Kempe seemingly says that a working quantum computer would require us to ask only $\sqrt{100}=10$ queries to get the answer we're seeking.

We don't understand how our brain works in processing information or what consciousness is. Penrose's proposal that consciousness arises from quantum effects in microtubular structures inside cells as part of an Orch-OR (orchestrated objective reduction) theory has recently made news. In early 2014, he and collaborator Stuart Hameroff claimed a discovery of quantum vibrations in microtubules by Bandyopadhyay in Japan confirms their hypothesis.[5] In this regard I have two comments.

First, as skeptics point out, a good model of how quantum coherence / entanglement is maintained by neural structures for needed times—given frequent collisions with water molecules in the hostile brain environment—is lacking. Yet, while some scoff, I feel quantum biology is an exciting field. In particular I'm intrigued by where using quantum random walks to create entanglement between spatially separated systems might lead, and in general how brains might interface with David Bohm's implicate order. Second, as to quantum vibrations in microtubules, fitting (standing) waves into specific structures has a long history in physics. Perhaps it began with early attempts to explain musical sounds produced by plucking strings in terms of standing wave patterns produced when waves traveling in opposite directions interfere.

Caitlin Matthews has likened using an oracle for divination to "stretching a musical string between an issue in physical reality and its correlate" in mind space, the unseen implicate or what she calls "subtle reality." Both her and Huang dismiss frivolous frequent use of oracles or consulting them on mundane matters. For Matthews, only if the issue raised with the oracle is "well aligned and connected" will the metaphorical result of plucking the string result in a pleasing, "resonant note." For her nonsensical oracle output or "a buzzing totally unresonant string" indicates that the question posed "lacks alignment and purpose."

Matthews' metaphor suggests a cause and effect in that asking the right question somehow produces a resonant response. In considering the physics behind this, Huang would merely point out that, given the response that must resonate is registered by a person, the complexities involved are such that this is a nonscientific domain matter! He feels the essence of what happens in our daily lives involves complexity. For him this is metaphorically modeled in the *I Ching* procedure "by the random element in the casting of a hexagram." He admits to having no explanation for Jungian synchronicity, other than coincidence. While he does not believe an oracle like the *I Ching* "can foresee the future in an objective sense," he nonetheless sees value in its use.

He feels that "to consult it" is "to solemnize the moment." He feels the function of an oracle "is to satisfy certain needs of the person seeking counsel (including the need to know the future)." Looked at this way, he says, "I have found that the *I Ching* works." He notes a key theme in the philosophy of the *I Ching* (sometimes called "The Book of Changes") is "all things run their cycle, and no situation remains immutable." Given this, Huang feels "it offers hope in the depth of despair." To that I'd add that consulting an oracle fosters a desirable "look before you leap" orientation.

I had planned to end this book right here—but it seems the universe had other plans. Seemingly, forces behind Jungian synchronicities (involving music and falling in love) demanded I continue!

Figure #10: The TFJD Oracle (T↔→Thinking, F ↔→ Feeling, J ↔→ Joining, D ↔→ Doing)

Instructions: 1) Obtain or fashion four colored dice, ideally colored white <=> T, red <=>F, yellow <=>J, and green <=>D.

2) Ask a question of the oracle. State if your (see step 5*) position is add + or subtract - (If no preference, males use +, females -)

3) Cast the dice rolling all four together. Using the color ID in step 1, record the four digit result = cast.

4) For any numbers 4, 5, or 6 that are rolled, subtract 3. Accept numbers 1, 2, or 3 as rolled. Record the four digit result = original. You now have two four digit results to compare: the "cast" and the "original." (Note the latter is your first TFJD code.)

5) Compare to find differences in the four column entries. If there is a difference in the T column, to that column's value in the original result (add or sub)* 1. If result = 4, record a 1; if result =0, record a 3. Record four digit value as result = changing to.

6) If there is no difference in T column, repeat step 5 for F column. If no difference in F column, repeat step 5 for J column. If there is no difference in J column, repeat step 5 for D column. Note if the result cast had only 1s, 2s, or 3s go to the next step.

7) If you still don't have a result = changing to, roll one die to get the column changing as follows: 1 or 2➔T, 3 or 4➔F, 5➔J, 6➔D. Using that, repeat step 5 adding or subtracting 1 to the value in the changing column, etc to arrive at result = changing to.

8) Use the chart below to find two worldview themes corresponding to four digit (TFJD) codes for "original" and "changing to" results. Study theme descriptions, songs in Part II. Based on what resonates with you, try to make sense of the oracle response.

1111 #7A Mysticism	2111 #11B Free Will	3111 #18B Dispassionate
1112 #20B Authoritarianism	2112 #29A The Self-Restrained Person	3112 #30 Intellectual Freedom
1113 #33A Servitude	2113 #35A Self Reliant Nonconformity	3113 #46A Technological Fix Mentality
1121 #11A Fatalism	2121 #39A Tough Love	3121 #5A Scientific Materialism
1122 #47B Pacifism	2122 #19A Economic Individualism	3122 #6 Scientific Method
1123 #15 Collective Cognitive Imperative	2123 #26A The Consumerist	3123 #22A Expansionism
1131 #5B Vitalism	2131 #31 Education For Democracy	3131 #4 Global Vision: The Big Picture
1132 #23B Enoughness	2132 #47A Attitudinal Fix Mentality	3132 #23A Sustainability
1133 #37A Proud Identification	2133 #48 Co-Operative Society Advocate	3133 #19B Corporate Capitalism
1211 #9B Apocalypticism	2211 #1A Humbly Unsure	3211 #20A Elitism
1212 #14A Moralistic God	2212 #52 Independent Living--Sick, Disabled	3212 #28B Healthy Orientation
1213 #26B More is Better	2213 #25 Anthropocentrism	3213 #45B Work Hard, Pay As You Go
1221 #14B Reincarnation	2221 #17B Gratitude & Forgiveness	3221 #42 Ethical Orientation
1222 #45A Borrowing Mentality	2222 #34 Valuing Traditions & Status Quo	3222 #50A Libertarian
1223 #24 Struggling With Sustenance	2223 #3 Focused Vision	3223 #13 Dancing With Systems
1231 #8A Monotheism	2231 #32 Valuing Human Rights	3231 #49B Socialism
1232 #8B Belief In A Personal God	2232 #16 Golden Rule, Mutual Help Ethic	3232 #49A Social Welfare Statism
1233 #7B Magic	2233 #44B Animal Rights	3233 #40 Environmental Economics
1311 #39B Scapegoating	2311 #36B Conspiracism	3311 #36A Cynicism
1312 #33B Addiction	2312 #2B I Know What's Best For You	3312 #1B Skepticism
1313 #28A Hedonistic Orientation	2313 #29B The Threatening Person	3313 #46B Militarism
1321 #9A Religious Fundamentalism	2321 #44A Sanctity & Dignity Of Life	3321 #10 Secular Humanism
1322 #17A Bitterness & Vengeance	2322 #50B Left Anarchist	3322 #22B Imperialism
1323 #18A Passionately Impulsive	2323 #41 Struggling With Self Esteem	3323 #43 Seeking Wealth And Power
1331 #2A The True Believer	2331 #21A Populism	3331 #37B Global Citizen
1332 #38 Valuing Family	2332 #21B Service To Others	3332 #51 Ethical Globalization
1333 #12 The Artistic Worldview	2333 #27 Belonging To Nature	3333 #35B Working For Change

Examples: #1: After asking question and stating + position, the roll of the dice in step 3 is white=4, red=5, yellow=3, green=2. So record result 4532=cast. Step 4: subtract 3 from values bigger than 3. So record result 1232=original. Step 5: compare 4532 and 1232 beginning with left hand columns. Note there is a difference in T, so take value in that column of original result and add 1 to it ➔ 1+1=2. The four digit original result has now become 2232. So record result 2232= changing to. Step 8: The worldview themes (from chart) are original = #8B Belief in a Personal God and changing to = #16 Golden Rule, Mutual Help Ethic.

#2: Position stated is -, dice give white=2, red=3, yellow=4, and green=6. So result 2346=cast. Step 4: subtract 3 from values bigger than 3. So result 2313=original. Steps 5 and 6: compare 2341 and 2313 beginning with left column. There's no difference in T or F; difference is in J so take value in that column of original result, sub 1 ➔ 1-1=0. Since the result is 0, from rule in step 5, 0 ➔ 3 So original result becomes 2333. So result 2333=changing to. Step 8: themes are original = #29B and changing to = #27

#3: Position stated is -, dice: white=1, red=3, yellow=3, and green=3. Per the note in step 6, we roll one die. This gives 3, showing change in the F column. To original result of 1333 we sub 1 in F column➔ 1233. So result 1233 = changing to. Step 8: we get themes from the chart as original = #12 Artistic Worldview and changing to = #7B Magic.

E. Strange Events That Shake Worldviews—Two Stories Involving Music & Love

If there was one person who I would have told you is a hard-core, confirmed skeptic (theme #1B) and scientific materialist (theme #5A), it would have been Michael Shermer, long-time publisher of *Skeptic* magazine. But after reading his October 2014 *Scientific American* column, I'll no longer make that assertion. The column, "Infrequencies," is subtitled "I just witnessed an event so mysterious that it shook my skepticism." I won't recount his story at length here, since I want to move on to my own story. So if you want more details, you'll need to track down the article and read it for yourself. Interestingly enough, music figures prominently in both his story and my story.

Shermer's involves a supposedly dead 1978 transistor radio suddenly coming back to life. The radio belonged to long dead Walter, who lived in Germany and had once helped raise his grand-daughter Jennifer. On June 25, 2014, in a house in California where family had gathered to celebrate Jennifer and Michael's marriage, just after they had said vows and exchanged rings, the radio came back to life. After noting Jennifer's world-view is built around skepticism, Shermer writes, "… these deeply evocative events gave her the distinct feeling that her grandfather was there and that the music was his gift of approval."

My own story is much more convoluted and involved. It starts in mid June, 2014, after I'd mostly finished writing the Part II songs. Ending months of house-hunting, I moved hundreds of miles from New Mexico to a mountain town in Arizona. There I basically knew no one. About three weeks after moving in, while cleaning the kitchen and standing on my tip toes, I felt a small object present on top of a kitchen cabinet. After grabbing a chair to stand on, I pulled the object down, wiped the dust off, and looked at it.

What I saw was a shock. Wrapped in plastic, there it was: an unopened three DVD music/video set, copyright 2003, titled "The Rolling Stones, 1962—present." Seemingly coincidentally, I happen to think of myself as one of the world's biggest Stones' fans. Some evidence: on July 16, 2012, in honoring the band's 50th anniversary, I posted on **Project Worldview**, as issue #25 of my *Worldview Watch* blog, "The Worldview Behind the Rolling Stones' Music." Despite having nearly all their LP albums and CDs dating back to the first one I bought in 1965, I had only one other Stones music video. And it's exclusively devoted to their 2005-2006 *A Bigger Bang* tour. So this mysterious object seemed to truly represent the best house-warming gift that anyone ever got! Of course the question was, "How did it get to where I found it?" I had bought the house from "Robert Randall"—someone I'd talked with about the house for but a few minutes—who certainly had no reason to connect me to the Stones.

The mystery grew dramatically given what happened on November 15, 2014. I was in the home of a woman I'd met eight days earlier — "Lena." (Her real name is the title of a Rolling Stones song. Eventually I'd fall in love with Lena and cherish her as the one who answered my "calling out to the universe," but back then I barely knew her.) We rather spontaneously decided to go see the just released movie *Interstellar*. (I had not been to a movie theater in well over a year.) The decision was made at 1:03 PM (the time on her computer screen) and the movie started at 2:20 PM. Seemingly there was time to eat a quick lunch and head from her house to the theater about six miles away. Pulling into the theater parking lot, I told her I thought we'd arrived in plenty of time, even saying, "I think it's about 2:05, but I could be wrong." I was. Lena's cell phone said it was 2:20 —where had the time gone? We had to hurry.

Fortunately the guy we bought tickets from told us the movie hadn't started yet—there were nine minutes of previews preceding it. After navigating the dark theater, settling into my seat, and turning my attention to the huge screen and impressive sound system, I realized a preview movie trailer (for *The Gambler*) was just starting. The song that then began to play (coincidentally?) is my all-time rock music favorite: "Gimme Shelter" by the Rolling Stones. (In that July 2012 blog issue I'd written: "Many rank 'Gimme Shelter' at the top of greatest classic rock songs.") After I enjoyed a minute of hearing it so loudly and clearly in the surround sound setting, I connected it with what I'd found in my new house four months earlier. I didn't have much time to reflect or be flabbergasted: *Interstellar* was starting.

I walked out of the theater nearly three hours later stunned by my emotional roller coaster ride, given all of my buttons it pushed. I was moved to tears several times as the main character (father /astronaut /time traveler) Cooper agonized over keeping the promise he'd made to his daughter Murph back on the dying Earth that his mission hoped to save. Somehow the movie successfully reconciled the cold impersonal equations of general relativity physics with the warmth and passion of human interaction / love.

The movie's elderly theorist Dr. Brand (played by Michael Caine) continually took me back to Caltech's Rip Thorne (the advisor who kept the movie plot within the bounds of the modern scientific conceptual framework). Several times I thought "When I get home I'm gonna pull out my massive 1000+ page graduate physics text *Gravitation*" (co-authored by Thorne). Some of the movies' "physics teaching moments" took me back to my career as physics teacher…

…Not the career I could have had as an astrophysicist had I chosen differently as a twenty two year old in 1973. What if I'd said "Yes" when Caltech Dept. Chair Jesse Greenstein seemingly offered me a place in their graduate program, instead of telling him, "No—I'm going to UC Santa Cruz." And then, months later, in one of the two biggest decisions I've made in my life—dropping out of that astrophysics Ph.D program, opting instead for a much different life, one that came to include doing lots of teaching. Should I have tossed the *I Ching* before making big decisions?

I told the story of agonizing over that decision in my 1990 *Coming of Age in the Global Village* book [1] (page 295). I'll never forget the elevator that I rode to see my advisor and professor Donald Osterbrock to tell him I'd decided to drop out. Interestingly enough, how one's weight changes in an elevator is often used in discussing how weight changes in a gravitational field and the equivalence principle in Einstein's theory of general relativity. And the first job Osterbrock had given me as his research assistant was reading a draft of a book he'd written about the interstellar medium.

Interstellar ends with Cooper again leaving to rescue someone who had earlier rescued him— someone who makes you leave the movie "thinking he's going to kiss Sleeping Beauty and live happily ever with her": astronaut, scientist and Dr. Brand's daughter, Amelia. The last scene where her face appears, emotionally takes me to my life's continual quest to find "Ms. Right" and the

other big agonizing decision of my life. In late July 2013, I decided to end my most recent marriage. Had I not made this decision I have no doubt this book you're reading would not exist.

My *Interstellar* experience, starting with "Gimme Shelter" and ending with "Ms. Right," made me wonder about the woman I'd shared the afternoon with. Did I have a future with Lena? Would I someday feel most at home wherever I found shelter in her arms? As for the movie plot, just as Cooper (aided by a black hole) moved through space and time to signal his daughter (by then herself a physicist), could similar higher dimensional / time travel explain how the Rolling Stones gift got placed for me to discover? I'll call that discovery Jungian synchronicity #1.

Jungian synchronicity #2 was a multi-faceted one: the "Gimme Shelter" song started playing at just the moment I sat down to watch a movie. Its plot was built around a scientifically acceptable mechanism that conceivably could explain what occurred in my new home: Jungian synchronicity #1—something I had no other way to explain except coincidence. And the way two synchronicities (and several other related seeming coincidences) fit together seemed to up the ante in deciding what to bet on. Should I go with random / rolling the dice wildly unlikely coincidence, or truly bizarre connectedness that the world's most brilliant physicists would struggle to explain?

As I (stupidly!) struggle to use the accepted scientific conceptual framework to explain these events, the movie seems to be teasing me. Pushing me to come up with something like the "inter-dimensional hypothesis"[2] that's been offered to explain events that others want to attribute to UFO visits by extra-terrestrial aliens. Or figuring out a scheme in which an unconscious version of me (or someone close to me?) somehow has superior knowledge, perhaps by mentally traveling through space and time to gather information, and is able to arrange my consciously experiencing what I now call Jungian synchronicity #1 and #2!

Perhaps the explanation will involve Mysticism (theme #7A) and ultimate "Oneness" through "which comes knowledge not available via normal human cognition or human senses?" After saying many leading physicists are comfortable with this theme—certainly David Bohm was—I'll add a disclaimer. Namely that physicists have struggled and so far failed to find convincing explanations for the physics of consciousness, Jungian synchronicities or how quantum physics processes seem to allow systems to behave like a good chess player — analyzing all possible moves and picking out the best one before it is made. And arguing that mystic states allow the seeker access to all times, past or future—like there's a tiny black hole in the brain, or a holographic model explains its operation —can bring much ridicule!

What if our decision-making, our selecting moves from many options, was sometimes backed by knowledge gleaned from the future? And after mentally-conducted experimentally probing reality in many different ways (in slightly different parallel universes?) we knew that we had made the best move? Put another way, suppose we have an oracle what provides perfect guidance in answering questions we pose for it? Some people seemingly have an intuitive sense that guides them, but a person possessing something vaguely resembling the ability that I've described, or that perfect oracle, would have more than good intuitive sense: he or she would have a sense of destiny!

Now back to the chase…Who was responsible for somehow perturbing the universe so that I followed a path that found me discovering the perfect gift in my new house, and months latter having the "Gimme Shelter" song signaling me I was in for a mind-bending, thought-provoking, emotionally wrenching movie experience? There are three candidates to consider here: 1) the realtor who showed me the house, 2) the person with me when I realized I'd somehow misplaced fifteen minutes of time as we headed to see *Interstellar* —my friend Lena, or 3) me.

The gift's dust covering, and her not owning up to it when I told her the story, ruled out the realtor. As for Lena, who I'd just learned has an interest in meditation and New Age spirituality, she is no doubt more intuitive, more "in tune with reality" in a metaphysical connectedness sense than I am. And has more power than I do, from a Magic (theme #7B) viewpoint, to "exercise power and control over" it. But she hardly seems the shaman or sorcerer type![3] That leaves one candidate: me.

How did I do it? Here are three possibilities. 1) Robert Randall and I telepathically connected during the brief time I saw him before buying the house. He sensed my being a big Stones' fan. He's not only paranormally gifted, but is kind and likes giving dusty old presents. Or 2) in a mystical state (while living in the house before discovering the gift) I used higher dimension connections between all humans to go back in time and communicate with either Robert Randall or a neighbor who once lived in the house. One of them is a Stones' fan. I implant a suggestion in his mind as to putting the desired object where it will become lost. Or 3) we create our own reality. I steered mine to the house —like the guy in *Close Encounters of the Third Kind* headed to Devil's Tower—because I knew the gift, and my destiny, was there. In a way, I've always known. Perhaps our whole lives, past and future, actually realized / potentially possible are stored in hologram-like fashion inside our brains. I tapped into this to make some good chess moves.

To me, all of these are unbelievable. And I now am left with three other possibilities: 4) a Personal God (theme #8B) is teasing me, 5) my house is haunted with playful vital spirits—see Vitalism (theme #5B), or 6) a chain of coincidences was involved. I won't accept any of these! The only thing I will accept is an experience-based feeling —actually two things I feel as I write this in mid December, 2014: 1) my worldview has been given a major shaking by the events I've described above, and 2) Lena and I are passionately in love. It's as if each of us has finally found that soulmate we've searched for our whole lives.

Given that the soulmate concept is one I've previously been a bit skeptical about, getting to know Lena has clearly perturbed my worldview with respect to this single concept. But what about the major worldview shaking in 1) above? Given what a powerful, transcending driving force love can be—touchingly illustrated in *Interstellar*—is the "soulmate connection" Lena and I feel in some way also behind it? I simply don't know!

My whole life's been a love affair, a "Lifelong Learning Parade" (theme #30 song). But suddenly "the storm is threatening." This structured learning parade that has long informed my worldview is being rained on. I'd come to think of my worldview like an old comfortable house I'd long lived in: it's home. But that house has been shaken off its foundation! Feeling very "Humbly Unsure" (theme #1A) has replaced comfortable. And in my mind I'm hearing music, music I've loved since I first heard it in 1969: "Gimme, gimme shelter …"

Part I—section A
1 Brooks, David "What Suffering Does" *NY Times* 4/7/2014
2 Carver, C. & Connor-Smith, J. "Personality & Coping" in *Ann. Rev. of Psychology* Vol. 61:679-707 Jan 2010
3 Matthews, Caitlin *Singing the Soul Back Home:Shamanism in Daily Life* Boston: Connections Book Publishing 2003
4 Cook, Stephen P. *The Worldview Literacy Book* Weed: Parthenon Books 2009 ISBN 978-0-9627349-1-5

Part I—section B
1 Tsien, Joe Z. "The Memory Code" *Scientific American* July 2007 pp 52-59
2 see for example: Quiroga, R, Fried, I, Koch, C, "Brain Cells for Grandmother" *Scientific American* Feb 2013 pp 30-35
3 Dobbs, David "The New Science of the Teenage Brain" *National Geographic* Oct 2011 pp 36-59
4 Rosenblum, Lawrence "Neuroscience: A Confederacy of Senses" *Scientific American* Jan 2013 pp 72-75
5 Arnsten, A, Mazure,C, Sinha,R, "This Is Your Brain in Meltdown" *Scientific American* Apr 2012 pp 48-53

Part I—section C
1 Schmidt, L and Trainor, L. "Frontal brain electrical activity (EEG) distinguishes valence and intensity of musical emotions" in *Cognition & Emotion* 15:4, 2001
2 Gosselin, N. etal. "Amygdala Damage Impairs Emotion Recognition from Music" *Neuropsychologia* 45:2 2007
3 Pinker, Steven *How the Mind Works* New York:W.W. Norton 1997 ISBN 0-393-31848-6
4 Zatorre,R and Salimpoor, V "Why Music Makes Our Brain Sing," *The New York Times* June 7 2013
5 Cook, Stephen P. "Imagining A Theory Of Everything For Adaptive Systems" in ed. Swan, L. etal *The Origin(s) of Design in Nature: A Fresh, Interdisciplinary Look at How Design Emerges in Complex Systems, Especially Life,* Dordrecht: Springer Science, 2012 ISBN 978-94-007-4155-3
6 Carter, Rita, *Mapping the Mind* London: Orion Publishing Group 1998 ISBN 1-841-88009-4
7 McNamara, Patrick "The God Effect" August 11 2014 post at http://aeon.co/magazine/psychology/dopamine-marks-the-line-between-religious-believer-and-fanatic/
8 see his 1976 book: Dawkins, Richard *The Selfish Gene*

Part I—section D
1 see for example: Balter, Michael "Why Are Our Brains So Big?" *Science* 5 October 2012 Vol. 338 pp 33-34
2 see Balter op cit.
3 DeDreu, C, Greer, L, Handgraaf, M, etal "Oxytocin Promotes Human Ethnocentrism" *Proceedings of the National Academy of Sciences* Jan 25 2011 Vol. 108:4 pp 1262-66
4 individualism is a social philosophy / belief system that places individual interests and rights above those of society, and individual freedom, self-reliance and independence above any social contract obligations
5 collectivism is a social philosophy / belief system that emphasizes the interdependence of every human being and values co-operation over competition
6 Dawkins, Richard *The God Delusion* Boston: Houghton Mifflin 2008 ISBN 0-618-91824-8
7 DeLude, Cathryn "A Common Brain Pathway for Anxiety and Social Behavior" *MIT News Office* Jan 15 2014 release
8 Bargh, John A. "Our Unconscious Mind" *Scientific American* Jan 2014 pp 30-37

Part I—section E
1 Jaynes, Julian *The Origin of Consciousness in the Breakdown of the Bicameral Mind* Boston: Houghton Mifflin 1990
2 created by American theologican Reinhold Niebuhr
3 a team led by Stan Floresco, Dept. of Psychology and Brain Research Centre, as reported in Nov 25 2013 news release

Part I—section F
1 Richter, G. *Portraits of the Greeks* London: Phaidon 1965
2 Trafton, Anne "Parts of Brain Can Switch Functions" *MIT News Office* March 1, 2011 release
3 Yuste, R. and Church, G. "The New Century of the Brain" *Scientific American* March 2014 pp 38-45

Part II—note in comment on page 31
1 *The UU Pocket Guide* p.55 Boston: Skinner House 2012

Part III—section A
1 see my hypothesis in this regard in Cook, S. "SETI: Assessing Imaginative Proposals" in *Life on Earth and Other Planetary Bodies* ed.A.Hanslmeir, etal. Dordrecht: Springer Science, 2013
2 Cook, S. "Coming of Age Under the Night Sky: the Importance of Astronomy in Shaping Worldviews" in ed. Tymienicka, A. and Grandpierre, A. *Astronomy and Civilization in the New Enlightenment,* Heidelberg:Springer Science 2011
3 *On the Phenomenology of the Consciousness of Internal Time (1893-1917)*, 1990[1928]. Brough, J.B.,tran Dordrecht: Kluwer.
4 Clarke, David and Clarke, Eric ed. *Music and Consciousness* Oxford:Oxford University Press 2011 ISBN9780199553792
5 Addis, Laird *Of Mind and Music* Ithaca: Cornell University Press 2004 ISBN 9780801489563
6 Sacks, Oliver "The Power of Music" *Brain* vol.129:10 2006
7 Pfeiffer, John *The Emergence of Society: A Prehistory of the Establishment.* New York: McGraw Hill 1977 0070497583
8 Storr, A. *Music and the Mind* NY: Random House 1993
9 as reported in Fields, Douglas "Why Can Some Blind People Process Speech Far Faster Than Sighted Persons?" www.scientificamerican.com/article posted Dec 13 2010
10 Syed, Matthew *Bounce* New York:Harper Collins 2010 ISBN 978-0-06-200474-1

Part III—section C
1 http://en.wikipedia.org/wiki/ACT-R retrieved 4/07/14
2 McNamara, Adam. "Can We Measure Memes?" *Frontiers in Evolutionary Neuroscience* vol 3:1 May 2011

Part III—section D
1 Huang, Kerson and Rosemary *I Ching* New York: Workman Publishing 1987 ISBN 0-89480-319-0
2 Penrose, Roger *Shadows of the Mind* Oxford: Oxford University Press 1994 ISBN 0-19-853978-9
3 Tegmark, Max "Importance of Quantum Decoherence in Brain Processes" *Physical Review E* Vol 61:4 April 2000
4 Kempe, Julia "Quantum Random Walks—An Introductory Overview" *Contemporary Physics* Vol 44 pp 307-327 2003
5 "Discovery of quantum vibrations in 'microtubules' inside brain neurons supports controversial theory of consciousness" www.sciencedaily.com/releases/2014/01/140116085105.htm

Part III—section E
1 Cook, Stephen P. *Coming of Age in the Global Village* Russellville:Parthenon Books 1900 ISBN 978-0-9627349-0-X
2 http://en.wikipedia.org/wiki/Interdimensional_hypothesis
3 after writing that, in "Lena's" library the author found an old edition of *Synchronicity: The Inner Path of Leadership* by J.Jaworski; Berrett-Koehler Publ SanFrancisco, CA 2011

CPSIA information can be obtained at www.ICGtesting.com
Printed in the USA
LVOW01s0414170115

423236LV00002B/3/P